How Regional Organizations Sustain Authoritarian Rule

How Regional Organizations Sustain Authoritarian Rule

The Dictators' Club

Maria J. Debre

Great Clarendon Street, Oxford, OX2 6DP,
United Kingdom

Oxford University Press is a department of the University of Oxford.
It furthers the University's objective of excellence in research, scholarship,
and education by publishing worldwide. Oxford is a registered trade mark of
Oxford University Press in the UK and in certain other countries

© Maria J. Debre 2025

The moral rights of the author have been asserted

All rights reserved. No part of this publication may be reproduced, stored in a retrieval system, transmitted, used for text and data mining, or used for training artificial intelligence, in any form or by any means, without the prior permission in writing of Oxford University Press, or as expressly permitted by law, by licence or under terms agreed with the appropriate reprographics rights organization. Enquiries concerning reproduction outside the scope of the above should be sent to the Rights Department, Oxford University Press, at the address above.

You must not circulate this work in any other form
and you must impose this same condition on any acquirer.

Published in the United States of America by Oxford University Press
198 Madison Avenue, New York, NY 10016, United States of America

British Library Cataloguing in Publication Data

Data available

Library of Congress Control Number: 2024943206

ISBN 9780198903604

DOI: 10.1093/9780198903635.001.0001

Printed and bound by
CPI Group (UK) Ltd, Croydon, CR0 4YY

Links to third party websites are provided by Oxford in good faith and
for information only. Oxford disclaims any responsibility for the materials
contained in any third party website referenced in this work.

The manufacturer's authorised representative in the EU for product safety is Oxford University Press España S.A. of El Parque Empresarial San Fernando de Henares, Avenida de Castilla, 2 – 28830 Madrid (www.oup.es/en or product.safety@oup.com). OUP España S.A. also acts as importer into Spain of products made by the manufacturer.

To my parents,

who have always supported and encouraged me.

Acknowledgments

This book has been a long time in the making. It started out as a PhD dissertation in 2014 during a time when I still had to convince people that authoritarian international cooperation was not just a fleeting phenomenon. Unfortunately, the world has changed drastically in the last 10 years and the geopolitical importance of authoritarianism is more pressing than ever. Along with political currents, this project also grew from a research idea into a proper dissertation, several journal articles, and now a book—and I am immensely grateful and want to give thanks to the people who have been part of this journey.

This book is therefore dedicated to Tanja Börzel, who believed in the project and provided me with my first academic home at Free University Berlin; to everybody who ever attended the Kolleg-Forschergruppe (KFG) "The Transformative Power of Europe" weekly Jour Fixe meetings and offered the best possible insights into doing, presenting, and understanding research in progress; to all the members of the Berlin Graduate School for Transnational Studies (BTS) who commented on draft chapters, shared office space, and talked about PhD life over coffee and wine; to all the wonderful people I met during my year as a Fox Fellow at Yale University who enriched my academic thinking immensely; to the members of the ERC Team "Decline and Death of International Organizations" at Maastricht University, particularly Hylke Dijkstra, who gave me space and time to turn the PhD into proper publishable research and taught me how to become a professional academic; to Potsdam University and the valuable advice I received on how to write a convincing book pitch from everybody at our monthly colloquia meetings; to Thomas Sommerer, who was the most supportive mentor I could have hoped for; to Stockholm University and Jonas Tallberg, who helped polish my book pitch; and, finally, to Marlene Hunger and Denise Klüber for invaluable research assistance during the last stretches of writing the book.

I would not be the researcher I am today without the support of many professional and personal friends that made the journey so very enjoyable: Laura von Allwördern, who turned into the most wonderful friend inside and outside of academia; Nina Reiners, who is my constant inspiration and role model as a researcher and person; Theo Vladasel, the best New Haven pub partner I could have asked for, who had to deal with my poor pool skills one too many times; Esther Versluis, who I admire forever for her most supportive leadership style; Daniëlle Flonk, who has become the most productive project partner; Helen and Seren, and Friday night dinners; Lea, who kept me on track during the last months of thesis writing; Maike, who will always pick up the phone and listen without judgment; and Linda and Jorid, for all the political discussions.

Finally, four people deserve particular recognition: my parents, Joseph and Monika, who have supported my academic journey and instilled my love for writing and reading; my partner, Juan, who had to watch me write for hours and days without looking up—I apologize for all the times I made us leave the house late because I "only" wanted to finish the next sentence or paragraph; and, finally, the newest addition to our family, my son Carlos, whose due date finally pushed me to finish the manuscript and send it off just in time for his arrival.

Contents

List of Figures	x
List of Tables	xii
Companion Website	xiii

1.	Introduction	1
2.	The Dictators' Club: Theorizing Regional Organization Membership and Regime Survival	19
3.	Patterns of Authoritarian Membership in Regional Organizations	42
4.	The Effects of Membership in Dictator Clubs on Regime Survival	67
5.	How Dictator Clubs Empower Autocratic Incumbents	92
6.	How Dictator Clubs Constrain Regional Challengers	118
7.	How Dictator Clubs Shield from External Pressure	144
8.	Conclusion	167

References	182
Index	217

List of Figures

1.1. Number of ROs across time, 1945–2020 (own depiction based on Polity (Marshall et al. 2018))   7

1.2. Autocratic density and homogeneity across time, 1945–2020 (own depiction based on Polity (Marshall et al. 2018))   9

1.3. Argument in brief   10

2.1. Causal mechanisms of regime-boosting regionalism   33

3.1. Development of number of ROs by regime type, 1946–2018 (own depiction based on Polity (Marshall et al. 2018))   48

3.2. Development of authoritarian density, 1946–2018 (own depiction based on Polity (Marshall et al. 2018))   49

3.3. Homogeneity and authoritarian density of ROs at foundation and death (own depiction based on Polity (Marshall et al. 2018))   51

3.4. Development of RO homogeneity, 1946–2018 (own depiction based on Polity (Marshall et al. 2018))   52

3.5. Development of authoritarian density by region, 1946–2018 (own depiction based on Polity (Marshall et al. 2018))   54

3.6. Number of autocratic and democratic ROs per state in region, 1946, 1990, 2010, and 2018 (based on own data and Polity (Marshall et al. 2018))   55

3.7. Lifetime density scores across select ROs (own depiction based on Polity (Marshall et al. 2018))   56

3.8. Number of ROs by economic, political, and security mandates per region and regime type, 1946–2018 (based on own data and Polity (Marshall et al. 2018))   59

3.9. Instances of democratic regime change and autocratic replacements across decades (based on Geddes et al. (2018) and own data)   63

3.10. Percentages of democratic regime change and autocratic replacements across regions (based on Geddes et al. (2018) and own data)   64

3.11. ROs with multiple failure events (based on Geddes et al. (2018) and own data), democratization (left) and autocratic replacements (right)   65

4.1. Kaplan–Meier survival estimates, democratization, and autocratic replacement (based on Geddes et al. (2018) and own data)   76

4.2. Kaplan–Meier estimator by regime type for democratization and autocratic replacements (based on Geddes et al. (2018) and own data)   77

4.3. Kaplan–Meier estimator by region for democratization and autocratic replacements (based on Geddes et al. (2018) and own data)   78

4.4. Average marginal effect, autocratic density (90 percent confidence interval) (own depiction based on Polity (Marshall et al. 2018))   81

4.5. Smoothed hazard function for democratization by autocratic density and homogeneity (own depiction based on Polity (Marshall et al. 2018))   84

7.1. Development of electoral democracy index for Nicaragua and Honduras, 1900–2023 (own depiction based on Varieties of Democracy (Coppedge et al. 2023))   145

List of Tables

3.1. ROs with a court or tribunal (based on own data)   60

4.1. ROs and autocratic survival (no democratization), 1945–2020   79

4.2. ROs and autocratic survival (no autocratic replacement), 1945–2020   86

5.1. Overview of cases   95

Companion Website

This book features a companion website that provides material that cannot be made available in a book, namely the Appendix. The reader is encouraged to consult this resource in conjunction with Chapters 3 and 4. Examples available online are indicated in the text with Oxford's symbol ⏵.

The companion website can be accessed by searching for this book in our online catalogue https://global.oup.com/academic. From the book's webpage you can follow the link to the companion website.

1

Introduction

On January 6, 2022, Russian-led troops entered Kazakhstan under a joint mission of the Collective Security Treaty Organization (CSTO) to aid the troubled regime of Kassym-Jomart Tokayev in repressing pro-democratic protestors. The troops were deployed under a peacekeeping mission to "guard strategic objects" because mass protests against high fuel prices were "hijacked by terrorist groups" (Satubaldina 2022). About 10 years earlier, the Gulf Cooperation Council (GCC) deployed a similar mission under the Peninsular Shield Force to suppress demonstrations calling for the end of the absolutist monarchy in Bahrain. The royal Bahraini family remains in power today.

In July 2009, the Uyghur issue first surfaced on the international stage. Deadly fighting had broken out between ethnic Han Chinese and Uyghur factory workers in Xinjiang's capital Urumqi. After several days of fighting and media blackouts, the death toll was in the thousands. Only days before the outbreak, all Shanghai Cooperation Organization (SCO) member states signed a new counter-terrorism treaty to allow for terror suspects to be extradited and re-transferred among member states with minimal evidence of crimes. In response to the Urumqi riots, around 70 cases of forcible returns of Uyghurs to China were reported by human rights organizations on exactly those charges of terrorism and separatism (HRIC 2011a, appendix D).

When Robert Mugabe was faced with possible election loss in 2008, he unleashed loyal security forces to target members of the opposition party MDC and areas where support for the party had been strongest, while the government moved against civil society organizations and electoral officials. The opposition candidate withdrew; Mugabe won the second election round with 85.5 percent of the votes. Faced with atrocities in their midst, Zambia and Botswana called for a regional intervention to stop bloodshed in Zimbabwe, but were faced with strong pro-Mugabe alliances and unanimity requirements during summitry meetings. Instead, an SADC-led mediation mission was initiated that negotiated a power-sharing deal with the opposition party to secure Mugabe in power.

How Regional Organizations Sustain Authoritarian Rule. Maria J. Debre, Oxford University Press.
© Maria J. Debre (2025). DOI: 10.1093/9780198903635.003.0001

2   How Regional Organizations Sustain Authoritarian Rule

During Uganda's 2016 general election, Museveni invited election observers from the African Union (AU), East African Community (EAC), Common Market for Eastern and Southern Africa (COMESA), and Intergovernmental Authority on Development (IGAD). All noted that the elections were conducted in a free, peaceful, and transparent manner, only noting technical shortcomings with regard to delayed openings of polling stations. None commented on the democratic quality of the elections. In response to claims of intimidations by the European Union (EU) mission and an opposition candidate under house arrest, Museveni responded: "I don't need lectures from anybody on how to organize elections ... those Europeans are not serious" (in Biryabarema and Makori 2016).

Daniel Ortega, former military junta leader of Nicaragua, returned to power during contested elections in 2007 and quickly reverted the country to autocratic rule. In 2018, peaceful protests turned into the "Mother's Day massacre" when Sandinista Youth paramilitaries attacked, looted, and ransacked the capital. The money to finance this repressive regime comes from a mafia-like network of companies set up by the members of the Bolivarian Alliance for the Peoples of our America (ALBA) to funnel drug and oil money toward socialist allies (Adams and Aburto 2018). The country has been subject to heavy international sanctions. Ortega's rule is still thriving.

These examples of interferences of regional organizations (ROs) on the side of authoritarian regimes are part of a broader pattern of autocracies successfully battling challengers with regional help. They exemplify the scope and variety of ways that ROs can help to tip the scale in the favor of authoritarian incumbents during politically contentious moments. ROs have had a helping hand in defending autocratic regimes from pro-democratic protestors, in co-opting political elites, in legitimizing flawed elections, in constraining regional enemies, and in shielding against the fallout from international sanctions. While regionalism has long been associated with the aspiration of states to promote democracy and human rights, it is important to recognize and understand this dark side of cooperation.

This book attempts to shed light on the questions of why, how, and under what conditions membership in ROs can help autocratic incumbent regimes secure their hold on power. I argue that authoritarian regimes sort into *dictator clubs*—that is, ROs with predominantly authoritarian membership. During moments of political instability, dictator clubs help to successfully defend against domestic, regional, and international challenges, thereby reinforcing autocratic rule across the globe. This happens via distinct causal chains. ROs redistribute resources toward authoritarian elites that raise the cost of challenging behavior for the opposition, ROs regulate appropriate behavior among fellow members to prevent regional interference on the side of dissenting actors, and ROs protect regimes in case of international pressure and thereby lower the cost of employing repressive tactics. ROs are thus responsible for reinforcing authoritarian rule across the globe in important ways.

The International Dimension of Authoritarian Survival

I am certainly not the first scholar to argue that international factors are important in explaining domestic regime developments. Apart from a large body of literature focusing on the democratization effect of RO membership (e.g. Hafner-Burton et al. 2015; Pevehouse 2005a; Simmons 2009), scholars in recent years have also highlighted an international dimension to authoritarian regime stability and survival. Early literature on this question pointed out the unintended effects of international democracy promotion with democratic patronage (Brownlee 2007a, 2012), corruption around foreign aid (Kono and Montinola 2013a), and legitimizing effects of international sanctions protecting incumbents in power (Escribà-Folch and Wright 2010; Peksen and Drury 2010).

Comparativists, however, had started to identify collaboration *between* autocratic regimes as potential international influences on domestic regime developments (Tansey 2016a; von Soest 2015). Initially motivated by the argument of ideologically driven autocracy promotion by "authoritarian great powers" (Gat 2007a) and the fear about the potential establishment of an "authoritarian international" (Silitski 2010a), these scholars turned to study how regional powers try to shape and sustain autocracy in their immediate neighborhood. Focusing on the activities of China, Russia, Venezuela, and Saudi Arabia, studies soon pointed out that these regional hegemons were actively engaged in bolstering neighboring regimes by providing financial handouts, military equipment, and advice on effective election manipulation or opposition repression (Bader 2014; Kneuer et al. 2018; Tansey 2016a; Vanderhill 2013).

But research has produced mixed results on the effects of authoritarian powers in influencing regime developments in their neighborhood. Vanderhill (2013), for instance, concludes that Russia's efforts to draw Ukraine into the authoritarian camp have been futile due to the strong counter-efforts of European powers to support liberal coalitions during the 2004 elections. The long-term effects of Russia's failed strategy to integrate Ukraine into its authoritarian camp became painstakingly obvious with its unlawful invasion of the country in 2022. This has also been highlighted by scholars of EU external relations, who argue that support by autocratic regional powers may sometimes cause unintended backlash effects that strengthen liberal actors in targeted neighboring autocracies (Börzel 2015). Both in Moldova and Georgia, Russian pressure rather led to the empowerment of liberal pro-Western actors that signed accession agreements with the EU than successful empowerment of pro-Russian politicians (Risse and Babayan 2015).

These mixed results are also due to the strategic nature of bilateral relationships. Just like democracies cooperate with autocrats where it suits domestic preferences, autocrats sometimes put friendly relations over regime type. Russia has allowed democratic regime change in Kyrgyzstan to install a pro-Russian, anti-Western government (Aris 2012), Saudi Arabia has supported democratic regime change in Egypt in 2011 in the hope of establishing more favorable relations with a government run by the Sunni Muslim Brotherhood (Odinius and Kuntz 2015), and China has actively built relations with a number of parties in Mongolia to avoid the rise of Sino-phobic actors in their neighborhood (Bader 2014).

Institutionalist international organization (IO) scholarship, in turn, focused on the activities of authoritarian ROs to resist democratization, highlighting that autocratic regimes often exploit ROs for "regime-boosting" purposes (Söderbaum 2004). A host of strategies has so far been discussed, often involving in-depth studies of single ROs or policy fields. In these studies, ROs are found to help consolidate national sovereignty (Acharya 2016), to legitimize regimes domestically (Debre and Morgenbesser 2017; Fawn 2013; Libman and Obydenkova 2018; Yom 2014), to engage in rent-seeking activities to buy the loyalty of crony elites (Bach 2005; Herbst 2007; Libman and Obydenkova 2014), or to pursue cross-border policing (Cooley and Heathershaw 2017; Dukalskis 2021). In these accounts, however, institutions often play a minor role: they are means for hegemonic powers to funnel resources and force their will or they are conceived as paper tigers that are used to signal democratic commitment to domestic and international audiences.

Large-N and comparative studies that take institutions more seriously and could attest to the systematic effects of ROs for authoritarian regime survival are so far in short supply. Where efforts to quantify results do exist, they remain focused on single regions (Obydenkova and Libman 2019). Comparative case studies, in contrast, often fail to clearly connect regional dynamics and domestic politics to theorize and empirically test how RO membership can actually increase the likelihood of incumbent survival (Kneuer et al. 2018; Obydenkova and Libman 2019). While this regional-domestic link has been amply theorized within the study of Europeanization (Börzel 2016; Börzel and Risse 2003; Schimmelfennig and Sedelmeier 2005), this is still lacking with regard to regionalism and domestic politics in non-democratic regimes.

This is where this book adds to existing scholarship. To begin with, the book is theoretically encompassing by combining IO theories and comparativist scholarship. While research on authoritarian resilience is mostly conducted within comparative politics or area studies, IO research usually focuses on regional and global dynamics. This is not to deny that there is a long tradition studying the domestic politics of international cooperation (Fearon 1998; Martin 2000; Risse-Kappen 2017). But this research usually focuses on domestic factors as independent variables influencing international outcomes, from conflict behavior (Russett and Oneal 2001; Weeks 2008) to trade liberalization (Mansfield et al. 2000) or IO institutional design (Grigorescu 2015; Simmons and Danner 2010; Tallberg et al. 2013, 2016). Where IOs in turn serve as independent variables, the domestic outcome of interest is usually democratic regime change and human rights performance (Hafner-Burton et al. 2015; Pevehouse 2005a; Risse and Sikkink 1999; Simmons 2009). By explaining both *why* and *under which conditions* RO membership can increase the likelihood of authoritarian regime survival, and developing a model that specifies *how* autocratic ROs strengthen regime stability through three distinct mechanisms, the book thus expands our theoretical knowledge on the relationship between international and domestic politics outside the democratization paradigm.

The book is also empirically comprehensive through its broad comparative scope. It maps membership of the population of authoritarian regimes in ROs across all major world regions since the end of the Second World War in 1945. It covers 119 regimes, 72 ROs, 6 regions, and 75 years. The conclusions on the role of dictator clubs in global governance are thus placed on a broad empirical foundation. Where previous studies have only focused on the most prominent dictator clubs or on the role of major powers, this book shows that different types of ROs produce effects and that different types of autocratic regimes profit from membership. The book shows that membership in dictator clubs substantially extends the time in power for authoritarian incumbent regimes. The overall autocratic quality of the RO is also more important than homogenous membership: dictator clubs can support incumbent survival even if membership is characterized by heterogeneity among the membership. Even regional courts cannot constrain incumbents, with more authoritative dictator clubs being just as likely to increase incumbent survival compared to intergovernmental institutions.

The results also show that dictator clubs do not equally protect against all types of threats. While regional resources help to deter democratization, they cannot protect incumbent leaders from being overthrown by their own elites. The comparative nature of the book also reveals additional mechanisms. The dominant narrative of ROs as toothless paper tigers does not necessarily hold up to empirical inspection. ROs are sites where resources are pooled and redistributed, where member state positions have to be negotiated and adapted, and where global politics are reshaped. ROs can thus actively empower and constrain domestic, regional, and international actors.

Finally, the book is also methodologically inclusive through its nested research design. It provides the first statistical test of the effects of RO membership for authoritarian regime survival based on original data. The book thereby manages to identify macro-dynamics with regard to the development of dictator clubs and their political effects on incumbent survival. Dictator clubs have consistently outnumbered democratic ROs across the globe and play a major role in organizing regional cooperation in the Global South. Statistical modeling based on survival analysis also reveals that, overall, dictator clubs reinforce authoritarian regime survival over time and across regions, and that the size of the effect is substantive: autocrats who are members in a dictator club are up to six times more likely to survive compared to those who cannot count on such regional support.

The book, however, goes further. It also attests to micro-dynamics, studying the processes that produce the identified macro patterns. Three chapters focus on isolating the theorized mechanisms by zooming in on crisis moments during which authoritarian incumbents faced particularly challenging threats to their survival. This selection strategy helps to highlight the role that ROs can play to increase stabilization of authoritarian regimes and can therefore help to rectify the endogeneity problem besetting the study of IOs as independent variables in statistical research. The selected cases span all regions of the Global South, covering different types of authoritarian regimes as well as different forms of challenges. In combination, they can attest to the prominent role that RO membership plays to tip the scale in favor of autocratic incumbents, thereby reinforcing authoritarian resilience.

Defining the Concept: The Dictators' Club

The past 70 years have seen a remarkable transformation in regime trends across the world. While the 1970s to early 2000s were characterized by a persistent wave of democratization (Huntington 1993), the last two decades both saw former liberalizers turn into hybrid regimes (Levitsky and Way 2010) as well as many established dictators stabilize their power (Svolik 2012).

The debate on the extent of an authoritarian counter-wave is still ongoing (see Lührmann and Lindberg 2019; Skaaning 2020; Tomini 2021 for a critical debate on the extent of global autocratization). But with Freedom House declaring 2021 to be the 16th consecutive year of democratic decline, only 20 percent of the global population today live in free societies and functioning democracies are again in the minority (Repucci and Slipowitz 2022).

At the same time, regional institution building around the world had reached a peak by the turn of the century. By that point, almost every country—democratic or autocratic—was a member of at least one RO, and a growing body of research investigated the emergence, design, and effects of regional institutions (Börzel and Risse 2016a). A look at the development of regionalism since 1945 reveals that autocracies are particularly eager to cooperate regionally (see Figure 1.1). Out of 71 ROs analyzed in this book, organizations dominated by authoritarian member states almost double those of democratic organizations today.

The functions and effects of dictator clubs, however, are not well understood. Once we move to ROs outside the liberal-democratic world, we know surprisingly little about institutional cooperation and its domestic consequences. Why would autocrats want to institutionalize cooperation in the

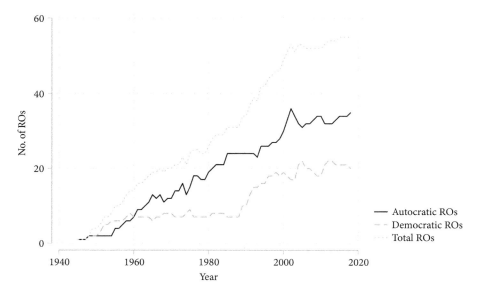

Figure 1.1 Number of ROs across time, 1945–2020 (own depiction based on Polity (Marshall et al. 2018)).

8 How Regional Organizations Sustain Authoritarian Rule

first place, thereby bearing possible sovereignty costs? Do dictator clubs differ from their democratic counterparts in terms of activities and design? And does membership in a dictator club produce domestic political effects?

This book is a response to these questions. Dictator clubs refer to ROs that are largely dominated by authoritarian member states. In statistical terms, dictator clubs are organizations with an autocratic density; that is, their membership is, on average, authoritarian. Authoritarianism, as further discussed in Chapter 2, is understood as a continuum in this book, dependent on the degree to which a regime holds free and fair multi-party elections and guarantees basic political and civil liberties. ROs, like regimes, can thus be more or less authoritarian depending on the overall composition of their membership.

Importantly, my concept of dictator clubs does not refer to the substantive content of RO charters and formal procedural rules. Dictator clubs can subscribe to democracy on paper, and in fact regularly exhibit shallow liberal norm commitment (Tallberg et al. 2020). They may still refrain from enforcing democratic elections among their membership or from protecting political and civil rights. In turn, democratic organizations can exhibit authoritarian practices. The North Atlantic Treaty Organization (NATO), for instance, scores relatively low in terms of transparency and offers basically no access for transnational non-governmental actors despite largely consisting of democratic members due to its security mandate (Grigorescu 2007; Tallberg et al. 2013). What I consider most important, therefore, is not necessarily the rules that are written out on paper but rather the practices that inform the cooperation between RO members and their political consequences.

Dictator clubs also differ profoundly from each other. There are those, like the GCC, that consist exclusively of highly authoritarian regimes without much development in terms of democratization or autocratization over their lifespan. These types of authoritarian ROs score high on autocratic density and homogeneity between member regimes. Then there are institutions that started out as dictator clubs but have seen a majority of their members democratize over time, like the Organization of American States (OAS). In between, there are hybrid ROs like the Organization of African Unity (OAU)/AU or the Economic Community of West African States (ECOWAS) that consist of a mix of hybrid regimes resulting in higher heterogeneity among their members.

Figure 1.2 shows the development of a select number of ROs across time, plotting the density (left axis) as well as the homogeneity (right axis) of their members based on the Polity IV measure (Marshall et al. 2018). Highly autocratic and highly democratic ROs, like the GCC and the EU, both have

Introduction 9

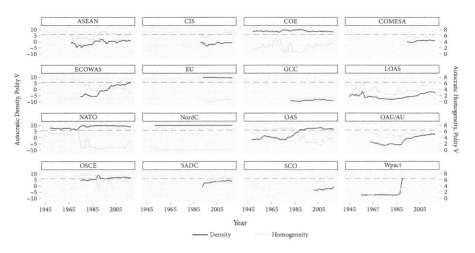

Figure 1.2 Autocratic density and homogeneity across time, 1945–2020 (own depiction based on Polity (Marshall et al. 2018)).

high homogeneity in common, while the democratic Organization for Security and Co-operation in Europe (OSCE) and authoritarian Southern African Development Community (SADC), for instance, share low homogeneity due to a mix of democratic and autocratic members. As long as their overall density falls below the threshold indicated in red in Figure 1.2 in a given year, I consider organizations as dictator clubs.[1]

The Argument in Brief: Dictator Clubs and Authoritarian Regime Survival

Having established how dictator clubs are defined, we can now move on to their political effects. This book attests to the important role that dictator clubs play in explaining domestic regime developments across the globe through their sorting and reinforcing effects (see Figure 1.3). The book establishes three important patterns with regard to the development, effects, and practices of dictator clubs over time and across regions.

First, democratic and autocratic regimes sort into distinct institutions. Regimes that successfully consolidated democracy during the third wave joined democratic clubs to lock in reforms (Mansfield and Pevehouse 2006,

---

[1] The threshold is set at a score of six on the polity scale, corresponding to the cut-off defined by the Polity project.

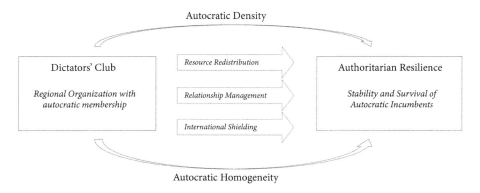

Figure 1.3 Argument in brief.

2008; Pevehouse 2005a; Poast and Urpelainen 2018). The democratic lock-in effect, however, mostly refers to the European and to a lesser extent also the Latin American experience. Former European dictatorships in the South like Spain and Greece, as well as the post-Soviet Eastern European states, joined the EU, the OSCE, and NATO to ensure successful democratization. Although the role of these organizations in preventing autocratization is currently under scrutiny (Kelemen 2020; Meyerrose 2020; Winzen 2023), their important role in supporting successful transitions during the third wave of democratization through membership and conditionality is undisputed. The OAS, in contrast, is one of the few examples of a RO that has successfully developed from a dictator club into a fully democratic institution, establishing institutional mechanisms to ensure democratic elections and establishing a broad human rights regime (Lohaus and Stapel 2022). The RO, however, is also unique in that highly democratic members (the US, Canada) and highly autocratic members simultaneously coexisted during previous decades.

In the rest of the world, few regimes are members in highly autocratic and democratic institutions at the same time. Exceptions are the OSCE, which was specifically enlarged with a democracy promotion agenda in mind (Galbreath 2007; Gawrich 2015), albeit lacking hard enforcement mechanisms (Kelley 2004). Many of the ROs in Sub-Saharan Africa, Eurasia, Asia, and the Middle East rather consist mostly of authoritarian members. Where regimes were able to successfully transition to and consolidate democracy in these regions, they remain in the minority. Overall, the homogeneity and authoritarian density among members of dictator clubs decreased over the years, but almost no ROs made a successful transition toward a fully democratic institution. Instead, the number of dictator clubs steadily rose over time, with more and more ROs founded by authoritarian regimes over the last decades.

Second, this sorting produces a reinforcing effect for regime type. Membership in dictator clubs alleviates future uncertainty associated with autocratic regime survival by protecting from domestic, regional, and international challengers. While political survival is a common goal to all regime types, strategies to achieve it differ significantly between democracies and autocracies. These differing domestic preferences also matter when it comes to international cooperation: while democracies tend to design and employ ROs to protect democratic governance in their region, autocracies will do the same with regard to stabilizing authoritarian rule.

Membership in a dictators' club significantly increases the likelihood of authoritarian regime survival over time and across regions. The effect is particularly pronounced with regard to autocratic density. Being a member of a highly autocratic dictator club increases the chances of survival by more than six times compared to membership in a RO with low autocratic density. Similarly, homogeneity among members matters but does not moderate the effect of density. Two similarly autocratic dictator clubs with varying diversity both still lower the hazard of regime failure for their autocratic members.

Interestingly, RO membership only protects from democratic challenges such as large-scale public demonstrations or oppositional dissent that aim to remove the authoritarian regime in power and establish an alternative democratic system. In contrast, membership in a dictators' club does not help to prevent successful autocratic challenges such as military coups that only aim to replace the current autocratic leader without changing the underlying power distributions. Democratic regime change as a threat often diffuses across regions and thus has potential ripple effects for other RO members, who try to prevent this type of challenge from crossing borders by offering solidarity to incumbent regime coalitions.

Finally, the reinforcing effect happens through three distinct mechanisms. First, RO membership creates *distributional consequences* for domestic politics. By pooling and redistributing material and immaterial resources, ROs can help boost domestic survival strategies of autocratic incumbents vis-à-vis domestic challengers. ROs can confer *legitimacy* to authoritarian incumbents by publicly supporting them, thereby preventing challengers from successfully contesting a dictator's right to rule. Material resources such as development aid can be used to *co-opt* key political, social, and business elites to prevent elite splits and intra-elite challenges. Finally, security cooperation in the military and intelligence field can boost domestic *repressive capacities* to constrain oppositional actors and dissidents or even quash large-scale protest. In total, autocratic incumbents gain more political security during crisis moments due to their membership in autocratic clubs.

Second, ROs engage in *relationship management* by regulating appropriate behavior among the members of the dictator club, thereby preventing them from unwanted interference in domestic affairs. Although authoritarian ROs exhibit varying degrees of authority in terms of pooled decision-making or delegated competences to their secretariats, autocratic clubs usually hold to their post-colonial origins and protect sovereignty and non-interference rights as central cooperation norms. Protecting sovereignty rights becomes particularly important in cases of heterogenous RO membership, where some members of the club might have democratized during the third wave. Given that democratizing states are particularly likely to lobby for conditionality rights for the RO to lock in democratic reform, protecting non-interference norms within ROs is essential for the remaining authoritarian regimes within the club. This constraining effect of institutionalized sovereignty protection allows autocratic incumbents to exercise costly domestic survival strategies against political challengers such as repressive tactics or election manipulation without the danger of democratic neighboring states interfering on the side of challengers.

Third, being a member of the club also helps to *shield* autocratic incumbents from the fallout of international pressure. Employing domestic survival strategies from electoral manipulation to violent repression are costly and often cause international condemnation or even (the threat of) sanctions. To prevent this type of pressure, members of the club often try to intervene in international fora to argue against measures carrying reputational or material costs. Should sanctions be enacted after all, ROs can step in and act as "black knights" and provide goods and service to help the sanctioned regime stay in power.

One important caveat should be mentioned here. ROs in the Global South of course serve other important functions apart from reinforcing authoritarian rule. Many of the ROs studied in this book have been created in the wake of post-colonialism to promote the sovereignty of newly independent states (Acharya 2016; Getachew 2019). ROs serve as mediators during intrastate conflicts to prevent the spread of negative externalities during civil war (Haftel 2012; Haftel and Hofmann 2017). ROs are also important actors to tackle humanitarian response after disasters. In fact, during the Covid-19 pandemic, ROs in the Global South were the primary organizations to successfully orchestrate early responses (Debre and Dijkstra 2021a). To argue that ROs sustain authoritarian rule does not negate that they might simultaneously fulfill important functions for their member states that we might consider as normatively good. This book, however, does not systematically test the explanatory power of different explanations for the emergence of regionalism or their institutional design, or the effect of ROs on other policy areas. Rather, it focuses on the consequences that different ROs have for regime developments in their member states.

The Research Design: A Mixed-Methods Approach

This book builds on a nested research design, combining statistical analysis with in-depth comparative case study research (Lieberman 2005a; Seawright 2016; Weller and Barnes 2016). While the quantitative analysis maps long-term dynamics among the population of authoritarian regimes and their membership in ROs and can engage in comparative hypothesis-testing, the qualitative components focus on tracing underlying processes in a select number of cases. The research design can therefore attest both to overall macro-dynamics and to micro-processes in an encompassing manner.

Data for the quantitative part comes from an original dataset including information on membership of 119 autocratic regimes in 72 ROs between 1946 and 2020. ROs are sampled from the Yearbook of International Organizations (UiA) database, and include all multi-purpose ROs with a political mandate across the globe. Authoritarian regime transitions are taken from the Autocratic Breakdown and Regime Transitions dataset (Geddes et al. 2014, 2018), which codes both instances of democratic regime change and autocratic replacements among the population of authoritarian regimes larger than 1 million inhabitants from 1945 to 2010. Based on this coding, I expand the data until 2020 for this book to allow for a more up-to-date analysis. The two main independent variables, autocratic density and homogeneity, are based on data from the Polity project (Marshall et al. 2018) as well as Varieties of Democracy (Coppedge et al. 2015, 2020). They are supplemented with original data on RO institutional design and mandates to account for RO authority.

This dataset is used to map the development of ROs across time and space with regard to their density, homogeneity, and authority. It also forms the basis of an extended survival analysis (Cox 1972). Survival models are a particularly well suited set of methods to analyze the time until the occurrence of an event, in this case the breakdown of autocratic rule. Survival models allow for competitive hypothesis-testing, estimating how a set of covariates change the underlying hazards of an event occurring at a specific point in time. They are also specifically advantageous to deal with issues of right-censoring, which is important since countries are only observed until 2020 but may not have experienced a breakdown event until that point in time.

The statistical relationships come alive in three subsequent chapters that test the proposed mechanisms in qualitative case studies. The cases covered in these chapters span four different regions, covering a wide variation of dictator clubs, from the homogenously autocratic GCC to the SCO, and from ALBA to the heterogeneous SADC. The qualitative in-depth analysis focuses on contentious moments in the lives of authoritarian members of these four ROs, where the survival of an incumbent regime was at stake. This allows me to better assess the role that the RO played in averting challengers and how different mechanisms produce stability and survival.

Data for the case study analysis comes from three different types of sources. Where available, I sourced official documents, statements, publications, and press releases provided by the RO and member states under analysis that are available online or through archives. I furthermore use media reporting by national, regional, and international outlets through the Nexis-Uni database to establish event timelines. Finally, reports by non-governmental organizations assessing situations during contentious moments on the ground like Amnesty International or Human Rights Watch are used to triangulate results.

Implications: Liberal Paradigm, IO Institutional Design, and the Crisis of the Liberal Order

What are the implications of these results for our understanding of democratization, authoritarian resilience, and the liberal international order? To begin with, scholars have mostly studied international influences on domestic regime developments from a liberal paradigm based on the experiences of democratic nation states in the Global North. Inspired by the *end of history* (Fukuyama 1989), a large body of literature around the turn of the century focused on the role of ROs in advancing democratization and improving the human rights performance of authoritarian regimes. According to liberalist understandings, ROs both serve *ex ante* and *ex post* functions (Martin 2000, 2017). They provide liberalizing member states with the opportunity to "lock in" democratic reform by changing the cost–benefit calculations of domestic elites, by offering the opportunity to signal credible commitments to other democracies, or by socializing key actors into democracy-accepting roles (Fearon 1997; Hafner-Burton et al. 2015; Pevehouse 2005a). But democratizing states also delegate authority to IOs to reduce uncertainty about a possible future reversal of policies. By delegating sanctioning capacity to IOs, they can commit future governments to human rights standards and prevent potential autocratic challengers from successfully reversing policies in the future (Moravcsik 2000; Simmons 2009; Simmons and Danner 2010; Tallberg et al. 2016).

An important contribution of this book is to shift the focus toward studying the role of ROs in sustaining authoritarian rule. Once we move to organizations that are largely dominated by authoritarian members, the functions of ROs also shift. While democratic ROs such as the EU, NATO, and the OSCE have traditionally engaged in promoting and protecting democracy at home and abroad (Schimmelfennig and Sedelmeier 2005; Whitehead 1996), dictator clubs, as this book shows, do the opposite. They help to alleviate future uncertainty associated with authoritarian regime survival by redistributing resources, constraining unilateral interventions of neighbors, and shielding from international pressure, thereby future-proofing authoritarian club members.

Second, regime type has been proposed as a major explanatory factor of regional integration outcomes by scholarship on institutional design of ROs and IOs (Acharya and Johnston 2007a; Börzel and van Hüllen 2015; Obydenkova and Libman 2019; Söderbaum 2004; Tallberg et al. 2016). These works show that authoritarian regimes tend to favor more intergovernmental and consensual forms of cooperation compared to democracies. Building on this scholarship, my book shifts the focus from questions surrounding the design of ROs to their domestic consequences. By offering both over-time comparative statistical evidence and in-depth case studies covering all major regions of the Global South, the book highlights the long-term domestic effects that different types of cooperative agreements have for regime trajectories.

Third, current debates in comparative and international relations scholarship circle around the crisis of the liberal international order due to endogenous challenges from within democracies. One camp argues that the rising authority of IOs paired with a technocratic style of decision-making diminishes IO legitimacy, thereby eliciting popular backlash (Börzel and Zürn 2021; Zürn 2018). Another camp sees growing multipolarity and declining US hegemony as a major driver of contestation from within, leading to disengagement from IOs (Choi 2021; Ikenberry 2011, 2020; von Borzyskowski and Vabulas 2019a). In contrast, this book takes an outside perspective. By highlighting the sorting and stabilizing effects of ROs, the book shows how developments outside the liberal camp further add to the global crisis of liberal internationalism. Dictator clubs normalize authoritarian practices at

16 How Regional Organizations Sustain Authoritarian Rule

home and abroad and serve as a regional stepping stone to further contest political liberalism on the international scene.

Plan of the Book

The theoretical argument of the book will be laid out in Chapter 2 to elaborate why, under which conditions, and how RO membership can help to increase the likelihood of authoritarian regime survival. To substantiate the theoretical argument, the book builds on a nested research design, combining statistical analysis with comparative case study research. Chapter 3 introduces the dataset and presents descriptive statistics on the development of dictator clubs across time and regions. The chapter pays particular attention to the development of ROs with regard to their density, heterogeneity, and authority, the three conditions hypothesized to affect domestic regime survival. It establishes that dictator clubs have become slightly less autocratic but more heterogeneous and authoritative over time. However, few ROs change category once established, turning from highly autocratic to fully democratic clubs. The chapter also presents an update on the Autocratic Breakdown and Regime Transition dataset by Geddes, Wright, and Frantz (2014, 2018), with new data coded on the population of authoritarian regimes for the decade 2010 to 2020.

Building on this dataset, Chapter 4 engages in survival analysis to study the extent to which membership in ROs prolongs the time in office for autocratic incumbents. The chapter presents the statistical modeling technique and introduces further independent variables that control for relevant alternative explanations pertaining to international- and domestic-level arguments from international relations and comparative authoritarianism research. The chapter then continues to investigate results from the different estimations and shows that across time and space, membership in ROs with higher autocratic density significantly reduced the hazard of experiencing democratic breakdown. Autocrats who are members of a dictator club have a six times lower likelihood of losing power because of democratic regime change compared to those who are not members of such an RO. In contrast, other international explanations including close relationships with authoritarian powers, authority of institutions, and diffusion of authoritarian practices cannot systematically account for authoritarian survival.

Chapter 5 turns to the first hypothesized mechanism of *resource redistribution*. It builds on a most-different system design to show how ROs help to prevent democratization during moments of political crisis. The chapter analyzes democratic challenges in Bahrain, Zimbabwe, and China, ranging from public protest during the Arab Spring to election loss of revolutionary parties in Southern Africa and ethnic dissident by Uighur minorities in Eurasia. By carefully tracing over-time development of these events, the chapter demonstrates that various regional resources employed by the GCC, the SADC, and the SCO helped to tip the scale in favor of autocratic incumbents by providing material and immaterial resources.

Chapter 6 investigates the second mechanism, *relationship management*. It shows how ROs prevent interference by regional challengers such as fellow RO member states, RO bureaucrats, and regional non-state actors on the side of democratic challengers, and why they do not protect dictators who face intra-elite challengers. Through a within-case design, the chapter explains how norms of sovereignty enshrined by the SADC, alliances between former liberation movements, and consensual decision-making constrained different regional challengers from successfully moving against the Mugabe regime. In 2002, South Africa and the SADC prevented the publication of the so-called "Khampepe report," an independent report on the electoral proceedings in Zimbabwe by two South African judges. In 2008, the SADC prevented Zambia and Botswana from militarily intervening on the side of the Zimbabwean opposition. Instead, the SADC helped to confer legitimacy to the troubled regime and brokered a deal with the opposition party to keep Mugabe in power. Finally, the SADC also intervened when the Tribunal decided against the Mugabe regime in a landmark ruling in 2008, and later reformed and heavily curtailed the rights of the court. In contrast, the SADC did not offer similar support to Mugabe when his own party cronies removed him from power in the 2017 military coup, but stayed on the sidelines once it was clear that Mugabe's former second-in-command would continue the rule of the dominant part. Factors that had previously played in favor of Mugabe—consensual decision-making, strong non-interference norms, and the solidarity of revolutionary parties—now played against the increasingly unpopular liberation hero. The dominant ZANU-PF party survived; Mugabe had to go.

Chapter 7 turns to the *shielding effect* of ROs. It analyzes how ROs help to decrease the cost of international sanctions in a most-similar system design. The chapter compares how Nicaraguan President Ortega was able to employ costly survival strategies ranging from electoral manipulation to protest repression through the help of ALBA and later the regional Central American development bank CABEI. While neighboring Honduras quickly faced regional and international pressure in response to a lifting of presidential term limits in 2015 and contentious elections in 2017, ALBA members intervened on the side of Ortega in international fora, provided unconditional financial support through the Petrocaribe agreement and development aid, and challenged the legitimacy of the OAS and its human rights mechanism in a lengthy reform process. With the help of regional allies, Ortega has since consolidated his authoritarian power and established a repressive regime in a former success story of democratization.

Finally, summarizing the relevant findings, the concluding Chapter 8 reflects on the important implications of these findings for the state of the liberal international order and for the future development of democracy across the globe. Regimes tend to form clubs and sort into distinct types of ROs that each work to reinforce a respective regime type. Even though countries in Latin America, Western Africa, or Southeast Asia have experienced democratization during the third wave, their continued membership in dictator clubs makes them prone to backsliding and re-autocratization and prevents them from developing meaningful regional instruments to protect democratic governance. In combination with growing challenges to democratic rule from within established democratic organizations by populist coalitions and a global retreat of US hegemonic power, the fate of democracy remains more unclear than ever.

2

The Dictators' Club

Theorizing Regional Organization Membership and Regime Survival

Why do autocrats decide to join formal organizations and bear the associated sovereignty costs? In what ways do autocratic regional organizations (ROs) differ from ROs with predominantly democratic membership? Does membership in ROs actually prolong the time in power for autocratic incumbents, and if so, does it help all incumbents equally? And how exactly can RO membership help incumbents increase their survival chances when faced with politically challenging situations?

In this chapter, I develop a theoretical framework to explain *why, how, and under which conditions* membership in ROs helps autocratic regimes secure their hold on power. I develop this framework in four steps. I first discuss the demand for in stitutionalized cooperation between authoritarian regimes rooted in functional considerations of authoritarian domestic survival politics. I continue with a discussion of the concept of regime type, the differentiation of stability and survival, and my conceptualization of survival politics of authoritarian regimes. Building on this conceptualization of survival politics, I describe the three distinct causal mechanisms of regime-boosting by which ROs strengthen autocratic incumbent regimes' survival strategies. Finally, I explain under which conditions RO membership can help to prolong time in power for autocratic incumbent elites by positing three hypotheses on the role of autocratic density, preference homogeneity, and international authority.

The Demand for Institutionalized Cooperation among Autocracies

Institutionalist international relations (IR) theory locates the demand for formalized cooperation on the systemic level, arguing that international organizations (IOs) help member states to solve cross-border issues, reduce

How Regional Organizations Sustain Authoritarian Rule. Maria J. Debre, Oxford University Press.
© Maria J. Debre (2025). DOI: 10.1093/9780198903635.003.0002

uncertainty, and create mutual gains (Abbott and Snidal 1998; Keohane 1984). Systemic institutionalist theorists mostly disregard the question of regime type. For them, interdependencies drive cooperation, and the question of whether autocracies and democracies might be equally willing and able to commit to formal cooperation is left untouched. However, due to informal and nontransparent politics, autocracies are considered to differ from democracies "in terms of their mutual suspicions and divergences, and inherent difficulties in working together as voluntary and mutually trusting partners" (Whitehead 2014, p. 23). Autocracies might thus be perceived as more likely to renege on their international commitments by democratic counterparts, which would impinge on the likelihood of cooperation even in cases of high interdependencies and potential mutual gains.

In power-based variants of systemic institutional theory, international cooperation is driven by a hegemon's international interest (Gilpin 1981; Ikenberry 2001). In this narrative, the regime type of the hegemon matters greatly. As Ikenberry argues, the United States was responsible for building an American-led liberal international order based on a web of multilateral institutions that not only served American domestic interests but also helped to spread liberal values globally (see also Kagan 2012). With declining US hegemony and rising illiberal powers, the liberal order is, however, increasingly considered to be in crisis (Ikenberry 2011, 2020; Kagan 2008). The extent of the crisis (Eilstrup-Sangiovanni and Hofmann 2019) and its main drivers (see, for instance, Goddard et al. 2024; Mearsheimer 2019; Zürn 2018 on different types of endogenous arguments) might be hotly debated. However, there is little disagreement that the liberal international order was always contested by illiberal powers, and that their role in building alternative orders and illiberal institutions is not well understood.

Approaches that incorporate domestic politics to explain the demand to form and join IGOs explicitly built on regime type in their argumentation. To domestic politics scholars, foreign policy preferences of states are driven by "two-level games" (Putnam 1988): governments try to cater to domestic coalitions by creating IGOs and delegating authority to an international agent (Koremenos et al. 2001; Moravcsik 1997; Voeten 2019). This argument has been taken up by the literature on democratization, arguing that IGOs and particularly ROs can help liberalizing member states to credibly commit to democratic policies domestically (Hafner-Burton et al. 2015; Moravcsik 2000). Since liberalizing regimes usually face high uncertainty regarding the credibility of their reform efforts during democratic transitions, they can join democratic ROs to signal to domestic audiences that they are committed to democratization (Fearon 1997; Mansfield and Pevehouse 2006, 2008; Martin 1993). Newly established democracies also benefit from membership in the long run because external monitoring and sanctioning mechanisms tie the hands of future governments and prevent policy reversals (Martin 2017; Pevehouse 2005a). To what extent this logic lives up to empirical realities is a matter of much debate: Meyerrose (2020), for instance, argues that IO assistance has contributed to current backsliding because it has prioritized executives and elections over other important democratic actors. Kelemen (2020) similarly shows that the European Union (EU) finds itself in an "autocracy trap" whereby the gains from an open single market now help autocrats like Orban to consolidate authoritarian rule.

However, domestic politics accounts only theorize why joining IGOs might be beneficial for democratic and liberalizing regimes without specifically addressing how autocracies might benefit domestically from RO membership. In the wake of the third wave of democratization, theorizing followed the trend of former autocracies joining democratic clubs. Against this backdrop, the main task was to study if and how IO membership could be beneficial to democratic regime change. Authoritarian cooperation, in contrast, was mostly characterized as dysfunctional (e.g. Mansfield et al. 2008; Gray and Slapin 2012; Gray 2018; see Acharya 2016 for a discussion on functionalism and its application to non-EU regionalism).

With rising numbers of authoritarian regional institutions, functionalist scholars started to suspect that there was rationality behind the dysfunctionality. They argued that ROs dominated by authoritarian regimes were never meant to engage in meaningful integration of markets, in providing public goods, or in protection of democracy and human rights (Acharya and Johnston 2007a; Börzel and van Hüllen 2015; Söderbaum 2004). When dictators like Mugabe and Gaddafi met during summitry sessions of the Organization of African Unity, they signaled to the world and their own constituencies that they are engaged presidents committed to regional integration and good governance—without, however, having to put pen to paper.

In these functionalist accounts, authoritarian ROs are intentionally "designed to fail" (Barnett and Solingen 2007). They are paper tigers that protect sovereignty by signaling commitment and averting international pressure. Summitry meetings are mostly for show (Söderbaum 2004a), conventions remain shallow without deeper norm commitment (Tallberg et al. 2020), and states refrain from any meaningful delegation of powers to regional agents (Acharya and Johnston 2007b). But these functionalist accounts provide too narrow a view of authoritarian ROs. After all, institutionalizing cooperation, even in the shallowest form, carries sovereignty costs

(Hafner-Burton et al. 2015). Why would autocratic regimes set up and join ROs and bear these costs when they could just as well rely on declaratory statements to signal the same commitment, but without the hassle of bargaining for and financing institutions with headquarters, bureaucracies, and regular meetings?

The argument advanced in this book is a functional approach that puts more emphasis on the domestic survival politics of authoritarian regimes. According to this perspective, authoritarian ROs are not only "cheap talk" meant to reduce international pressure by maximizing national sovereignty. ROs are also a means to actively further member states' strategic and normative domestic preferences (Voeten 2019), one of which is political survival (Bueno de Mesquita et al. 2003). ROs, according to this perspective, are opportunity structures that actively constrain and empower different domestic and international actors by redistributing resources and offsetting costs associated with achieving political survival. Thereby, authoritarian ROs play a much more central and active role in reinforcing authoritarian rule across the globe compared to conceptualizations in mainstream functional accounts.

This view of ROs as opportunity structures stems from rationalist scholarship that investigates the constraining effects of international institutions for domestic and foreign politics of member states. Goldstein (1996), for instance, shows how the North American Free Trade Agreement (NAFTA) has served the US presidency to constrain Congress as a veto player and Aspinwall (2009) argues that NAFTA has empowered civil society actors in less-developed member states while simultaneously constraining executive authorities. In a similar vein, scholarship on Europeanization conceptualizes domestic changes in member states as differential empowerment of some actors over others through resource redistribution (Börzel and Risse 2003).

This is also applicable to ROs in non-democratic settings where autocratic players want to constrain political challengers with the help of ROs. For autocratic incumbents, taking advantage of RO membership becomes particularly important when domestic, regional, or international actors challenge their hold on power. During these moments of political upheaval, additional regional support strengthening survival strategies can help to tip the scale in favor of incumbent regimes, thereby making an important contribution to mitigate threats and increase the likelihood of survival. To autocrats, RO membership thus helps to alleviate future uncertainty by actively contributing to strengthening domestic and international survival strategies.

Authoritarian Regimes and Political Survival

Democracy, Autocracy, and Regime Transitions

The last statement opens two important questions: what exactly do I mean when talking about political survival and survival strategies of authoritarian regimes, and how should we define regimes and the difference between democracy and autocracy in the first place? A straightforward definition of autocracy is problematic because authoritarianism is often understood negatively either in contrast to totalitarianism (Linz 2000) or in terms of a residual category encompassing all non-democratic forms of rule (e.g. Cheibub et al. 2010).[1] Additionally, it is also disputed whether measurements should consider democracy as a continuous variable reaching from liberal democracy to totalitarianism—that is, encompassing autocracy—or as two dichotomous categories of democracy versus autocracy (Köllner 2008).

In principle, I regard democracy as an institutional quality that is a matter of degree. Dichotomous conceptualizations fail to recognize that both within the category of democratic states and among all non-democratic countries we can observe large differences in democratic quality (Coppedge et al. 2011). As Coppedge et al. convincingly argue, binary measures put countries such as Sweden and Turkey in the same democratic category, while both show obvious variation in the quality of elections, competition, or civil and human rights protection. Likewise, countries like Saudi Arabia and Tanzania are both considered as different variants of autocratic rule, although the degree of participation and political freedom varies greatly between the two.[2]

Following Dahl's (1971) definition of polyarchy, I thus consider the two basic qualifying criteria of democratic systems to be public contestation (i.e. competitive elections) and inclusiveness (i.e. broad suffrage), advanced by basic political and civil rights. Depending on the degree of those criteria, all regimes can be sorted on a continuum, encompassing democratic, autocratic, and totalitarian forms of rule. Thus, democracy and autocracy form part of a larger category of political rule, broadly understood as who holds power (public vs. small elite).

---

[1] While some differentiate between the terms authoritarianism (a form of government in which power is concentrated on a small group) and autocracy (power lies within one person), I will use both terms interchangeably.

[2] The Democracy and Dictatorship (DD) index by Cheibub, Ghandi, and Vreeland (Cheibub et al. 2010), for instance only, differentiates between democracy and dictatorships based on the contested election of the chief executive and legislature, without making any more qualifying criteria to qualitative differences within both broad categories.

With continuous conceptualizations of democracy, one of the central questions is how to define the threshold between democratic and non-democratic forms of rule. Inductive approaches include methods such as factor or latent-variable analysis (Coppedge et al. 2011, p. 250), while others, such as the method employed by the Polity Project, rely on pre-determined forms of aggregation and categorization (Marshall et al. 2018). Some conceptualizations of democracy from the literature on democratization consider a turnover of government in a democratic election or even an alternation as basic criteria of a successful transition toward democracy. Such a conceptualization has, for example, been introduced by Cheibub et al. (2010) to differentiate between instances of liberalization and democratic consolidation. Yet, this criterion is highly questionable given the fact that democratic turnover is not a regular feature of many consolidated democracies (e.g. Wahman et al. 2013, p. 22). The important aspect of reaching a threshold of democracy is that the opposition has the possibility of competing in elections, which is captured by the concept of competitiveness. As I am also not primarily concerned with processes of democratic consolidation, but only with potential instances of autocratic breakdown, a turnover or alternation rule as a qualifying criterion for the threshold is unnecessary.

To further define power relations within democratic and autocratic systems, we need to clarify the term regime, understood as the specific set of formal and/or informal rules for choosing leaders and policies (Geddes et al. 2014, p. 314ff.). According to Fishman, "a regime determines who has access to political power, and how those, who are in power, deal with those who are not" (1990, p. 428). This conceptualization of regime follows the argument by Bueno de Mesquita et al. (2003) that the leadership group that makes the key policy decisions is central in understanding the functioning of political systems.

However, Bueno de Mesquita et al. define the size of the leadership group (*winning coalition*) in relation to the *selectorate* as the central aspect to understanding survival in power. In contrast, I follow Geddes, Wright, and Frantz (Geddes et al. 2014, p. 335) in their argument that we need to primarily focus on the interests represented within the leadership group, as well as the power distribution and decision-making procedures that define who can rise to power to differentiate between different regime types, and their ability to survive. If we can define whose interest is represented within the leadership group (e.g. public, military, royal family), and who can become part of the leadership group, we can better differentiate not only between democratic and autocratic regimes but also between democratic and autocratic sub-types. Finally, while the differentiation between autocratic and democratic systems is a matter of degree, the differentiation between different types of autocratic regimes does not correspond to a variation in degree, but is a matter of categorization. In fact, degrees of democratic quality can vary both within and between types of authoritarian regimes, as they do between different types of democracy (Geddes et al. 2014, p. 319).

To conclude, according to the above definitions of democracy, autocracy, and regime, a political system would be considered autocratic when a certain threshold condition—that is, minimal public contestation and inclusiveness—is not met. That is to say, the executive leadership group is chosen by undemocratic means, and the people who can rise to power are limited to the elite whose interest is represented in the leadership group. In a democratic regime, the interest represented in the leadership group is that of the general public and any citizen can potentially rise to power. Furthermore, depending on whose interest is represented in an autocratic regime, we can further differentiate between different *types* of autocratic regimes, such as military, party, personal, or monarchy. This means that a regime that primarily draws its leadership from military ranks is considered a military regime, a regime that relies on hereditary succession would be considered a monarchy, and so forth.

To illustrate the differentiation between types of regimes, consider the example of Egypt. At its foundation, Egypt was an autocratic monarchy under King Farouk. When the king was overthrown by Nasser in 1952, Egypt turned into a so-called triple-threat party-personal-military regime. The differentiation is made according to the main interests represented within the leadership group, which changed from those of the royal family under Farouk to those of the dominant party (the National Democratic Party), the military, and the autocratic leader himself under Nasser. Even though the autocratic leadership went from Nasser to Sadat and Mubarak in subsequent decades, the principles of interest representation in the leadership group did not change until the popular uprisings in 2011. Thus, the same type of regime was in power from 1952 until 2011. With the ousting of Mubarak, a democratic regime was established that allowed for democratic elections of a new leadership group. With the military coup in 2013, the regime type changed again to autocratic military.

Regime Stability and Survival

Now that we have defined the main difference between democracy, autocracy, and authoritarian regime types, we can move on to define what we mean when we talk about regime stability and survival. In the literature, stability and survival are frequently used interchangeably with persistence, durability, longevity, endurance, stability, or resilience, often without much specification of underlying concepts. Political stability can refer to several underlying concepts and operationalizations, such as the absence of violence, governmental longevity, the absence of structural change, the existence of a legitimate constitutional regime, norm-conforming behavior, or a combination defining stability as a multifaceted societal attribute (Dowding and Kimber 1983; Hurwitz 1973). Regarding authoritarian stability, studies mostly operationalize the concept as referring to longevity, meaning the average time dimension during which regimes ruled a country uninterruptedly (e.g. Brownlee 2007b).

Yet, this conceptualization is inadequate. Simply equating stability with the time a regime has been in power doesn't correctly reflect the basic notion of the concept. First, longevity equates any change of regime or government with a loss in stability, and is thus unable to differentiate between voluntary and forced changes (Hurwitz 1973). Second, longevity as mere duration in office is a very static measure that may rather be indicative of resistance to adapt—which could be considered the exact opposite of stability (ibid.). In contrast to these conceptualizations, I understand stability as the ability of a political system to effectively deal with challenges and demands from the environment, and to effectively adapt to them (Easton 1965). To use Dowding and Kimber's (1983, p. 238f) more specific definition:

> Political stability is the state in which a political object exists when it possesses the capacity to prevent contingencies from forcing its non-survival, that is, from forcing a change in one or more of that object's criteria of identification.

Thus, political stability describes the ability of a political system or any part of it to effectively deal with real or potential threats to one or more of its most basic characteristics. For instance, since the identifying criterion of authoritarian rule is the absence of minimal conditions of public contestation and inclusiveness, an autocratic system can be considered stable when it has the capacity to deal with any threat that might force a change of rule toward minimally democratic elections with broad suffrage. A specific kind of authoritarian regime can in turn be considered stable if it has the capacity to uphold the rules that define whose interests are represented in the leadership group. For instance, a monarchical regime would be stable when it has the capacity to effectively deal with threats to its royal rule emanating, for example, from other elite groups such as the military.

While stability can be understood as the status quo, stabilization refers to the process toward achieving (more) stability (Gerschewski 2013). I argue that the process of stabilization in authoritarian regimes can be conceptualized as building the capacity to effectively enact survival strategies that deal with internal and external threats. Survival strategies can be thought of as the "game plan" of autocratic regimes to ensure a hold on power. They encompass strengthening institutional (polity), regulative (policy), and procedural (politics) capacities to prevent threats from materializing, and to successfully deal with challengers during moments of political upheaval.

It is further necessary to distinguish the concept of stability from the concept of survival. Although approaches and models to authoritarian resilience are manifold, they all share one similar axiomatic assumption: the most important goal of any person or group in power is political survival (Bueno de Mesquita et al. 2003). Survival refers to "the continuity of those elements by which that object is identified" (Dowding and Kimber 1983, p. 237). To illustrate the difference, a democratic regime is stable if it has the capacity to deal with potential or acute threats to one or more of its basic identifying criteria, for example institutional checks that prevent an incumbent government from limiting regular, free, and fair elections. The democratic regime survives as long as those identifying criteria are upheld; it breaks down when minimal conditions of contestation or inclusiveness are no longer met. Thus, stability refers to a property of regimes, stabilization is the process by which this property is strengthened, and survival refers to the successful outcome of this process.

According to Dowding and Kimber (1983), stability and survival are not dependent on one another; that is, stability is not a necessary condition of survival. A political system may not have the capacity to deal with a threat, but if that threat never occurs, the system can survive in a state of unstable persistence (p. 241). While I agree with their argument that stability is not a necessary condition of survival, I would nonetheless argue that a state of latent instability reduces the probability that a system may survive in the future (unless the threat is highly unlikely to ever materialize). Therefore, I assume that stability increases the probability of survival in the future.

There are three possible outcomes that survival can potentially refer to:

(1) Simply put, survival means that the autocratic leader stays in power. When he[3] is replaced, this would count as an instance of breakdown.

---

[3] Throughout the book, I refer to autocratic leaders in the male form, given that there are basically no female autocratic leaders, either historically or in the present.

However, just because a leader is removed from power, this does not necessarily mean the end of autocratic rule or a change of regime type. Often, an autocratic leader is simply replaced by a different leader, mostly even from the same elite group. This frequently happens in monarchies, where a new king or queen follows the previous one based on a clearly defined hereditary line of succession to ensure the continuity of the current regime. Leadership survival will therefore not be considered as an instance of regime survival going forward.

(2) Survival can also mean an absence of democratic system transition. To investigate the phenomenon of resilient authoritarianism, most studies inspired by democratization research are interested in instances of transition from an autocratic to a democratic regime. The moment of transition thus marks the instance of authoritarian breakdown and the beginning of democratization. In the following, I will refer to this type of survival as autocratic system survival, and breakdowns as democratic regime change, or *democratization*.

(3) Lastly, survival can also refer to a lack of autocratic replacements. Since Geddes's (2003) study on the effect of regime type on durability, many studies are also concerned with variation in resilience of different types of authoritarian regimes. In this literature, survival hence refers to autocratic regime survival; that is, the absence of transitions from one type of autocratic regime (e.g. monarchy) to another (e.g. military). In the following, this type of autocratic regime change will be referred to as *autocratic replacements*.

In summary: authoritarian resilience as an umbrella concept refers to both stability and survival capacity of regimes. Stability denotes the capacity of a system to deal with threats to its basic identifying criteria, while survival is understood as the continuity of these criteria. I assume that stability and survival are not entirely independent concepts but that stability is a facilitating factor that increases the probability of survival in the future. Stabilization in turn refers to the processes of strengthening institutional, regulative, and procedural regime capacities to deal with potential and real threats. Finally, authoritarian survival can refer to three outcomes: leadership survival in office, autocratic regime survival (no autocratic replacements), and autocratic system survival (no democratization).

Authoritarian Survival Strategies

Given that the main difference between democracies and autocracies lies in regular contestation of free and fair elections and constraints on power execution presented by the guarantee of civil and political liberties, strategies to achieve political survival also differ profoundly between both regime types. Democratic parties and politicians need to win elections and therefore have to provide common goods to a large number of citizens to achieve reelection, while also promoting and protecting free and fair elections, the rule of law, and civil liberties at home and abroad (Bermeo 2016; Bueno de Mesquita et al. 2003; Lührmann and Lindberg 2019). Liberalizing regimes are particularly often challenged by disenfranchised autocratic elites that aim to reverse reforms and regain control and therefore look for support to consolidate democracy (Moravcsik 2000). Autocracies, in contrast, cater to a much smaller group of politically and economically relevant elites, and are thus better off providing club goods to ensure the loyalty of the winning coalition, while repressing dissidents and public protestors that aim to topple the current regime (Geddes et al. 2018; Gerschewski 2013; Svolik 2012).

According to this perspective, politics in authoritarian regimes are characterized by strategic political elites who strive for political survival by mitigating the double dilemma of authoritarian rule: simultaneously achieving control over the population and establishing appropriate power-sharing arrangements with societal elites (Svolik 2012). The first problem refers to the relationship between the dictator or small ruling elite and the larger population. Although popular uprisings only represent a small percentage of authoritarian regime breakdowns (Svolik 2012, p. 5), they nonetheless occupy a major concern in most autocracies, and have recently gained particular relevance since the massive protests toppling and destabilizing leaders during the Arab Spring and the Color Revolutions.

Threats of popular uprisings by the masses can potentially be mitigated in two forms, often employed in concert: garnering support through legitimation and applying coercion through repression. *Legitimation* is directed toward creating diffuse support from the population and is achieved by offering claims to legitimacy that justify the division between ruler and ruled (Beetham 1991). While the most popular type of legitimation today is the creation of democratic institutions (Levitsky and Way 2010; Schedler 2006), legitimation can also rest on providing alternative narratives based on tradition, ideology, or output (Dukalskis and Gerschewski 2017; von Soest and Grauvogel 2017).

Repression can be exerted through soft (i.e. non-violent restriction of rights and creation of fear) and hard (violent) means to coerce the population and oppositional actors into rule-conforming behavior and discourage them from challenging the incumbent elites (Escribà-Folch 2013), often executed by a variety of coercive institutions (Bellin 2004). Yet, repression alone is an insufficient strategy for creating stability and ensuring survival, since violent forms of coercion tend to decrease legitimacy and unite the opposition (Tanneberg et al. 2013; Wintrobe 1998). To successfully manage this dilemma, autocracies thus have to combine optimal degrees of (soft) repression to retain diffuse support from the public gained through legitimation with strategies that aim to create loyalty among the elites through co-optation (Acemoglu and Robinson 2006; Josua and Edel 2014).

Co-optation ties to the second problem described by Svolik, which is the relationship between the dictator and his fellow political supporters. Historically, coups represent the most common cause of non-constitutional exits from office for authoritarian leaders (Svolik 2012, p. 5).[4] Co-optation therefore involves tying key political and societal groups to the incumbent. This can be achieved in a number of ways. Formal institutions like legislatures, dominant parties, and manipulated elections serve to tie elites but also oppositional groups to the autocrat and the leadership group (Blaydes 2011; Gandhi 2008; Gandhi and Przeworski 2006, 2007; Schedler 2006; Wright 2008), to regulate intra-elite power sharing (Boix and Svolik 2013; Myerson 2008), and to divide the opposition (Gandhi and Reuter 2013; Lust-Okar 2005). Co-optation can also be achieved by informal means through patronage, loyalty networks, and corruption (Svolik 2009; Wintrobe 1998).

Although these three strategies are often considered to be directed at the population, opposition, and intra-elite groups, respectively, they are to some extent cross-cutting. Legitimation can, for instance, also be aimed at justifying power positions to the rulers themselves (e.g. Barker 2001 on the concept of self-legitimation); co-optation can target the masses or particularly important societal groups through social spending (Lucas and Richter 2013);[5] and coercion can just as well be directed to violently oppress or intimidate opposition leaders, parties, and civil society actors (Levitsky and Way 2002).

These perspectives prioritize authoritarian responses to domestic challengers that might endanger survival. However, in a globalized world, authoritarian regimes are also increasingly challenged by international actors. I therefore expand the taxonomy of survival strategies to address specifically

---

[4] Coups have in fact decreased as a major cause for democratic breakdown in the last decades, having been replaced by "executive aggrandizement"; that is, a slow demise of democratic quality and expansion of executive function of democratically elected leaders (Bermeo 2016). This has changed somewhat in recent years with a number of coups in Western Africa. Coups thus remain a highly relevant threat category for authoritarian leaders that ROs also respond to (Boutton 2019; Cottiero 2023; Hohlstein 2022).

[5] The concept of mass co-optation is to some extent contested since it overlaps with the concept of output-based legitimation; that is, garnering diffuse support through providing welfare, security, or efficient governance structures. However, I define mass co-optation as a short-term payment strategy to react to specific events, while output-based legitimation rolls out on a long-term basis.

how authoritarian regimes mitigate threats from two specific types of international challengers. First, a wave of international democracy promotion starting in the 1990s put new pressures on authoritarian regimes. Foreign policies of the US, the EU, and European states increasingly included conditionality clauses in economic cooperation and financial, military, and development aid, while institutionalizing their democracy promotion programs (Burnell 2000; Carothers 2004; Hobson and Kurki 2012; Whitehead 1996). Since the 1980s, election monitoring has become a global norm, requiring many dictators to hold regular elections to show compliance with the norm (Hyde 2011; Kelley 2012). When dictators are too overtly engaged in anti-democratic practices and human rights violations, democratic states and international organizations increasingly issue targeted sanctions against regime elites (Drezner 2011; von Borzyskowski and Vabulas 2019b; Weber and Schneider 2022) while transnational non-state actors engage in naming and shaming campaigns (Hafner-Burton 2008; Murdie and Peksen 2013; Peksen et al. 2014). Dictators also have to fear diffusion of democratic norms and values, thereby inspiring waves of protest movements endangering their hold on power (Brinks and Coppedge 2006; Gleditsch and Ward 2006; Greenhill 2015; Weyland 2010).

Democracy promotion efforts and exerted pressure often vary greatly across regions and regimes depending on the degree of linkage to democratic powers and vulnerability to external pressure (Brownlee 2012; Levitsky and Way 2006). Scholars have repeatedly questioned the effects of the democracy promotion paradigm in terms of actual democratic transitions (Diamond 2002a; Heydemann and Leenders 2011), particularly given the current debate on an authoritarian counterwave (Lührmann and Lindberg 2019; Skaaning 2020; Tomini 2021). The debate on sanction effectiveness is likewise divided on the likelihood that punitive measures can increase the likelihood of democratization (Peksen and Drury 2010; von Soest and Wahman 2014).

These mixed findings on effects do not negate the fact that many autocrats have made concerted domestic efforts to minimize challenges stemming from international pressures. Incumbent regimes have become sophisticated in staging manipulated elections (Hyde 2011; Levitsky and Way 2010; Schedler 2006), in offsetting costs of international sanctions through increased legitimation efforts (Grauvogel and von Soest 2014), and in acquiring alternative revenues through criminal networks (Andreas 2005). They have created governmental civil society organizations to react to growing pressure for civil society participation (Glasius et al. 2020) and partly reformed economies to conform to international restructuring programs (Heydemann 2007; Hinnebusch 2012). All these tactics amount to a survival strategy of *international appeasement*: autocratic regimes aim to signal compliance with demands for democratic reform to international actors, while at the same time employing diversion strategies at home to offset costs.

A second threat to authoritarian regimes stems from external influences into domestic affairs by immediate neighbors. As post-colonial nations, authoritarian regimes in the Global South are often highly influenced by experiences of colonialism and great power rivalry (e.g. Acharya 2001). But threats of intervention are not necessarily only stemming from the West. In Sub-Saharan Africa, spill-overs from civil wars into neighboring states cause negative externalities for whole regions, increasing the likelihood of inter-state war (Salehyan 2008). In Central Asia, newly established states face contentious borders both with a post-Soviet Russia and rising China (Aris 2011; Jetschke and Katada 2016). Popular uprisings tend to spread across borders into neighboring regimes, causing destabilization of whole regions (Gleditsch and Ward 2006; Weyland 2010). Newly established democracies can be overly motivated to signal their democratic commitment to international partners by providing incentives or applying pressure on autocratic states to initiate further regime change in their environment (Moravcsik 2000; Pevehouse 2005b). Finally, RO bureaucracies themselves might engage in agency slack (Hawkins et al. 2006; Heldt 2017) to expand mandates and powers, and try to move against troubling member states.

These experiences tend to make post-colonial states more susceptible to interventionist policies. In consequences, foreign policies of post-colonial states are often driven by sovereignty and non-interference norms. Amitav Acharya and Ian Johnston, for instance, find in their edited book on comparative regionalism that "the design of regional institutions in the developing world has been more consistently sovereignty-preserving than sovereignty-eroding" (2007a, p. 262) in comparison to regionalism in the Global North. This is not to say that interpretations of sovereignty and conceptions of legitimate intervention are uniform across the Global South (see, for instance, Coe 2015 for temporal and spatial variation of sovereignty norms in the Global South). But generally, Acharya and Johnston conclude that "the more insecure the regimes, the less intrusive are their regional institutions" (Acharya and Johnston 2007a, p. 262). Thus, a final survival strategy can be entitled *sovereignty protection*: concerted efforts by authoritarian regimes to promote sovereignty as a norm of IR that helps to protect domestic affairs from unwanted external interference.

Mechanisms of Regime-Boosting Regionalism

We can now attempt to return to the initial question: Why would autocracies be interested in institutionalized forms of cooperation given the assumption that their main preference is achieving stabilization and political survival? The answer is that the demand for participation in ROs is driven by the hope of incumbent regimes that they can profit from RO membership in terms of increasing their likelihood for regime survival. Just as democratizing regimes use RO membership to lock in democratic reform and ensure consolidation, autocrats use ROs to actively strengthen survival strategies and thereby increase the likelihood of regime survival.

This section lays out how exactly RO membership adds to incumbent survival. As Figure 2.1 shows, ROs can contribute to each survival strategy outlined above, amounting to three distinct causal mechanisms of regime-boosting that help to mitigate domestic, regional, and international challengers, respectively: *resource redistribution* to strengthen legitimation, repression, and co-optation vis-à-vis domestic actors, *relationship management* to ensure non-intervention of regional neighbors, and *shielding* from international pressure to lower the cost of appeasement politics.

First, RO membership can help to tap into *resource redistribution* and thus be a means to secure access to pooled regional resources to mitigate domestic challengers during moments of uncertainty. RO membership thus opens

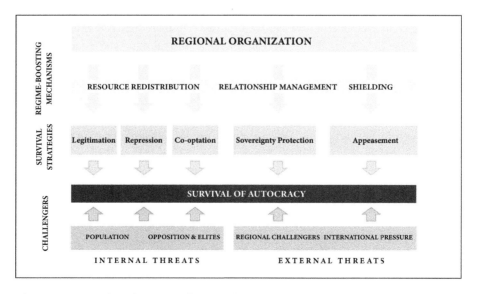

Figure 2.1 Causal mechanisms of regime-boosting regionalism.

access to both material resources such as financial redistributions, market access, military equipment, intelligence sharing, and technical support, but also to ideational support such as diplomacy, information, and identity discourses. During moments of political turmoil, these additional resources can make a substantial difference to tip the scale in favor of autocratic incumbents. In contrast to short-lived alliances or bilateral relations, formalizing these pooling measures within a RO represents a higher level of commitment to support the existing non-democratic status quo among member states in times of political turmoil.

Regionally pooled resources can essentially be used to strengthen the domestic survival strategies outlined above. ROs can generate legitimacy by helping regimes to present themselves as democratic and part of a regional ideational group. Legitimacy in autocratic regimes either rests on presenting incumbents as quasi-democratic or by recurring to alternative legitimation strategies based on traditional values or ideology (Dukalskis and Gerschewski 2017; von Soest and Grauvogel 2017). RO "shadow election monitoring" (Kelley 2012) has emerged as a highly effective way to award autocratic incumbents international recognition for highly flawed elections by praising their democratic quality without actually engaging in meaningful monitoring activities (Debre and Morgenbesser 2017). Additionally, ROs often represent ideational communities with common value systems such as Eurasianism in the post-Soviet space (Laruelle 2008), the "ASEAN Way" in Southeast Asia (Acharya 2003), pan-Arabism in the Middle East (Korany 1986), or the Shanghai Spirit in Central Asia (Ambrosio 2008). By drawing on those regional values and identities, autocratic incumbents strengthen alternative domestic legitimation narratives while critical actors are cast as part of an illegitimate out-group (Debre 2021; Hellquist 2015).

ROs also provide material benefits in the form of economic support, financial redistributions, and development aid or bureaucratic positions that can be employed to strengthen the co-optation of key elites. The literature on regionalism in Sub-Saharan Africa shows how ROs help to sustain patrimonial networks by accumulating diplomatic positions to reward politicians, business elites, and military personnel with reputable jobs and to capture rents such as tariff revenues by undermining trade liberalization (Bach 2005; Hartmann 2016; Herbst 2007). Additionally, development assistance, especially from new South–South donors, is of particular interest to authoritarian regimes to increase rent-seeking capacities, especially given the fact that all types of development assistance are often intentionally or unintentionally blind to regime type and can thus be easily exploited (Bruszt and Palestini 2016; Kararach 2014; Kono and Montinola 2013a). Even the suggestion of economic regionalism without meaningful liberalization might be enough in the short term ensure the loyalty of key business elites (Collins 2009).

Finally, regional security cooperation and intelligence sharing may help to boost the repression of popular uprisings and oppositional actors. Many ROs such as the Economic Community of West African States or the Association of Southeast Asian Nations (ASEAN) have developed security capacities over time, or have been specifically founded as security institutions, such as the Shanghai Cooperation Organization (SCO). Autocratic regimes might be particularly interested in increased intelligence cooperation. In Central Asia, for instance, the SCO Regional Antiterrorism Structure has played a major role in helping member states to criminalize legitimate opposition by blacklisting, extradition, and denial of asylum for political opposition (Cooley and Heathershaw 2017). Similarly, cross-border policing has become a popular instrument among Gulf Cooperation Council (GCC) members to better pursue and prosecute critical activists independently of their physical location (Yom 2016). While military interference to safeguard an incumbent regime comparable to the 2011 GCC intervention in Bahrain remains the exception, joint military maneuvers can still be used to signal military strength to potential challengers. Finally, simply having the opportunity to learn from other incumbent regimes about "worst practices" within an institutionalized setting with regard to crisis management can strengthen successful repressive strategies (Yom 2014).

Second, ROs help to *manage relationships* with neighboring countries by regulating appropriate behavior among the members of the dictator club, thereby preventing them from unwanted interference in domestic affairs. Protecting sovereignty rights becomes particularly important in cases of mixed RO membership, where some members of the club might have democratized during the third wave. Given that democratizing states are particularly likely to lobby for conditionality rights for the RO to lock in democratic reform, protecting non-interference norms within ROs is essential for the remaining authoritarian regimes within the club. This constraining effect of institutionalized sovereignty protection allows autocratic incumbents to exercise costly domestic survival strategies against political challengers such as repressive tactics or election manipulation without the danger of democratic neighboring states interfering on the side of challengers.

Findings from recent research on international authority indeed show that many autocratic ROs in the Middle East, Sub-Saharan Africa, and Central and Southeast Asia are equipped with less authority, particularly with regard to pooled decision-making procedures compared to democratic ROs in the Global North like the EU (Hooghe et al. 2017, 2019). Sovereignty protection is a major driver to explain this type of institutional design including informal and consensual forms of decision-making and strong norms protecting sovereignty and non-interference. As Acharya and Johnston conclude in their edited volume on RO institutional design in the Global South, "one common feature of these regional 'ways' is that notwithstanding geographic, cultural, and political differences and the time lag in their evolution, the emphasis on sovereignty and non-interference has remained a powerful constant" (Acharya and Johnston 2007b, p. 246).

Third, being a member of the club also helps to *shield autocratic incumbents* from the fallout of international pressure and decrease the cost of appeasement strategies. First, as envisioned in mainstream functionalist accounts, autocrats can upload norms on good governance, democratic elections, and human rights to the RO by signing treaties and installing responsible regional commissions and bureaucratic entities charged with furthering liberal norms (Börzel and van Hüllen 2015). ROs thereby act as signaling devices that promise norm commitment without member states having to follow through on domestic implementation. At the same time, mock compliance strategies will not always successfully deter international actors from threatening the use of sanctions where dictators need to openly employ survival strategies during political crisis moments. While fellow autocratic RO members can try to intervene in international fora like the United Nations Security Council to argue against measures carrying reputational costs or sanctions, this strategy is limited given term limits and the distribution of voting powers in the Council.

Should reputational measures such as shaming campaigns or economic and political sanctions be enacted during political crisis moments, ROs can help to offset their cost in two ways. First, they can engage in regional legitimation campaigns that help autocratic incumbents paint reputational and coercive measures as politically motivated actions of Western leaders, thereby intensifying rally-round-the-flag effects. These effects occur where autocracies managed to incorporate sanctions into their legitimation strategies because they increase in-group cohesion, brand sanctions into general criticism of the nation, and build connections to foundational myths (Grauvogel and von Soest 2014). ROs can potentially help to strengthen all three mechanisms: they can use international sanctions to increase regional cohesion among RO members, thereby preventing unilateral moves against sanctioned states; they can brand critical opponents as Western puppets, thereby de-legitimizing dissidents across the region; and they can sell sanctions as Western interference, thereby de-legitimizing their use as unfit with regional values.

Second, ROs can step in and act as "black knights" and provide goods and services when sanctions are not only threatened, but enacted. Black knights or sanction busters refer to strategic third parties such as states or firms that provide a sanctioned target with subsidies and assistance to buffer the negative impact of coercive measures and obtain economic and political benefits in return (Early 2011; Hufbauer et al. 2009). Sanction-busting is considered a major problem undermining the effectiveness of sanctions because it provides sanctioned entities with the necessary resources to uphold their rule (Early 2011; Tolstrup 2015).[6] In fact, increased repression and corruption often follow sanction episodes because targets need to ensure regime stability and survival under conditions of international pressure (e.g. Hafner-Burton 2008; Peksen and Drury 2010). In these cases, ROs can provide necessary financial subsidies, alternative markets, and technical assistance that allow regimes to step up their co-optation of elites and repression of dissidents.

The Supply of Regime-Boosting Mechanisms by Regional Organizations

Now that we have understood why autocrats institutionalize cooperation and how ROs might strengthen stability and survival, we can turn to theorize under what conditions RO membership is likely to yield the desired results. Three supply-side conditions make the relationship between RO membership and regime survival more likely.

First, RO membership is only going to yield results where preferences of member states are more aligned. Since democracies, transitioning regimes, and autocracies differ in terms of their survival politics, they are also going to disagree over the design and function of ROs. Consequently, the composition of membership of an institution in terms of regime type is an important dimension to determine the outcomes of cooperation. The more democratic a regime, the more it is likely to employ ROs to jointly provide common goods to their selectorates, to spread and protect norms of good governance and human rights, and to funnel resources to liberal coalitions to assist them in consolidating democratic transitions. In contrast, autocracies should have higher preferences to employ institutions to redistribute resources that help to strengthen autocratic incumbent elites vis-à-vis domestic challengers, and to protect regimes from external intervention and pressure to democratize.

---

[6] Democratic sanctions can, however, sometimes be successful even in the presence of black knights because targets make limited democratic concessions to increase their bargaining position vis-à-vis the black knight (Sejersen 2019; von Soest and Wahman 2014).

Following this line of argumentation, we can reasonably expect that ROs with higher autocratic density among members should be more likely to provide the theorized mechanisms. The more ROs are dominated by autocracies, the better autocratic executives can exploit the RO to strengthen their survival strategies, and to constrain challengers. The more ROs are dominated by democracies and liberalizing regimes, the more they should be likely to disturb the preferences of autocratic members, and try to enforce and incentive behavior via the RO that conforms with democratic governance. In fact, previous research shows that ROs that are dominated by more democratic members are more often equipped with enforceable democracy and conditionality clauses, as well as judicial control mechanisms that can provide for credible commitments and constrain future reversals of democratic reform in member states (Pevehouse 2005b, 2016; Schimmelfennig 2016). Efforts to redistribute resources toward liberal elites have also been a central goal of EU accession and neighborhood policy (Schimmelfennig and Sedelmeier 2005), while democratic coalitions have used IGOs and bilateral and multilateral trade agreements to spread human rights and good governance provisions (Greenhill 2015; Hafner-Burton 2009). International donor organizations comprising member states with lower levels of corruption are also more likely to adopt and enforce anti-corruption standards and refrain from diverting money to corrupt states (Ferry et al. 2020; Hafner-Burton and Schneider 2019). We can thus expect the following:

H1: The higher the autocratic density of an RO, the higher the likelihood of survival for autocratic incumbent members.

Second, average levels of autocracy among member states do not represent the full picture. Similarity is not merely captured by how autocratic the RO membership is on *average*, but also by its *diversity*. It would follow that an RO with a diverse set of autocratic and democratic members (e.g. the Economic Community of West African States (ECOWAS)) will serve neither the autocratic nor the liberalizing states well, while an RO with a similar average density but more homogenous members (e.g. CIS) will be more likely to add to authoritarian stability and survival. We can thus expect homogeneity of membership within autocratic ROs to produce a higher likelihood of autocratic survival. Thus, homogeneity should function as a moderator of the effect of density on survival. We can thus formulate a second hypothesis:

H2: The higher the autocratic homogeneity of an RO, the higher the likelihood of survival for autocratic incumbent members.

Finally, the above argumentation also implies that ROs without more delegation to regional agents should be more likely to provide benefits to autocratic regime survival. Since autocrats want to gain additional support and prevent unwanted external interference through RO membership, they are very aware of possible unintended consequences resulting from entering into legally binding forms of cooperation. Thus, they will try to avoid such consequences by making specific institutional design choices to hold tight on the reins of power without delegating too many enforcement competences to RO bureaucracies or installing majority voting procedures.

However, functional pressures as well as the size of an institution will often make delegation and pooling necessary, thereby leading to variation in regional authority levels across authoritarian ROs (Hooghe et al. 2019). RO bureaucracies with agenda-setting or enforcement powers, for instance in the form of regional courts or dispute settlement mechanisms, might in fact punish member states for employing autocratic survival strategies and thus increase the costs of repressive and manipulative tactics (e.g. Alter and Hooghe 2016; Jetschke and Katada 2016). In a similar vein, empowered bureaucrats with agenda-setting power might push for the adoption of stricter democratic regional standards or block the redistribution of resources to regimes that have come under political pressure through agency slack (Hawkins et al. 2006; Heldt 2017). Democratic neighbors might also try to use the RO to bargain against autocratic incumbents where voting procedures allow for majority decision-making or to support oppositional actors and interfere in domestic affairs unless sovereignty protection has become an institutionalized norm of cooperation. Thus, ROs with less delegated and pooled authority should be more likely to serve autocratic member states during political turmoil and help them stay in power. We can therefore expect the following:

H3: The lower the authority of an RO, the higher the likelihood of survival for autocratic incumbent members.

Two final questions have to be answered before moving on to test these hypotheses. First, why is the theory outlined in this chapter directed specifically at ROs, not at any IGO? I expect that the hypothesized effects should play out particularly within ROs instead of global IGOs. I understand *regions* as a category between the national and the global that describes the social construction of a geographically contiguous space. In other words, regions are not structurally and exogenously given entities (Söderbaum 2013). This means that definitions and boundaries of regions can both change over time and be subject to feelings of cultural, political, or historical belonging that transcend geography. I understand ROs as the formal and institutionalized cooperative relations among at least three states within a region (Börzel and Risse 2016b). ROs are thus defined by regionally limited membership and represent related sets of formal and informal rules that define the behavior of member states of an RO by enabling or constraining actors.

As such, ROs consist of geographically and culturally proximate members, and can thus be particularly well employed to further domestic preferences without the confounding influence of international-level dynamics. ROs tend to be community-oriented, involving fewer numbers and more interaction compared to task-specific and universal membership IGOs that deal with global coordination problems (Hooghe et al. 2019). Thus, ROs are also closer to domestic and regional political events, so the proposed causal processes should work more easily.

Second, why expect that dictator clubs are only concerned with upholding the status quo, not with promoting autocracy, even beyond their membership? The original debate on authoritarian international behavior had been motivated by fears of ideologically driven autocracies, promoting autocracy akin to democracy promotion efforts by democratic states (Gat 2007b; Kneuer et al. 2018; Silitski 2010b). China's international activity is likewise debated as a threat to the rules-based liberal international order, with China promoting alternative illiberal norms internationally (Flonk 2021; Hackenesch and Bader 2020; Kagan 2012).

I agree with other scholars that the international behavior of authoritarian regimes is—mostly—strategically motivated by preventing regime change at home, not with ideologically promoting authoritarianism abroad (Tansey 2016b; von Soest 2015; Way 2015). After all, China is only contesting liberal norms internationally where it maximizes its own domestic preferences, but keeps engaged in policy fields where international cooperation is beneficial to the Communist party (Weinhardt and ten Brink 2020; Weiss and Wallace 2021). Autocrats in Eurasia and Southeast Asia usually exploited distinctive *illiberal* regional orders like the ASEAN Way or Eurasianism to normalize autocratic practices at home and limit the reach of democracy promoters and human rights activists (e.g. Ambrosio 2009; Laruelle 2008; Russo and Stoddard 2018a). This logic has somewhat been called into question with the Russian invasion of Ukraine, where ideological expansionism seems to trump strategic motivations (Bluhm 2022; Kragh 2022; but see also Mearsheimer 2014, 2022 for the realist geopolitical argument).

It also seems difficult to transfer concepts from democracy promotion such as conditionality, transnational advocacy, and democracy promotion to the study of external influences on autocracy due to the low legitimacy of authoritarianism as a form of political rule (also see Tansey 2016b for a similar argument). While democracy promoters can state outright that their policies are intentionally designed to further democracy as the normatively best form of rule, there is no evidence that authoritarian ROs seem to be able to do the same. On the contrary, even autocratic ROs such as CIS, the Arab League, or ASEAN prescribe to some aspects of good governance, even if only to pay lip service to domestic and international audiences (Börzel and van Hüllen 2015).

Additionally, it becomes somewhat difficult to disentangle where autocracy promotion actually starts. In his book on the international politics of authoritarian powers, Tansey (2016a), for instance, considers both Germany's and Italy's support for Fascism as well as the Soviet Union's efforts to prop up satellite regimes as instances of autocracy promotion, while post-Cold War cases such as Venezuela's support for Bolivarianism, China's foreign policy of Peaceful Coexistence, or Saudi Arabia's advancement of Sunni-Wahabism and absolute monarchy are interpreted as instrumental efforts of democracy resistance. While Fascism is clearly defined by its totalitarian opposition to any form of competitive electoral system, oppositional positions, or liberal values, Communism as such is not fundamentally defined in terms of non-democratic political rule but as a utopian ideology aimed against capitalist economy. Communism has become synonymous with totalitarian rule during the twentieth century, but the Soviet Union's efforts at establishing like-minded regimes in the face of American neo-liberal democracy can be interpreted just as instrumental as current Russian foreign policy that aims at securing Russian geopolitical status in Eurasia and preventing pro-Western governments from taking office.

What flows from this debate is the differentiation between motivations for cooperation that aim either to expand a regime's zone of influence or to protect the regime domestically. In the former case, we would expect an expansion of regionalism to include more states over time, and concerted efforts to ensure new members become or stay authoritarian. In the latter case, regionalism is mostly inward-looking, intended as a means to prevent a change in status quo at home. Both motivations can coexist. However, the latter will be the focus of further empirical tests in this book, while the former has to remain a matter for future research.

3
Patterns of Authoritarian Membership in Regional Organizations

Many research contributions have shed light on authoritarian institutions in various world regions and moments in time, but we still know little about how these institutions compare globally. As a first step in the empirical analysis of the book, this chapter lays out patterns of authoritarian membership in regional organizations (ROs) across space and time. Thereby, it provides answers to three main questions. First, how widespread are dictator clubs? Do we see major variation between different world regions with specific regions driving the development or a global phenomenon of authoritarian institutional cooperation? Second, what is the historical perspective? Are dictator clubs a recent phenomenon or a development that dates back in time? What have been important periods of change, and do more recent forms of authoritarian institutions compare to those that were founded in the Cold War period? Third, are dictator clubs homogenous organizations with similar types of authoritarian members or rather a mix of different types of autocracies and democracies? And do they all look the same with regard to form and function?

While the first part of this chapter is dedicated to answering these guiding questions, the second part will continue with mapping the dependent variable: autocratic regime failure. Here, I will present the Geddes, Wright, and Frantz (GWF) dataset, *Autocratic Breakdown and Regime Transition*, as well as my update, which extends the 1945–2010 data to 2020. This part will show where democratic regime change and autocratic replacements have taken place around the world, particularly in the last 10 years, which regimes seem to be the most stable, and which ROs had to deal with the most types of failures. Before moving on to map both the main independent and dependent variables, the chapter will first discuss dataset design, particularly sampling of ROs and measurement of authoritarian density, homogeneity, and authority.

How Regional Organizations Sustain Authoritarian Rule. Maria J. Debre, Oxford University Press.
© Maria J. Debre (2025). DOI: 10.1093/9780198903635.003.0003

The Design of the Dataset

To start, a note on RO sampling is in order. Previous efforts to identify the population of ROs have resulted in samples including between 35 (Hooghe et al. 2017) and almost 100 (Jetschke et al. 2016) organizations, with most studies arriving at a number around 60–70 (Haftel 2012; Panke et al. 2015; Panke and Stapel 2016; Powers and Goertz 2011). Many of these datasets purposely focus on major organizations with a "more detectable footprint in the primary and secondary records" (Lenz et al. 2015), thereby often excluding dead organizations or those from the Global South (Debre and Dijkstra 2021b; Knecht and Debre 2018).

Since these are exactly the institutions of interest for this book, I build an adjusted sample that is tailored to the requirements of the theoretical considerations laid out in the previous chapter, namely multi-purpose ROs active between 1945 and 2020 that have a political, economic, or security mandate and can thus affect domestic political change in a broad and meaningful way. Sampling of ROs is primarily based on the *Yearbook of International Organizations* (YIO) database (Union of International Associations). ROs are understood as formal and institutionalized relations among at least three states within a region. Geographically defined membership can refer to both neighboring states and socially defined proximity (e.g. Arctic Council for states with littoral access to the Arctic Pole, the Shanghai Cooperation Organization for Eurasian states, or Asia-Pacific Economic Cooperation (APEC) for states with littoral borders with the Pacific). Furthermore, ROs have to be multi-purpose institutions and can be both alive or dead; that is, dissolved at some point before the study period ends in 2020. This results in a sample of 72 ROs, with 17 of these dead and 55 currently alive spread over six main world regions (Europe, Asia, Middle East and North Africa (MENA), Sub-Saharan Africa, Latin America, and Soviet space/Eurasia). More detailed information on the sampling procedure and categorization can be found in the Online Appendix.

Measuring Dictator Clubs: Autocratic Density, Homogeneity, and Authority

Dictator clubs are defined as organizations with a predominantly autocratic density, which refers to the average degree of authoritarianism among the members of an RO. To measure density, this book uses average autocracy scores of all members of an RO in a given year. RO membership is based on the Correlates of War (COW) Intergovernmental Organization (v.3) dataset (Pevehouse et al. 2020).[1] Where ROs are not part of the COW dataset, or membership data is missing, membership was based on further research on the YIO or RO websites.

Density scores are a commonly used way to measure the democratic quality of institutions in the international organizations (IO) literature and are often included as predictor variables in statistical modeling (e.g. Debre and Dijkstra 2021b; Pevehouse 2005a; von Borzyskowski and Vabulas 2019a). To compute density scores, I employ the polity2 variable from the Polity IV project (Marshall et al. 2018) both for conceptual and organizational reasons. Based on the continuous understanding of regime type reaching from highly democratic to highly autocratic laid out in the previous chapter, the *polity* measure is a fitting operationalization to assess regime type. The polity project's unit of analysis is polity, understood as "subsets of the class of 'authority patterns'" (Marshall et al. 2016, p. 1). This definition is similar to my understanding of regime as the set of formal and informal rules that determines power relations between people. The polity variable is a combination of the democracy and autocracy authority patterns of each polity unit measured between 1800 and 2018. It combines both democratic and autocratic authority patterns into one continuous polity variable, which is then scored on a scale reaching from −10 (very autocratic) to +10 (very democratic). Regimes with a score lower than +6 are considered autocratic; regimes with a score higher than +6 are democratic.

While democracy is understood as a system with effective preference articulation by citizens, institutionalized constraints on the executive, and guarantee of civil liberties, only the institutional aspects (competitive political participation, openness of executive recruitment, constraints on chief executive) are coded (Marshall et al. 2016, p. 14). Autocracy, in contrast, refers to systems with low competitive participation, openness of executive recruitment, and executive constraints (ibid., p. 16). Other indices either use a more minimalist conception of democracy that is only based on contestation (e.g. Cheibub et al. 2010; Przeworski et al. 2000) or work with a far broader concept including civil and political rights (e.g. Freedom House). As a robustness check, data from Varieties of Democracy, particularly the Electoral Democracy Index (EDI), will be used as an alternative measurement throughout the statistical analysis with results provided in the Online Appendix. While Varieties of Democracy has the advantage of coding different aspects of democratic governance, the dataset was not fully available at

---

[1] See the Online Appendix for more information on differences from the COW dataset.

the start of this project. Therefore, the following descriptive statistics and the subsequent analysis in Chapter 4 rely on the polity data.

To differentiate between autocratic and democratic ROs, two operationalizations are chosen. I adopt the threshold commonly used by polity and define ROs with an average density score above 6 as democratic; all other ROs are considered dictator clubs. ROs are coded as democratic or autocratic according to their lifespan density (i.e. the average polity score of all members from their year of foundation to the death of the RO, or the end of the study period in 2018) or according to yearly density levels. Density scores based on the polity measure were only calculated until 2018 due to data availability. Both approaches have advantages and disadvantages. While lifetime scores can tell us something about the long-term orientation of organizations, they miss important variation when parts of the membership transition between regime types. In the following, I will therefore use both measures to understand the regional dispersion, historical trajectories, and functional variations of autocratic ROs.

Additionally, we also want to understand how different the regimes are within dictator clubs with regard to their autocracy scores. This autocratic homogeneity measure basically indicates how diverse the regimes are in each organization. It is operationalized in terms of the standard deviation—that is, the mean dispersion—between the autocracy scores of an RO. A higher score signifies more variety in terms of democratic and autocratic features among the members, which could make it harder for the group to stick together. In simpler terms, being part of a dictator club with regimes with similar autocracy scores (like the Central Africa Economic and Monetary Community (CEMAC)) might make it easier to get support to resist democratization or autocratic changes compared to support from a club with equal density but more heterogenous membership (like the Economic Community of West African States (ECOWAS)), where democratic and autocratic members have different policy expectations on the role the RO should play.

The third key factor this chapter will trace across dictator clubs is the power that is accorded to the RO as an agent to intervene in the domestic affairs of member states. This is measured in terms of how much authority is delegated to regional courts and tribunals. Where RO members have set up judicial constraints with the power to rule on political matters concerning human rights, and also in response to individual complaints by constituencies or non-governmental organization (NGO) groups, the ability of regimes to use the RO to redistribute resources toward troubled members might be constrained. Therefore, the last section of the first part in this chapter will

46 How Regional Organizations Sustain Authoritarian Rule

highlight where, when, and which types of ROs have installed courts and tribunals.

Mapping Dictator Clubs

This section will lay out the principal patterns that describe the historical trajectories, regional variation, and major functions accorded to dictator clubs. In each subsection, I will make use of the three main concepts operationalized above and draw on autocratic density scores, both yearly and lifetime measures, as well as homogeneity and RO authority to compare and contrast both democratic and autocratic institutions, as well as dictator clubs, among themselves.

Historical Trajectories

The analysis of the evolution of ROs between 1946 and 2018[2] corroborates that dictator clubs are the most numerous forms of regional institutional cooperation across the globe. Figure 3.1 (top) depicts the overall growth of democratic and autocratic ROs based on yearly density scores, picking up on the divergent development of democratic and autocratic ROs over time. While democratic ROs have been the subject of a host of different literatures, autocratic ROs are in fact a much more prevalent type of regional institution across the globe. In fact, by 2018, the number of autocratic ROs almost doubled that of ROs in terms of democratic density, with 20 ROs with a density over +6 on the polity measure and 38 with a density below this threshold.

The evolution depicted in Figure 3.1 (top) reveals three distinct phases. During a first phase until the 1960s, only a few ROs existed, and most of the existing ones were located in Europe with the foundation of the North Atlantic Treaty Organization (NATO) (1949), the Council of Europe (CoE) (1949), the European Coal and Steel Community (ECSC) (1952), and finally the European Community (EC) (1958). Several ROs outside Europe saw their foundation during that time as well: the League of Arab States (LAS) as the first major Global South institution (1945), the Organization of American States (OAS) (1948) driven by a US desire to unite Latin America against Communist regimes, and the important Warsaw Treaty Organization (WTO) (1955) as a counterinstitution to the West's NATO alliance.

---

[2] Because of data availability, density scores based on the polity measure are only calculated until 2018.

At the start of the 1960s, a second phase began. Decolonialization coincided with the establishment of new states and numerous ROs in the Global South that were an expression of post-colonial independence and a joint pursuit of sovereignty. Many of the well-known ROs were founded during this time, including the Organization for African Unity (OAU) (1961), the Association of Southeast Asian Nations (ASEAN) (1967), ECOWAS (1975), the Southern African Development Coordination Conference (SADCC) (1980), and the Gulf Cooperation Council (GCC) (1981). In Europe, this phase was mostly characterized by increasing integration within established institution, with the exception of the establishment of the Organization for Security and Cooperation in Europe (OSCE) (1975), which was specifically founded to foster cooperation with the Soviet bloc.

A third phase of development can be identified after the end of the Cold War starting in the 1990s. Here, we can see a distinct rise in newly founded democratic institutions until the early 2000s, among them the reformed European Union (EU) (1992), but also the Common Market of the South (MERCOSUR) (1991), the Central American Integration System (SICA) (1991), the Andean Community (1996), the Union for the Mediterranean (UfM) (1995, an EU–MENA cooperation initiative emerging out of the Barcelona Process), and the Arctic Council (1996) to regulate relationships between states bordering the Arctic region. But the mid-1990s also saw the establishment of new dictator clubs, particularly organizations situated in the post-Soviet region that was now about to be rebranded as Eurasia and needed to redraw borders and establish relationships between newly independent former Soviet satellites. Among these are the Commonwealth of Independent States (CIS) (1991) as a quasi-successor to the disbanded WTO with its security arm, the Collective Security Treaty Organization (CSTO) (2002), as well as the Eurasian Economic Community (EAEC) (2000) and the Shanghai Cooperation Organization (SCO) (2001). Likewise, new and mostly economic and developmental ROs were being established in Sub-Saharan Africa, among them the Common Market for Eastern and Southern Africa (COMESA) (1994), the West African Economic and Monetary Union (UEMOA) (1994), and the Community of Sahel-Saharan States (CEN-SAD) (1998).

Interestingly, this is also a time when we see dictator clubs becoming more heterogenous in their membership (Figure 3.1, bottom). When disaggregating dictator clubs into highly autocratic ROs with a density below −6, which corresponds to Polity's category as fully autocratic and thus many highly autocratic members, we can see a distinct drop in 1990. At the same time, dictator clubs with less autocratic members corresponding to Polity's anocracy category (between −6 and +6) increased dramatically, as we can see from the hybrid RO category in Figure 3.1. This is mostly due to the third wave of democratization, which saw numerous regimes liberalize, easing up on hard repression and grave human rights violations, and introducing somewhat free and fair elections. This development has been amply described in the literature as the rise of electoral, hybrid, or competitive authoritarianism (Diamond 2002b; Levitsky and Way 2010; Morse 2012; Schedler 2006) and mirrors the composition of Global South ROs during this time.

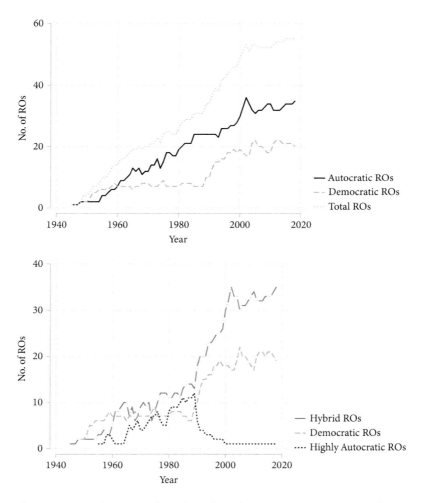

Figure 3.1 Development of number of ROs by regime type, 1946–2018 (own depiction based on polity (Marshall et al. 2018)).

Patterns of Authoritarian Membership in Regional Organizations   49

This development during the third phase might lead to the conclusion that the phenomenon of dictator clubs saw its end by the 1990s. This, however, is far from true. If we look at the development of the average density of democratic and autocratic ROs over time as depicted in Figure 3.2, we can notice two interesting points. First, while dictator clubs have become, on average,

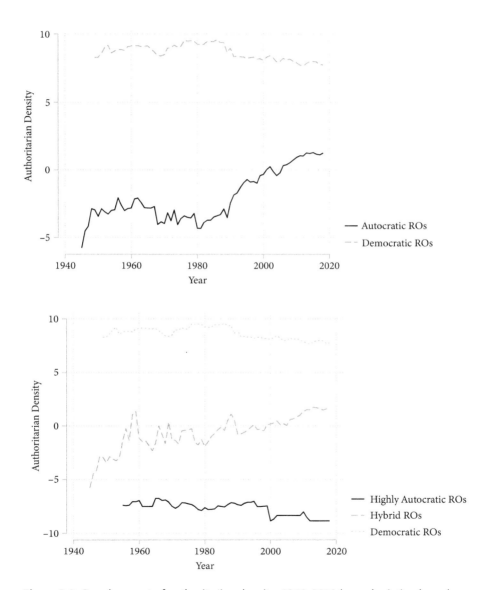

Figure 3.2 Development of authoritarian density, 1946–2018 (own depiction based on polity (Marshall et al. 2018)).

less autocratic since the 1990s, their average is still well below the democratic threshold of +6, reaching an all-time high of 1.9 in 2016 and falling again to 1.2 in 2018 (Figure 3.2, top). If we disaggregate dictator clubs again in highly autocratic and hybrid institutions, we see that highly autocratic clubs have, in fact, become even more autocratic until 2018 (Figure 3.2, bottom). Hybrid ROs made up of a majority of anocracies have only become slightly less autocratic in the same time frame, increasing their average density from −0.7 to about 1.7 from 1990 to 2018 (Figure 3.2, bottom). While hybrid ROs and their members might thus seem to be developing into more democratic clubs, in reality most of them have rather entered a phase of stalled democratization and electoral autocracy, thereby remaining firmly in the autocratic camp.

A second important point to note in Figure 3.2 is that democratic clubs have become somewhat less democratic during the same time. During the 1990s, this development is likely due to new Eastern European members becoming part of established European ROs. While democracy clauses forced these countries to substantially reform their systems to be able to become part of democratic clubs, the quality of democracy was not necessarily on the same level as that in established consolidated members in western Europe and North America. Starting in the mid-2000s, however, the further decline was likely caused by a period of democratic backsliding that particularly engulfed established democratic powers (Cassani and Tomini 2020; Lührmann and Lindberg 2019; but see Little and Meng 2023 for an alternative argument). The subsequent rise of populist right-wing parties, their success at the ballot box, and the limitations that these governments put on institutional checks and balances and established freedoms since 2010 have led to a distinct crisis of democratic organizations across the globe in the last decade (Copelovitch and Pevehouse 2019; Ikenberry 2018; Walter 2021a).

Finally, the second measure, autocratic homogeneity, can tell us more about the variety and dispersion of members among democratic and autocratic clubs over time. Mean values of the density measure are sensitive to outliers, and could in fact also indicate that many of our dictator clubs, particularly those in the hybrid category, are made up of some regimes that remain highly autocratic and some highly democratic members. It is thus prudent to also look at the homogeneity of ROs in terms of the standard deviation between polity scores of all members. Remember that low scores on the measure indicate strong homogeneity, while high scores indicate high heterogeneity of regime types. Figure 3.3 shows boxplots[3] of the

---

[3] Boxplots depict the interquartile range through box lengths, with the median as a bold line, as well as whiskers to signify the highest and lowest values. Dots represent outliers.

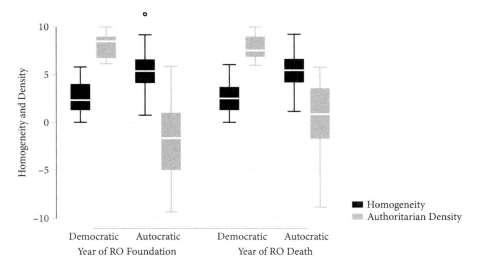

Figure 3.3 Homogeneity and authoritarian density of ROs at foundation and death (own depiction based on polity (Marshall et al. 2018)).

average homogeneity scores of autocratic and democratic ROs at their respective years of foundation and year of death.[4] Three points are important. First, autocratic clubs are more heterogenous compared to their democratic counterparts, with a median homogeneity score of 5.5 in contrast to democratic clubs at 2.4. This might, on the one hand, be due to the measurement of the polity variable, where autocracies include a wide 15-range scale from −10 to +5, while democracies only range on a five-point scale from +6 to +10. It might, however, also signal that democratic clubs often institute entry requirements that ensure conformity of members to democratic standards (Martin 2017; Schimmelfennig 2003; Schneider 2008). These types of entry requirements are notably absent in dictator clubs.

Second, we can also conclude that both democracies and autocracies sort into their respective institutions. A median of 5 for autocratic ROs on the homogeneity index indicates that, on average, regimes in a dictator club deviate about five points on the policy scale. Thus, it is impossible that many of the dictator clubs have an equal number of highly democratic and highly autocratic members given the 15-point polity scale and the mean density scores. Similarly, a median of 2.4 for democracies signifies that democracies tend to only cooperate regionally with other democratic members. Some ROs with an average density around the +6 threshold might be made up of anocracies and democracies and could sensibly be categorized as either type. However,

---

[4] ROs that are still alive are coded in 2018.

only a few ROs actually cluster around this threshold (see also Figure 3.7). In fact, there are only a handful of ROs (OSCE, Southeast Asia Treaty Organization (SEATO), BSEC, UfM, and IOC) where membership is significantly diverse, usually because of membership of EU member states or the US and Canada. There is only one notable outlier among dictator clubs in terms of homogeneity at foundation, which is the Indian Ocean Commission. This RO was founded by democratic Mauritius as well as autocratic Seychelles and Madagascar in 1982, thus causing the outlier at 11 points of dispersion. This dispersion, however, disappeared over time, with the institution gaining new democratic members and established authoritarian members consolidating democratization processes over time, eventually turning the RO into a fully democratic club.

Third, there seems to be a reinforcement effect of membership in the respective clubs. Both in autocratic and democratic ROs, homogeneity is at the same median level at foundation and death, while density only changes slightly for both types of institutions, indicating that there is little change, overall, over time (Figure 3.3). This reinforcement effect of RO membership also becomes evident when we take a look at the development of RO homogeneity over time. As we can see from Figure 3.4, both dictator clubs and democratic ROs became more homogenous until the 1990s in terms of their membership, but turned slightly more heterogeneous since then. This

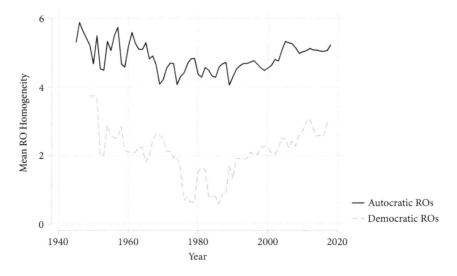

Figure 3.4 Development of RO homogeneity, 1946–2018 (own depiction based on Polity (Marshall et al. 2018)).

development is much more pronounced in democratic institutions, though, with an increase from one to three points of dispersion between 1990 and 2018. In contrast, dictator clubs hover between two and three throughout the observation period. This loss in homogeneity again signifies the crisis of liberal democracy, with many democratic clubs not being able to contain populist right-wing and autocratic actors (e.g. Kelemen 2020; Meyerrose 2020). Similar developments might be at work in dictator clubs, with numerous regimes becoming more authoritarian again in recent years, turning former democratization hopefuls like ASEAN or the Southern African Development Community (SADC) back into fully fledged autocratic clubs (Debre and Sommerer 2023).

Dictator Clubs across World Regions

To better understand how dictator clubs vary and change over time, this subsection will unpack the distribution between regions in more detail. Looking at the distribution of dictator clubs across world regions, we can note that the phenomenon is mostly a Global South occurrence, with Latin America as an outlier case.[5] Figure 3.5 depicts the development of density scores for six main regions. As we can see, density in Europe remains at an overall high, although the region has seen a slight decline since the 1990s for the reasons outlined above. Until the 1990s, MENA, Sub-Saharan Africa, and Eurasia were the main drivers of authoritarian institutions, with both Asia and Latin America remaining at a medium level. The 1990s saw an opportunity and shift for many regions, with increases in density across all regions. However, the only lasting change happened in Latin America, where overall density remains at an all-time high comparable to Europe since 1990. Sub-Saharan Africa has seen an equal increase but remains, on average, on an autocratic level. Eurasia has seen a very drastic quick democratization with the dissolution of the Soviet Union and a democratization of most members of the WTO within a short time period around 1990. But the institution was disbanded in 1991. Newly sovereign autocratic members joined the Commonwealth of Independent States, while democratizing regimes gained accession and ultimately full membership of the EU, leaving their association with the Soviet space and newly constructed Eurasia behind.

The following comparisons turn to the concept of lifespan density scores to better contrast and compare dictator clubs across regions. According to this

[5] On coding of regions, see above and the Online Appendix.

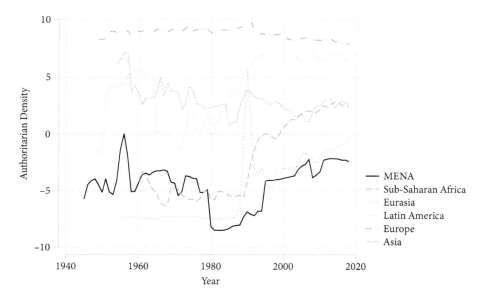

Figure 3.5 Development of authoritarian density by Region, 1946–2018 (own depiction based on Polity (Marshall et al. 2018)).

measure, 52 out of the total of 72 ROs in the dataset can be coded as autocratic over their entire lifespan, with 37 of these ROs still alive in 2018 and 15 dead. In absolute numbers, most ROs in 2018 exist in Sub-Saharan Africa (16), Latin America (13), and Europe (10), with Asia (7), MENA (5), and Eurasia (4) lagging. However, when comparing the number of ROs per state in each region, the picture looks a little different and regions converge (see Figure 3.6).[6] Latin America now has the most ROs relative to the number of states in the region, with Sub-Saharan Africa in second place. The other regions are characterized by relatively similar levels averaging at around 0.3 ROs per state, with MENA lagging behind. A cursory look at the number of ROs at the end of the Cold War shows that both Latin America and Eurasia have seen a larger increase in terms of numbers of ROs per state since the 1990s. In 1945, by contrast, only one RO had so far been established globally—the LAS.

The distribution of dictator clubs across world regions depicted in Figure 3.6 highlights again that the phenomenon is mainly driven by four regions: Sub-Saharan Africa, MENA, Asia, and Eurasia. Because of the clustering of

---

[6] The number of states per region has been calculated based on the comprehensive case list of all regimes (autocratic and democratic) in Geddes et al. (2014) and my own continuation, and their years of independence as defined in this dataset.

autocracies within these four regions, autocratic ROs also bulge there: Sub-Saharan Africa, Asia, and the Middle East each have only one democratic RO in 2018 (IOC, APEC, and UfM), mostly due to the membership of Western democratic states, while Eurasia has none. In contrast, there are only three ROs with an overall autocratic character in Europe (GUAM, BSEC, and OSCE) compared to seven highly democratic ROs. Here, the categorization of the OSCE as autocratic might seem surprising, given that one of its main functions is democracy promotion. However, the OSCE represents one of the hybrid threshold organizations discussed above. The OSCE was specifically founded with the intention of security cooperation between former Soviet states and European members and has therefore always had a highly heterogenous membership with regard to regime types. Thus, a formal mandate of democracy promotion sits uneasily with the continued membership of some highly autocratic members across Eurasia up to the present. At the same time, the average authoritarian density of the OSCE saw a shift from autocratic to democratic after 1990 (see also Figure 3.2), highlighting the diverging categorization of some institutions depending on the type of measurement used.

The distribution of autocratic and democratic ROs in Latin America mirrors the turbulent past and present of the region characterized by military

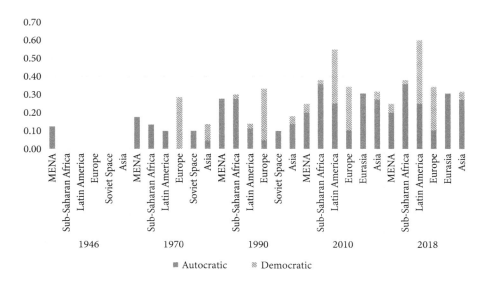

Figure 3.6 Number of autocratic and democratic ROs per state in region, 1946, 1990, 2010, and 2018 (based on own data and Polity (Marshall et al. 2018)).

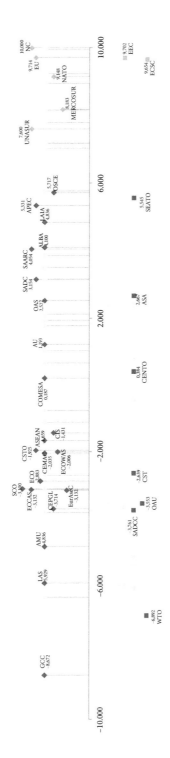

Figure 3.7 Lifetime density scores across select ROs (height of line no substantive meaning; own depiction based on polity (Marshall et al. 2018)).

dictatorships in the 1970s and 1980s, broad democratization, recent instability, populist governments, and democratic backsliding in diverse countries from Argentina to Bolivia, Brazil, Honduras, Nicaragua, and Venezuela. Still, we see a slight majority of democratic ROs in 2018, but also the biggest change since 1990 where most ROs were still autocratic. While some of the older Latin American ROs such as the Latin American and Caribbean Economic System (SELA), LAIA, and the OAS exhibit an overall autocratic density due to the long autocratic past of many of their members, newer ROs on the continent such as MERCOSUR, UNASUR, and the Pacific Alliance can be characterized as democratic. In contrast, only one of the newly founded ROs in Latin America—ALBA—is autocratic due to the membership of Venezuela, Cuba, and Nicaragua, three of the remaining firmly autocratic regimes in Latin America to date.

To further understand the distribution of density scores across different ROs, Figure 3.7 depicts the distribution averaged across the lifespan of organizations for select prominent ROs. Clearly, the GCC represents the most autocratic club to date, with only highly autocratic members across the lifespan of the organization. Most autocratic ROs cluster around a medium autocratic density score (e.g. SCO (-3.1), ECOWAS (-2), ASEAN (-1.6), CIS (-1.4)). The field thins out toward the threshold of 6, with the OAS ($+2.5$), SADC ($+3.1$), ALBA ($+4.1$), and LAIA ($+4.8$) among the least autocratic institutions. Only a few organizations remain on the democratic end of the continuum. Because of its broad membership including many non-democratic post-Soviet regimes, the OSCE ($+5.7$) hovers around the threshold but does not qualify for the category of democratic RO. Latin American organizations such as MERCOSUR ($+8.1$) and UNASUR ($+7.6$) remain in the middle field of democratic ROs. The Nordic Council and the EU, in contrast, are the most democratic ROs with almost perfect scores of $+10$ and $+9.7$, despite some prominent cases of backsliding on the European continent in recent years. Historically democratic ROs are also mostly European-based, with the Southeast Asian-focused SEATO as a threshold case, because many European states were also members (e.g. France, the UK).

Mandates and Authority of Dictator Clubs

In this final subsection, we will turn to analyze the third main independent variable, authority of ROs, and investigate the main formal functions evident from mandates of dictator clubs as well as institutionalized constraints. Figure 3.8 (left) shows the distribution of the main objectives across regions and RO types (on coding of functions, see the Online Appendix). Economic ROs still represent the most common type across all regions (36), corresponding to the historical development of regionalism in terms of economic cooperation (e.g. Söderbaum 2016a). Security ROs are far less common, in contrast, with only six ROs in total, while political ROs feature quite prominently across all regions (30). Security ROs are most common in Europe and Eurasia, mirroring the strong security focus of transnational politics in the post-Soviet space. Both Latin America and Europe feature more political than economic ROs, while the Middle East has a similar number of political and economic institutions. Again, this mirrors the main focus of transregional relations in these regions. In particular, the European region has historically focused on economic, political, and security matters simultaneously, which can be seen by the relatively equal distribution of ROs across political, economic, and security objectives.

In Sub-Saharan Africa, in contrast, regional projects have predominantly been framed in terms of economic cooperation, although this focus does not necessarily match the main interdependence problems of the region, which are largely security-related with low levels of economic interdependencies (Börzel and Risse 2016c, p. 629). Surprisingly, though, there are no explicit security ROs in Africa. Rather, political and economic ROs seem to have gained strong security elements to deal with transnational security threats over time. Both ECOWAS and the African Union (AU) have, for instance, developed competences for automatic suspension and military intervention to safeguard democracy and human rights.

The main cooperation logic evident from mandates also differs between democratic and autocratic institutions, as is evident from the right-hand panel in Figure 3.8. While both dictator clubs and democratic ROs form political ROs at about equal rates (22 percent vs. 19 percent), most dictator clubs have been founded with a clear economic mandate. This seems to be primarily driven by the various sub-regional economic communities in Sub-Saharan Africa that formed around a specific post-colonial developmental mandate, as well as economic cooperation in Asia. Both regions, however, have also been heavily incentivized by foreign actors, particularly the EU and the US, to form economic regional clubs (Engel and Mattheis 2021; Stapel et al. 2023). Interestingly, security ROs feature somewhat more prominently among dictator clubs, with historic organizations such as the WTO, the Central Treaty Organization (CENTO), a Middle Eastern military alliance also known as the Baghdad Pact, and SEATO dominating the field. In contrast, only two such clubs are still active, both in Eurasia: the CSTO

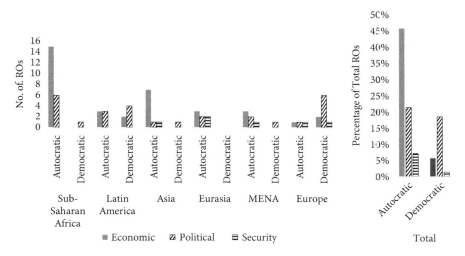

Figure 3.8 Number of ROs by economic, political, and security mandates per region and regime type, 1946–2018 (based on own data and Polity (Marshall et al. 2018)).

and the SCO. Both have been described as counter-institutionalization to the Western-dominated NATO (e.g. Allison 2018; Aris 2011).

While most of these ROs, both democratic and autocratic, have broadened their policy scope over time (Hooghe et al. 2017, 2019; Panke et al. 2020), dictator clubs seem to be particularly active in the economic and political arena. This also corresponds to the findings presented in Chapters 5 to 7: dictator clubs are particularly engaged in redistributing resources through economic cooperation and supporting each other politically by offering resources to legitimize elections, to constrain oppositional actors, and to protect against foreign interferences. In contrast, traditional military cooperation for external defense purposes is less common. Instead, military interventions by dictator clubs are employed to strengthen the internal security of member regimes in trouble, as the GCC intervention in Bahrain discussed in Chapter 5 highlights (see also the literature on coup-proofing through military cooperation, particularly in Sub-Saharan Africa: Boutton 2019; Cottiero 2023). Dictator clubs also use covert methods of intelligence cooperation meant to repress dissidents at home and abroad, as we can see from the Uighur case in China (on this, see also recent studies on transnational repression by Dukalskis et al. 2022; Lemon and Antonov 2020).

While informal practice might be very important for the functioning of dictator clubs, the presence of formal institutional constraints is still an important dimension to consider. Authority delegated to a regional court

60 How Regional Organizations Sustain Authoritarian Rule

or tribunal could, in fact, endanger the ability of dictator clubs to support their own and empower oppositional actors to lodge complaints. While we might expect dictator clubs to refrain from delegating this type of authority to regional agents, many autocratic ROs in the sample have, in fact, done so over the last decades, as is evident from Table 3.1. As we can see, 20 ROs from

Table 3.1 ROs with a court or tribunal (rows highlighted red were autocratic from the start) (based on own data)

IO Acronym	Full Name	Start	End	RO Type at Start
AU	African Union	2006		Hybrid
ANDEAN	Andean Community	1983[a]		Democratic
ASEAN	Association of Southeast Asian Nations	2004		Hybrid
BENELUX	Benelux Union	1974		Democratic
CARICOM	Caribbean Community	1996		Hybrid
CEMAC	Central Africa Economic and Monetary Community	2000		Hybrid
SICA	Central American Integration System	1994		Democratic
COMESA	Common Market for Eastern and Southern Africa	1998		HYBRID
CIS	Commonwealth of Independent States	1994		Hybrid
COE	Council of Europe	1998		Democratic
EAC	East African Community	2001		Hybrid
ECOWAS	Economic Community of West African States	2001		Hybrid
EU	European Union	1993		Democratic
LAS	League of Arab States	2003		Autocratic
OSCE	Organization for Security and Co-operation in Europe[a]	1994		Democratic
OAU	Organization of African Unity (succeeded by AU)	1987		Autocratic
OAS	Organization of American States	1979		Hybrid
SADC	Southern African Development Community	1992	2012	Hybrid
MERCOSUR	Southern Common Market	2004		Democratic
OECS[b]	Organization of Eastern Caribbean States	2001		N.A.

[a]The foundation of the Andean Court of Justice predates the formal foundation of the RO; the court was part of the Andean Pact, a multilateral treaty preceding the Andean Community.
[b]A majority of member states are not covered by Polity or Varieties of Democracy (V-Dem) due to their small population size. Thus there is no lifetime density for the OECS and ACS.

the sample of 72 ROs have established standing courts and tribunals with broader mandates than simple trade dispute resolution between two member states, with only 7 out of these 20 representing democratic institutions. In fact, autocratic regimes have been found to accede to human rights treaties and international courts at similar rates compared to democracies in order to legitimize their regimes and signal commitment to international norms (e.g. Lohaus and Stapel 2022; Simmons and Danner 2010). We can also see this in the data presented in Table 3.1. Most of the dictator clubs that have installed courts are in the hybrid category and founded courts and tribunals during the third wave of democratization until the mid-2000s.

This pattern will also become more evident from the empirical analysis. As we will see in Chapter 6 in the case of the SADC, a tribunal with a human rights mandate was established in 1992 in the wake of an international decade of liberalization to satisfy international donors and NGOs. The tribunal was empowered to hear cases from individual petitioners, and also on human rights matters. However, the SADC member states did not expect the tribunal to actually rule against sitting governments and subsequently limited the powers of the court when it challenged the Zimbabwe regime in a landmark case in 2008, thereby factually removing its power in 2012. Agents empowered by dictator clubs on paper can thus "run amok" (Hulse and van der Vleuten 2015) and contribute to an empowerment of oppositional actors, thereby threatening the functioning of dictator clubs in meaningful ways.

Mapping Authoritarian Regime Failure

Now that we have understood the historical development, regional dispersion, and variation in terms of functions and authority among dictator clubs, this section will turn to map the dependent variable of this book: autocratic regime survival. As discussed in the previous chapter, I understand survival as two possible outcomes: autocratic regime survival (no autocratic replacements) and autocratic system survival (no democratization). Autocratic replacements refer to transitions from one type of autocratic regime to a different type of autocratic regime, while democratization refers to system breakdowns leading to subsequent democracy. To measure both types of outcomes, I take the binary variables on transitions from the GWF dataset, "Autocratic Breakdown and Regime Transitions" (Geddes et al. 2014), which covers the timespan 1945 to 2010. This dataset was chosen because it is the only one available also covering regime transitions between autocratic states, thereby not simply focusing on instances of democratization.

The GWF dataset includes country-year observations for every country that has experienced autocratic rule at some point between 1945 and 2010 and has a population bigger than 500,000. Only autocratic country-years are included. A country enters the dataset either in 1945 or at the year of RO foundation if it has always been autocratic, or in the year following an instance of democratic breakdown. It exits the dataset either when it turns democratic or when it enters a phase that is neither autocratic nor democratic (i.e. not independent (occupied by foreign troops), the government doesn't control the majority of the state resources, or the country ceases to exist). Thus, democratic country-years and country-years that are neither democratic nor autocratic are not included in the dataset. The onset of autocracy can either occur through non-competitive or non-inclusive elections or a change of electoral rules preventing such elections in the future. The end of an autocratic system is defined by experiencing an instance of democratization that encompasses competitive and inclusive elections for the executive. The end of an autocratic regime is defined as all instances when a group with different rules for choosing the leader takes power (e.g. by coup, rebellion, or civil war). The final variables are dichotomous measures, indicating survival (0) or autocratic or democratic breakdown (1).

To update the dataset, both variables have been extended to the year 2020 based on the GWF codebook. A detailed list and explanation of the coding decisions for every country can be found in the Online Appendix. This update resulted in 17 new cases, with 14 cases of democratic regime change and 3 cases of autocratic replacements. Figure 3.9 shows the distribution of cases across decades since 1945. The graph reveals the continuing development of decreasing numbers of both democratic transitions and autocratic replacements in the last decade. This might be predominantly due to a decline in military regimes in the last decades that have a much lower likelihood of regime survival due to their transitionary function as a bridge toward civilian rule or turnover to other autocratic leadership groups (Bermeo 2016; Geddes et al. 2014, 2018).

Both types of regime change also vary considerably across regions (see Figure 3.10). While almost all autocratic regimes in the West have democratized until 2020, with the exception of Hungary's reentry as an autocracy in 2018, the percentage is lowest in the MENA region. Other regions in the Global South have seen between 30 and 50 percent of their regimes democratize. In contrast, autocratic replacements are similarly common in Latin America, MENA, and Sub-Saharan Africa. In Latin America, this was due to military dictatorships changing hands with personalist leaders back and forth, while MENA has seen a higher number of replacements of monarchies

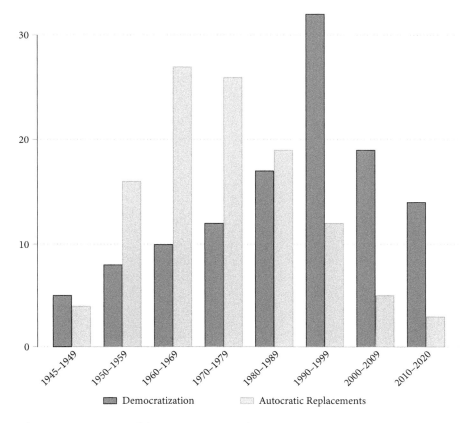

Figure 3.9 Instances of democratic regime change and autocratic replacements across decades (based on Geddes et al. (2018) and own data).

with populist or military regimes. In Sub-Saharan Africa, coups have been quite common, particularly in western and central Africa, with different party leaders changing hands with the help of loyal militaries. While autocratic replacements have become more common again in Sub-Saharan Africa in recent years, most of the instances of military coups in the region happened after the end of the study period in 2020.

Finally, it is also interesting to gauge the stability of authoritarian regimes. While some regimes consolidate their new form of democratic or autocratic rule over the long run, for a range of regimes this is not the case. On the contrary, we see a number of regimes re-enter the dataset several times after democratic regime change, with Haiti (5), Thailand (4), and Peru (4) leading the score on the democratic breakdown side, and Bolivia (6) and Guatemala (5) on autocratic replacements. This also has consequences for ROs, as depicted in Figure 3.11. As becomes evident, both the OAS and OAU

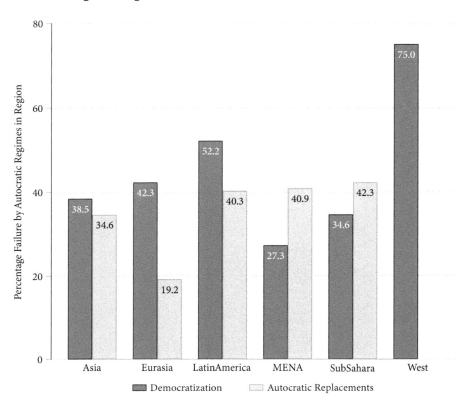

Figure 3.10 Percentages of democratic regime change and autocratic replacements across regions (based on Geddes et al. (2018) and own data).

have seen a host of democratic and autocratic replacements, which is also due to their large size. The Latin America and Caribbean Economic System (SELA), though, has experienced the most drastic form of democratization, including several of the Latin American regimes with multiple democratic re-entries. On the autocratic replacement side, the LOAS features as the institution most prominently affected by autocratic replacements. But as we will see in Chapters 4 and 6, ROs do not help to prevent against these types of leader changes because they rarely involve actual regime change.

Conclusion

As the data presented in this chapter has shown, dictator clubs are a ubiquitous phenomenon even after the wave of democratization in the 1990s. Highly autocratic clubs have become even more autocratic since the 1990s, while more hybrid institutions with medium-density scores have mostly retained members that have introduced elections and liberalized civil and political freedoms, but still hold a tight grip on the central tenets of power. A notable exception is Latin America, where we have seen former ROs with a number of highly autocratic military regimes like the OAS turn into fully fledged democratic institutions. While Latin American ROs today, like all democratic institutions, are struggling to contain autocratization processes among their membership, we cannot yet discern a large-scale descent of democratic clubs into the authoritarian camp.

The chapter has also highlighted that autocratic and democratic regimes sort into distinct clubs. Homogeneity is higher among democratic institutions, potentially because many have introduced strict entry requirements

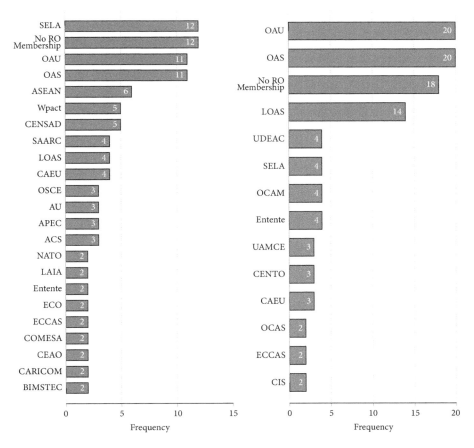

Figure 3.11 ROs with multiple failure events (based on Geddes et al. (2018) and own data), democratization (left) and autocratic replacements (right).

based on democratic governance while dictator clubs do not have these types of formal entry requirements. Overall, few institutions exist with an equal number of autocratic and democratic members, and the ones that have heterogenous membership do so because established democratic and often Western states have joined together with autocratic regimes, as in the OSCE. We have also learned that there seems to be a reinforcement effect because ROs usually retain their autocratic and democratic densities and homogeneity from foundation to death.

In terms of functions, many dictator clubs have developed out of an economic-developmental mandate, or have specifically been founded as political institutions. Few explicit security organizations exist in both camps, and dictator clubs with a security mandate usually rather focus on internal security, not traditional military external defense pacts. Finally, a range of dictator clubs have established institutional constraints in the forms of courts, often to signal commitment to an evolving democracy norm since the 1990s. As will become evident in the later analysis, these types of institutional constraints can become a major threat to the survival and legitimacy of member states, and can empower dissidents and oppositional actors on the domestic and regional scene.

Finally, the chapter has traced the development of democratization and autocratic replacements over time and across regions. Both types of regime changes have become less numerous in the last decade between 2010 and 2020, following a similar trend that started in the mid-2000s. This is similar to findings from other democracy research, which highlights the ebbing wave of democratization and an equally expanding wave of autocratization (Lührmann and Lindberg 2019).

4
The Effects of Membership in Dictator Clubs on Regime Survival

In the previous chapter, I showed how dictator clubs are a common regional arrangement particularly in the Global South, but that there is significant variation in terms of their membership composition over time and across regions. I also discussed global trends with regard to authoritarian regime survival and failure between 1945 and 2020, and introduced an update to the Autocratic Breakdown and Regime Transition dataset (Geddes et al. 2014, 2018). In this chapter, I now focus on exploring the domestic consequences that membership in dictator clubs has for the likelihood of survival of authoritarian incumbent regimes. To this end, this chapter presents results from survival analysis (Cox 1972), a set of models that can be used to assess the influence of different factors on the hazard of an event occurring over time.

In Chapter 2, I hypothesized that membership in regional organizations (ROs) can positively influence the spell of authoritarian incumbent regimes under three conditions. First, where preferences of members are more aligned and autocratic density is higher, the likelihood of ROs being able to successfully support incumbent members under political duress is also higher. Second, membership should also be more likely to yield effects when the homogeneity of members is higher. Where ROs comprise both highly autocratic and highly democratic members, the effect of autocratic density should be dampened. Third, ROs that have been equipped with higher levels of authority might also be more likely to interfere on the side of challengers and block RO support to the autocratic incumbent.

In this chapter, the effects of these three conditions on the likelihood of authoritarian regime survival will be tested while controlling for alternative domestic and international explanations. As operationalized in Chapter 3, I understand the dependent variable authoritarian regime survival as two distinct outcomes: regime failure due to democratic transitions and regime failure due to autocratic replacements. Both outcomes usually follow distinct types of threats. While election loss or a change of formal

---

How Regional Organizations Sustain Authoritarian Rule. Maria J. Debre, Oxford University Press.
© Maria J. Debre (2025). DOI: 10.1093/9780198903635.003.0004

rules is more likely to usher in democratic regime change, military coups and revolutions are more likely followed by a replacement with another autocratic regime (Geddes et al. 2014, 2018). The two outcomes will therefore be tested in separate models because they rarely represent competing risks.

Sampling of ROs is based on the *Yearbook of International Organizations* (YIO) as laid out in more detail in Chapter 3 and the Online Appendix. ROs are defined as the formal and institutionalized cooperative relations among at least three states within a region (Börzel and Risse 2016b). Accordingly, all international governmental organizations (IGOs) listed in the YIO with (1) regionally defined membership, (2) at least three member states, and (3) a formal secretariat are included. Additionally, only ROs that comprise political and/or security as policy fields are selected because the theorized mechanisms cannot work in purely task-specific technical ROs that do not cover matters of high politics. Policy fields of ROs were coded based on the RO profiles in YIO. A list of all ROs covered by the dataset can be found in Table A11 in the Online Appendix.

This chapter is structured in four sections. I begin with a section on the operationalization of variables included in the analysis. I will briefly summarize the main variables making up the dataset as introduced in Chapter 3 and will then motivate and explain the choice of control variables that have been identified by previous literature to significantly affect authoritarian regime survival. In a second section, I will then outline the dataset design and model specifications to explain the setup used for survival analysis. In a third section, I will present the statistical results and robustness tests, which can be found in the Online Appendix. The chapter concludes with an in-depth discussion of the results, implications for theory, and connection to further case-based findings in the following three chapters.

Operationalization of Variables

The existing literature is rich in causal explanations to account for the survival of authoritarian regimes. Quantitative tests usually include a range of domestic factors but rarely include international variables in the analysis. The intention of this chapter is to specifically model and assess the institutional environment of authoritarian regimes and their explanatory power while controlling for other important international and domestic variables identified by previous scholarship. The following subsection explains the choice and operationalization of included predictor variables.

Dependent Variable: Autocratic and Democratic Regime Breakdown

The dependent variable measures two types of breakdown events that can end the survival spell of an autocratic regime: autocratic regime breakdown due to autocratic replacements (*autrep*) and autocratic system breakdown due to democratization (*democ*). Autocratic replacements refer to transitions from one type of autocratic regime to a different type of autocratic regime (e.g. a change from monarchical to military rule after a successful coup), while democratization refers to system breakdowns leading to subsequent democracy. To measure both types of outcomes, I take the binary variables on transitions from Geddes et al. (2014). Since the Geddes et al. dataset ends in 2010, I have updated their data until 2020 (see Chapter 3 and Online Appendix). The extension yields additional 14 cases of democratic regime change and three cases of autocratic replacements. Ten regimes experience autocratization and re-enter the dataset between 2010 and 2020. One new country, South Sudan, enters the dataset in 2012 after gaining independence in 2011.

Autocratic replacements have only recently been included into the study of stability and survival, while previous analyses have mostly dealt with democratization. However, separating both types of breakdowns makes a big difference when analyzing drivers of survival because it helps to separate if and how predictor variables help to deter against replacements by a rivaling autocratic group or against democratic challengers, and can thus offer more fine-grained information on underlying processes. The influence of resource wealth on authoritarian survival has, for instance, been a topic of debate for years, with some authors arguing that it does destabilize autocracies (Ross 2001a, 2012), while others could not find effects on autocratic failure (Haber and Menaldo 2011). However, when separating both types of regime breakdowns, analysis shows that resource wealth does in fact have a positive effect on survival by lowering the likelihood of replacements by a rivaling autocratic group, but that resources do not help to deter democratic challengers to prevent democratization (Wright et al. 2015).

Independent Variables: Autocratic Density, Homogeneity, and Authority

I construct three predictor variables to test the argument that membership in a more autocratic but less authoritative RO should increase the probability of authoritarian regime survival. The first predictor variable, autocratic density (*autdensity*), represents the average autocracy score of the most autocratic RO in which state i is a member based on the Polity IV data (Marshall et al. 2018). Autocratic density is constructed by computing the average *polity2* score of all member states of a RO in which country i is a member in year t, without the score for country i. The final score for each country is achieved by transforming the Polity score so that the final range runs from 1 (highly democratic) to 21 (highly autocratic), with 0 signaling no membership. ROs with a score of 6 and higher are consequently considered as autocratic, including the category of anocracies. I expect that membership in more autocratic ROs should reduce the probability of both types of breakdown events, and that the effect is more pronounced the higher the autocratic density of an RO.

Following the argumentation on the democratizing effects of ROs (Pevehouse 2005a), theoretically, it should be enough to be a member of one highly autocratic organization for the effect to work. If a country is a member of several autocratic ROs of which one or more turns more democratic, the country can still profit from the most autocratic RO to stabilize its rule. Thus, theoretically it should be enough to look at the most autocratic RO of which country i is a member of at a given point in time to see if it affects survival. However, membership in an additional RO that comprises more democratic members might still counteract the effects of the autocratic RO membership, thereby biasing estimation results. To account for possible changes in density scores across all RO memberships, I also test if results remain similar when including the average density across all RO memberships in a given year (*avgdensity*).

The second main predictor variable, autocratic homogeneity (*homogeneity*), measures the diversity of regimes within ROs. This diversity can best be captured by measuring the dispersion of Polity scores within autocratic ROs, which is expressed as the standard deviation in statistical terms. Thus, I calculate the standard deviation of all scores of all member states of each RO in year *t-1*. To capture autocratic homogeneity, I use the score corresponding to the most autocratic RO chosen for variable AutDensity for each unit under analysis. Thus, the variable measures the homogeneity of the most autocratic RO membership in a given year for country i under analysis. Higher values correspond to more diversity between members in terms of their autocratic and democratic characteristics, and should thus reduce the likelihood of regime or system survival, due to lower preference similarity. Additionally, homogeneity might also moderate the relationship of autocratic density and survival. Consequently, higher homogeneity should increase the effect of autocratic density on authoritarian regime and system survival, due to even higher preference similarity. Put simply, membership in an autocratic RO that is highly homogeneous (e.g. the Central Africa Economic and Monetary Community (CEMAC)) should be more likely to help prevent democratization and autocratic replacements compared to membership in an equally autocratic but less homogenous RO (e.g. the Economic Community of West African States (ECOWAS)).

The third main predictor variable measures the authority of a RO proxied by the degree of delegation awarded to regional courts. The presence of a regional court has been argued to be a major international driver of democratization processes because they can sanction non-compliant member states and thereby empower democratic coalitions over autocratic elites (Alter 2014; Alter and Hooghe 2016). In contrast, ROs without a regional court have no enforcement capacity over member states, and should thereby protect them from interference in domestic politics by independent judges.

While we might expect dispute settlement mechanisms to be endogenous to regime type, with more autocratic ROs having a lower likelihood of being endowed with more authority, this is empirically not the case. As we have seen in Chapter 3, a range of dictator clubs have established regional courts and tribunals with some form of bindingness in their decision-making power over time. In fact, authority of ROs is mainly explained by two factors that are not necessarily related to regime type. First, functional pressure to cooperate often leads to task-specific institutions with specific contracts, open membership, and low authority. In contrast, transnational identity will drive institution-building with open contracts, limited membership, and higher authority (Hooghe et al. 2019). Unfortunately, more fine-grained measures of RO authority are currently not available for the sample of ROs employed in this book. The Measuring International Authority dataset by Hooghe et al. (2017) only captures a small subsection of the sample, while the dataset employed by Zürn, Tokhi, and Binder (2021) only covers the 30 most important IGOs globally. I therefore include a binary variable that measures if the RO under investigation has a regional court (standing or ad hoc) with some authority over human rights and good governance matters (*authority*). This excludes dispute settlement mechanisms that only have jurisdiction if called upon for trade-related inter-state disputes.

In a first step, ROs with a permanent or ad hoc court were identified based on the variable dispute settlement taken from Hooghe et al. (2017) and ROs with a court coded as 1. Those ROs not covered by the Hooghe et al. dataset were coded based on the collection of RO courts in Alter (2014) and Alter and Hooghe (2016) and further supplemented by an online search on the respective RO website for all those ROs covered in the sample of this study that are not included in either of those works. I expect that membership in ROs without a regional court should increase the probability of both types of breakdown events.

Alternative Explanations

To control for alternative explanations, I further include predictor variables pertaining to international- and domestic-level arguments from the international relations (IR) and comparative authoritarianism literature. First, power-based approaches such as hegemonic stability theory suggest that regional institutions are only epiphenomenal to the underlying power asymmetries within a region (Gilpin 1987). States thus join international institutions such as ROs to bandwagon with regional powerhouses that wield substantial economic and military power and are willing to act as the "regional paymaster" (Mattli 1999, p. 5). To assess if survival is more likely where an autocratic power dominates a region, I include a variable to test for the effect of regional power asymmetries (*hegemon*). I understand a regional autocratic power as the state with the highest share of material capabilities in a region, with at least 20 percent of all regional power capabilities based on the Correlates of War (COW) National Material Capabilities dataset (Singer 1988). The variable is a dummy coded 1 if country i is a member of a RO with any of the autocratic regional powers as members.

A further realist implication flows from balance-of-power theory, which argues that international anarchy results in internal and external balancing to protect states from aggression by a dominant power (Waltz 1979). Since balance-of-power should lead to a stable international system, I would expect higher likelihoods of breakdowns with the end of the Cold War. To capture this change in the international system, I include a dummy variable (*coldwar*), coded 0 before 1990 and 1 afterwards.

Contagion offers a second international alternative to explain regime dynamics. Diffusion approaches treat events such as regime transitions as open to interdependent decision-making rather than purely endogenous or functional processes of rational actors (Glasius et al. 2020; Gleditsch and Ward 2006; Greenhill 2015; Hyde 2011). These interdependencies play out particularly strongly on the regional level as waves of regime breakdowns such as the Color Revolutions or the Arab Spring have shown. To control for these types of interdependencies, I include a binary indicator coded 1 if a state in the region has experienced a democratic regime change (for the dependent variable democratization) or autocratic breakdown (for the dependent variable autocratic replacements) in the previous year.

To control for alternative explanations identified by the comparative authoritarian resilience literature, I include three variables pertaining to the most important domestic-level factors. First, the institutionalist literature argues that institutional variation between regimes can account for differences in survival (Gandhi 2008; Geddes 2003; Hadenius and Teorell 2007). In essence, this literature finds that regimes with institutionalized dominant parties and legislatures are more stable because they constrain actors by containing conflict amongst elites, and by binding them to citizens through established patronage networks (Pepinsky 2014). To capture the effect of regime type on survival, I include a categorical variable based on the definition of regime type in the Geddes, Wright, and Frantz dataset that codes each regime as either military, personal, party-based, ormonarchy.

Second, both economic growth and economic crisis have been identified as important factors to the survival and breakdown of autocracies and democracies, although the literature is divided on the direction and causality of the relationship (Cheibub and Vreeland 2011). While modernization theory argues that economic wealth can induce democratic regime transitions (Gasiorowski 1995; Lipset 1959), its critics posit that economic growth rather stabilizes autocratic systems (Huntington 2006; Moore 1966; O'Donnell 1973) or that the relationship is dynamic and dependent on degree of growth (Przeworski et al. 2000). To control for the possible effect of economic growth on regime survival, I include annual growth rates (growth) based on logged GDP per capita taken from the updated Maddison project (Bolt and van Zanden 2020; Maddison 2010).

Finally, structural factors, most importantly resource wealth, have been argued to produce positive effects for autocratic survival. The literature on rentier state theory argues that governments reliant on external revenue from natural resources can act more autonomously from society since they are not dependent on taxation (Beblawi and Luciani 1987; Mahdavi 1970). Instead, rentier states can offer benefits and sustain coercive institutions to alleviate pressure for democratization (Ross 2001a, 2012). While the resource curse argument is disputed (Haber and Menaldo 2011), not including resource wealth as a control variable could produce biased results, since all studies do find some effect of resource wealth on regime dynamics.

I include two alternative variables to account for resource dependency. First, I include total resource income per capita (*resources*) taken from

74 How Regional Organizations Sustain Authoritarian Rule

Haber and Menaldo (2011), which is available from 1800 to 2006. Second, I include total natural resource rents as a percentage of GDP (*dependence*) from the World Bank, which is available from 1970 until 2020 (World Bank 2023). Since both measures are slightly different (resource wealth vs. resource dependence), I employ them in alternative models. I expect that rising levels of resource rents make autocratic replacements more likely, but do not significantly affect the likelihood of democratization (Wright et al. 2015).

Model Specifications

To estimate effects, I employ survival analysis (Cox 1972), which is a particularly well-suited set of methods to analyze the time until the occurrence of an event, in this case the breakdown of autocratic rule. Essentially, survival models estimate how covariates change the underlying baseline hazard of an event occurring at time t, given that the subject under analysis has survived until this point in time. The models are advantageous to deal with issues of right-censoring, which is important since countries are only observed until 2010, but may not have experienced a breakdown event until that point in time.

Countries enter the risk-set with the first autocratic year and exit the year after a democratic breakdown event with countries that are still autocratic at the end of the study period in 2018 right-censored. Years in which a country was not independent (foreign occupation) or in which the central government did not control a majority of the territory (failed state) are excluded. When a country ceases to exist, it exits the dataset in the year following its abolishment. Since countries can theoretically undergo several instances of regime change and backsliding over time, the data is in multiple failure-time format, with countries that experience re-autocratization entering the risk-set again the year after the event.

In total, 55 regimes remain autocratic at the end of the study period. Twenty-six autocratic regimes re-enter the dataset at some point after previously undergoing democratic regime change, with 11 out of those 26 experiencing more than one instance of re-autocratization (amongst those, Haiti, Peru, and Thailand are the least stable regimes with five and four instances of re-autocratization each; see also Chapter 3). Thirty-seven countries experience autocratic replacements, with 17 experiencing more than one instance (at the top are Bolivia and Guatemala, with six and five autocratic replacements, respectively; see Chapter 3). In total, the dataset includes 114 cases

The Effects of Membership in Dictator Clubs on Regime Survival   **75**

of democratic regime change and 112 cases of autocratic replacement for the study period 1946–2018.

I estimate stratified Cox proportional hazard models with robust standard errors following a conditional risk-set approach (Prentice et al. 1981).[1] Cox models work with random hazard functions based on time since study entry and stratify units on the number of preceding failure events. This approach is chosen to account for multiple ordered failure events. First, failures are assumed to be ordered since countries are not at risk of a second failure event if they have not experienced a preceding moment of breakdown. Second, countries are stratified by number of preceding failure events, since a country that has previously undergone a breakdown should theoretically have a different underlying hazard of experiencing a recurring failure compared to countries that have been stable over longer time periods without any failure events. Finally, time is counted from the first time a country enters the risk-set to account for the overall time a country has been under autocratic rule. As a robustness check, models without stratification and models counting time from previous failure events are estimated and reported in the Online Appendix.

Testing the Results

Before investigating the results from the Cox regression analysis, it is helpful to look at the baseline survival rates of democratization and autocratic replacements using the Kaplan–Meier estimator (see Figure 4.1). The estimator depicts the survival function among the population of autocratic regimes, with downward steps signifying probabilities of survival until that point in analysis time, in this case, years since establishment of the autocratic regime. For both democratization and autocratic replacements, regimes are relatively volatile for about 50 years, with median survival times at about 40 until democratization and 30 until autocratic replacements. However, some regimes manage to survive exceptionally long without undergoing any form of breakdown event. Among those are regimes such as Mexico (85 years until democratization), South Africa (84 years until democratization), Ethiopia (85 years until autocratic replacement), Nepal (105 years until autocratic replacement), and Saudi Arabia (83 years of uninterrupted rule until 2010).

---

[1] The proportional-hazards assumption of Cox models essentially assumes that hazard ratios of all subjects are proportional over time. Results from the proportional-hazards tests for both dependent variables are reported in Tables A9 and A10 in the Online Appendix. The assumption is not violated.

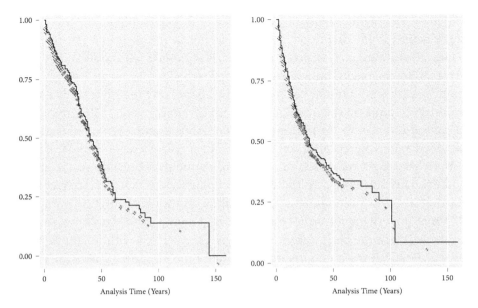

Figure 4.1 Kaplan–Meier survival estimates, democratization, and autocratic replacement (based on Geddes et al. (2018) and own data).

While the study period begins in 1946, some autocracies that have been independent sovereign states before that date enter the risk-set with the first independent autocratic year and are thus not left-censored. Thus, survival times can exceed the time of the study period. Because data is not left-censored, the dataset includes one extreme outlier—Oman—with 268 years of uninterrupted autocratic rule since the establishment of an independent Sultanate in 1742. The country is therefore excluded from the following analysis to avoid bias of results.

Further tests show interesting variation in baseline hazards for different regime types (Figure 4.2). With regard to democratization as a failure event, we can observe that monarchies are among the most stable regime types, although they only make up a small portion of the regimes in the dataset. Regimes with the longest uninterrupted tenure include monarchies such as Nepal (105 years), Ethiopia (85 years), and Saudi Arabia (93 years). In contrast, party, personal, and military regimes are much more short-lived. Military regimes remain among the most susceptible to democratic failure because they are often established as interim regimes to safeguard orderly transfers to democratic rule. Party regimes are more stable with a median survival time of 60 years compared to personal regimes with a median of only 30 years.

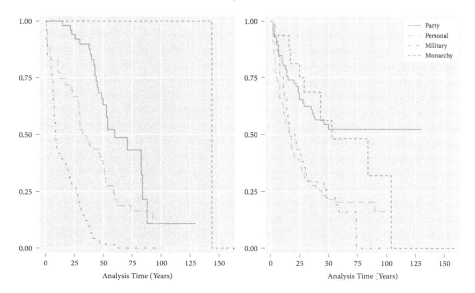

Figure 4.2 Kaplan–Meier estimator by regime type for democratization and autocratic replacements (based on Geddes et al. (2018) and own data).

In contrast, monarchies are more volatile to autocratic replacements. This is due to many monarchies having been replaced by personalist regimes such as Egypt in 1952, Ethiopia in 1974, Libya in 1969, and Iran in 1979. Party-based regimes remain more stable in the face of intra-elite challengers because they are able to integrate and co-opt elites through institutional co-optation (Blaydes 2011; Gandhi 2008). Personalist and military regimes are the most susceptible to being overturned by intra-elite challengers with a median tenure of only 20 years.

Interesting variation can also be observed for different regions (see Figure 4.3). While autocracies in Latin America only have a mean survival time of 20 years, facing both high risks of democratization and autocratic replacements, autocracies in Eurasia, the Middle East and North Africa (MENA), and Asia remain somewhat more stable. In fact, some of the most volatile regimes with more than three instances of re-autocratization or autocratic replacements come from Latin America, as we have also seen in Chapter 3. Sub-Saharan Africa shows a relatively high propensity for autocratic replacements and scores similarly to Asia and Eurasia with regard to the risk of democratization. Three autocracies existed in core Europe (Spain, Portugal, and Greece[2]), all democratizing without ever having faced

---

[2] East Germany as well as Eastern European countries were coded as part of the Soviet space until 1990.

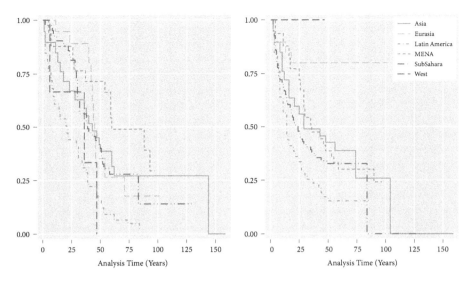

Figure 4.3 Kaplan–Meier estimator by region for democratization and autocratic replacements (based on Geddes et al. (2018) and own data).

autocratic replacements. In 2018, one new autocracy in Europe—Hungary—entered the dataset again after democratizing with other post-Soviet states after the fall of the Soviet Union and becoming a full member of the European institutional system in subsequent years.

Effects on Likelihood of Democratization as Regime Failure Event

Turning to the effects of survival modeling, Table 4.1 reports results from estimations of democratization as a regime failure event. Model 1 reports results on the three main predictor variables Autocratic Density, Homogeneity, and Authority, Model 2 includes further international-level predictors, Models 3 and 4 represent fully saturated models with alternative specifications of the resource variable, Model 5 is a parameterized model including the interaction effect between Autocratic Density and Homogeneity, and Model 6 includes Average Density and overall homogeneity as the main regional predictors to account for density and homogeneity across all RO membership.

Overall, Table 4.1 reveals several important insights about the effect of RO membership on survival. First, across time and space, membership in ROs with higher autocratic density significantly reduces the hazard of experiencing democratic breakdowns. The results remain consistent across all model

The Effects of Membership in Dictator Clubs on Regime Survival 79

Table 4.1 ROs and autocratic survival (no democratization), 1945–2020

	(1)	(2)	(3)	(4)	(5)	(6)
Autocratic Density	**−0.0546**[**]	**−0.0575**[**]	**−0.0579**[*]	**−0.0988**[**]	**−0.0748**[*]	
	(0.0184)	(0.0212)	(0.0246)	(0.0308)	(0.0342)	
Homogeneity	**0.210**[***]	**0.202**[***]	**0.135**[**]	**0.124**[*]	0.0834	
	(0.0423)	(0.0426)	(0.0491)	(0.0601)	(0.100)	
Authority	−0.0522	−0.122	−0.585	−0.195	−0.596	−0.537
	(0.262)	(0.274)	(0.546)	(0.319)	(0.540)	(0.561)
Hegemon		0.324	0.223	0.443	0.223	0.368
		(0.278)	(0.314)	(0.426)	(0.315)	(0.307)
Cold War		0.206	0.0118	0.606	0.0152	−0.183
		(0.291)	(0.317)	(0.331)	(0.320)	(0.317)
Contagion		−0.897[**]	−0.770	−0.701	−0.762	−0.861[*]
		(0.310)	(0.450)	(0.408)	(0.447)	(0.437)
Regime Type						
Party			−0.641	−0.354	−0.640	−0.572
			(0.339)	(0.342)	(0.338)	(0.352)
Military			**1.347**[***]	**0.993**[**]	**1.352**[***]	**1.367**[***]
			(0.335)	(0.319)	(0.335)	(0.347)
Monarchy			**−34.28**[***]	**−33.79**[***]	**−34.95**[***]	**−33.29**[***]
			(0.612)	(0.692)	(0.610)	(0.571)
Growth			**−3.705**[**]	**−5.584**[***]	**−3.703**[**]	**−4.132**[**]
			(1.273)	(1.024)	(1.272)	(1.263)
Resources			−0.0703		−0.0735	−0.0741
			(0.0461)		(0.0475)	(0.0454)
Dependence				−0.0178		
				(0.0109)		
AutDensity[*] Homogeneity					0.00696	
					(0.0118)	
Average Density						**−0.140**[**]
						(0.0427)
Homogeneity (all)						**0.470**[**]
						(0.151)
N	4882	4882	3165	2951	3165	3165

Stratified Cox proportional hazard models with robust standard errors in parentheses and coefficients reported. Bold entries indicate statistically significant values. [+] $p < 0.1$, [*] $p < 0.05$, [**] $p < 0.01$, [***] $p < 0.001$

specifications and controls. In the fully saturated Models 3 and 4, including alternative specifications of the control for resource rents, we can see that autocratic density has a significant and negative effect on the hazard of regime failure. Survival models report the hazard of a failure event occurring at point t in time. Where coefficients are negative, they decrease the hazard, thereby reducing the likelihood of experiencing democratization. Where coefficients are positive, they increase the hazard, thus having a negative effect on the likelihood of survival. The models thus show that membership in a dictator club can have lasting and positive effects for autocratic regimes, with membership in more autocratic clubs also translating into more support to stay in power during troubled times.

The effect on authoritarian survival also remains the same when including the average density across all RO memberships. Model 6 shows that an inclusion of the average density across all ROs that a country is a member of in a given year likewise reduced the hazard of democratization significantly. This indicates that autocratic regimes rarely seem to be members of both very autocratic and democratic ROs, but are rather members of a number of dictator clubs. The models thus offer strong support for Hypothesis 1 on the effect of autocratic density to explain the absence of democratization as a failure event.

Both results are quite stunning. First, it is interesting to note that both specifications of the main variable autocratic density, the autocratic density score of the highest RO membership as well as the average density score across all ROs, both significantly reduce the hazard of democratic regime change. This points to sorting effects of RO membership, with autocratic regimes mostly joining dictator clubs instead of a mix of ROs with both democratic and autocratic memberships. In fact, the mean of Autocratic Density (11.07) and Average Density (10.12) is very similar, highlighting that all memberships of a regime are usually in relatively similar types of ROs with regard to membership. This finding makes sense in light of findings from the democratization literature that newly democratic regimes tend to join ROs with a democratic density to signal their commitment to domestic regime change to domestic and international audiences and consequently profit from their membership by stabilizing democratic governance. While some autocratic regimes are also members in ROs with a democratic density (e.g. Russia and previously the Soviet Union in the Organization of Security and Cooperation in Europe (OSCE)), membership in the opposite club is not common, and does not induce regime change. The low impact of institutions such as the OSCE or the Council of Europe (CoE) have in fact been repeatedly shown by literature highlighting that in the absence of hard conditionality, soft mechanisms of influence are unlikely to yield to change in authoritarian regimes (Escribà-Folch and Wright 2010; Kelley 2004).

Second, membership in more homogenous ROs also significantly decreases the hazard of experiencing a democratic breakdown, providing first support for Hypothesis 2 on the effect of homogeneity. ROs with a more homogenous membership thus stabilize regimes. As shown in the work on democratization, democratic clubs will do so with regard to locking in democratic reform, while more homogenously autocratic clubs will be more likely to prevent democratic regime change. Interestingly, the interaction of homogeneity and density in Model 5 does not seem to create effects on the hazard of failure. While autocratic density remains significant, homogeneity and the interaction term are both not significant. This also becomes clearer in Figure 4.4, which plots the marginal effect of autocratic density with rising homogeneity. As Figure 4.4 shows, the marginal effect of density does not change across different homogeneity levels, pointing to the overall importance of density as the main regional predictor of survival.

These findings suggest that membership in a dictator club is enough to enjoy significant benefits of cooperation, regardless of whether some regimes in the club might have liberalized or even become full democracies over time. The constraining effects of democratic membership in a dictator club will become clearer in the case study of the Southern African Development

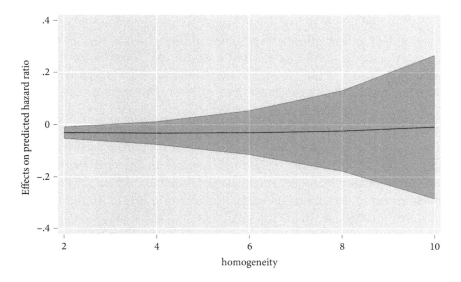

Figure 4.4 Average marginal effect, autocratic density (90 percent confidence interval) (own depiction based on Polity (Marshall et al. 2018)).

Community (SADC) in Chapter 6. It shows that in spite of membership in a heterogenous RO like the SADC that consists of a range of democratic countries like Botswana, Zambia, or even powerful South Africa, authoritarian Zimbabwe was continuously able to garner diplomatic support. In fact, solidarity and unity between former members of the liberation struggle had become the guiding norm of the RO, despite the fact that SADC had a formal democracy clause and even institutionalized a regional tribunal with sitting judges and a human rights mandate at its foundation in 1992.

This last empirical observation on the role of courts is also evident in the statistical analysis: the authority of ROs does not seem to be significantly related to domestic regime dynamics. This remains the same over all alternative model specifications, as well as those reported in the Online Appendix. In contrast to the hypothesized relationship, being a member in a more authoritative RO that has been equipped with a court does not constrain autocratic incumbents in power and increase the likelihood of regime change. This might be because courts in dictator clubs are equipped with co-opted elites, or because their powers are restrained as in the case of the SADC once they actually use their powers against incumbent governments. We thus have to reject Hypothesis 3 on the constraining effect of regional authority.

It is of course possible that the estimated effect of autocratic density is not due to membership in the organization but rather due to diffusion between neighboring states. While the models do control for contagion of breakdown events, they might omit controlling for other forms of bilateral diffusion. To mitigate this potential omitted variable bias, I add a variable capturing the percentage of autocracies in a region (*diffusion_regional*). The results are reported in Table A1 in the Online Appendix. The variable does not achieve significance in both models, while autocratic density remains significant, although at a slightly lower significance level. This seems to suggest that the effect of autocratic density on survival is due to something related to RO membership and not just a matter of regional diffusion.

This result also holds for the end of the Cold War. While pressure on autocratic regimes to democratize might have increased since the 1990s due to more conditionality included in international treaties, the establishment of a global norm of democratic governance, and an increase in international democracy promotion actors, autocracies are not more likely to experience democratic regime change after 1991. As becomes evident in Chapter 7, which focuses on the case of the Ortega regime in Nicaragua, this might be because dictator clubs like the Bolivarian Alliance for the Peoples of our America (ALBA) can help to ease international pressure to undertake democratic reforms, and provide unconditional financial and diplomatic support that allows autocratic regimes to employ otherwise costly survival strategies such as electoral manipulation or large-scale repressions.

The finding that membership in more autocratic and more homogenous ROs is the the most significant international-level predictor to explain regime survival is striking. The finding highlights the importance of studying formal cooperation between authoritarian regimes, as well as arguments by the regime-boosting literature that autocracies profit from RO membership in terms of strengthened regime security and prolonged survival. In fact, being a member of a highly autocratic RO (one standard deviation above the mean density score of 11) increases the mean probability of survival from around 40 years in a low-density RO (one standard deviation below the mean density score) to 70 years. Similarly, being a member of a highly homogenous RO increases the likelihood of survival from 30 to around 50 years. Figure 4.5, depicting the hazard function dependent on the level of density and homogeneity, highlights these effects. While the risk of democratization generally increases until about 40 years of existence, the hazard remains significantly lower in high-density and highly homogenous ROs compared to ROs with low density and homogeneity. Generally speaking, membership in a highly autocratic homogenous ROs makes survival for members with similar numbers of past democratic failures more than six times more likely compared to membership in a RO with mean density and homogeneity scores.

The findings are particularly important considering that the literature on the international dimension of authoritarian resilience has so far mostly argued that regional powers have a stabilizing effect on neighboring autocracies and often work through ROs (Tansey 2016a; Tolstrup 2015; but see Bader 2015 for similar results on Chinese external interference). However, it seems that the presence of a regional power does not systematically influence the survival times of autocratic incumbents, nor does it offer protection vis-á-vis democratic or autocratic challengers. In fact, recent research even suggests that attempts at influencing neighboring regimes can sometimes even lead to unintended effects, whereby autocratic powers inadvertently turn liberal reform coalitions toward Western partners instead of tying them to their camp (Börzel 2015). In consequence, this finding suggests that the institutional commitment between a critical mass of like-minded regional allies seems to be the key factor affecting survival.

This finding will also become clear when looking at the role that ROs have played in recent cases of political turmoil within authoritarian regimes, as we will see in the following three chapters. Saudi Arabia, for instance, was only able to send troops to support neighboring Bahrain as part of the Gulf

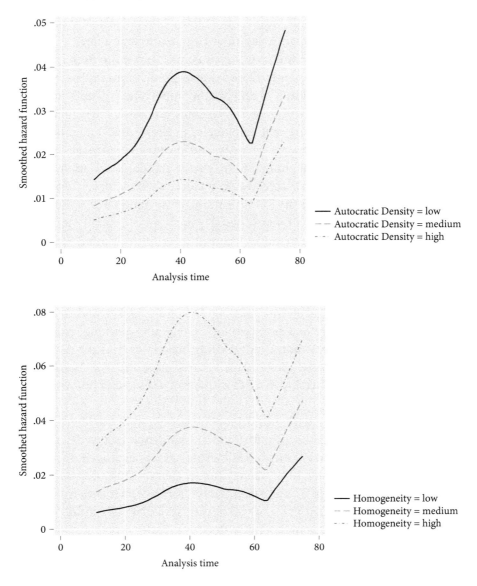

Figure 4.5 Smoothed hazard function for democratization by autocratic density (top) and homogeneity (bottom) (own depiction based on Polity (Marshall et al. 2018)).

Cooperation Council (GCC) Peninsular Shield Force during the Arab Spring crisis in 2011, which provided the legitimacy of an institutionalized military framework. Bahrain's King Hamad officially asked for GCC forces to assist in managing protestors, with Kuwait and the United Arab Emirates also contributing to the joint mission (Bahrain News Agency 2011e). In contrast, Saudi Arabia acted much more hesitantly during the 2018 diplomatic crisis with Qatar where two of the GCC member states, Kuwait and Oman, remained neutral. It had to rely on unilateral diplomatic sanctions and was unable to employ the GCC to further its own interests. Similarly, member states of the SADC were restrained by the institutional norm of solidarity during the election crisis in Zimbabwe in 2008, with none of the critical powers being able to push for regional sanctions or unilateral interference outside of the SADC framework, as we will see in Chapter 6.

Domestic explanations stay mostly in line with previous research. Regime type is significantly related particularly to democratization, with monarchies as the most stable regime type compared to the omitted category (personal) and military regimes as the least stable category because they carry inherent instabilities that will eventually lead to elite splits (Geddes 2003; Hadenius and Teorell 2007). However, the effect for monarchies is not stable across different model specifications (see the Online Appendix), which can be due to the relatively low number of cases in the overall population. Finally, growth significantly reduces the hazard of experiencing democratic regime change, while resources do not seem to have a significant effect on the hazard of democratization.

Effects on the Likelihood of Autocratic Replacements as a Regime Failure Event

In this section, I now turn to the results on autocratic replacements, which are reported in Table 4.2. All six models are set up in parallel to the estimation on democratization as a failure event. Interestingly, membership in ROs with higher autocratic density and homogeneity has no effect on the hazard of experiencing autocratic replacements. Across all model specifications, all three regional-level variables, autocratic density, homogeneity, and authority, cannot systematically explain variation in regime tenures of autocratic incumbents. RO membership thus does not seem to protect from challenges from within the elites such as military coups. Instead, membership in more autocratic ROs only produces a system-boosting effect: it protects from democratic challengers aiming for a larger systemic change in the underlying power distributions between ruler and ruled, while not protecting from autocratic challengers that aim to change the power distribution within the ruling elite.

86 How Regional Organizations Sustain Authoritarian Rule

Table 4.2 ROs and autocratic survival (no autocratic replacement), 1945–2020

	(1)	(2)	(3)	(4)	(5)	(6)
Autocratic Density	0.0301 (0.0220)	0.0323 (0.0238)	−0.0107 (0.0388)	−0.0408 (0.0401)	−0.0274 (0.0377)	
Homogeneity	0.0536 (0.0509)	0.0562 (0.0481)	0.114* (0.0564)	−0.0437 (0.0819)	0.0190 (0.142)	
Authority	−0.172 (0.372)	0.140 (0.378)	0.504 (0.424)	0.344 (0.426)	0.461 (0.424)	0.622 (0.418)
Hegemon		−0.125 (0.251)	−0.108 (0.357)	0.318 (0.425)	−0.148 (0.368)	−0.0695 (0.373)
Cold War		**−0.778*** (0.367)	−0.446 (0.424)	−0.492 (0.470)	−0.445 (0.420)	−0.480 (0.417)
Contagion		**−1.097*** (0.491)	**−1.135*** (0.464)	**−0.174** (0.597)	**−1.116*** (0.474)	**−1.203*** (0.487)
Regime Type						
Party			−0.430 (0.363)	−0.249 (0.413)	−0.440 (0.362)	−0.441 (0.361)
Military			**−0.660*** (0.290)	−0.246 (0.437)	**−0.628*** (0.286)	**−0.586*** (0.296)
Monarchy			0.0410 (0.494)	−1.076 (0.853)	0.0204 (0.493)	−0.00613 (0.514)
Growth			**−6.164***** (1.655)	**−7.254***** (1.630)	**−6.250***** (1.622)	**−5.960***** (1.674)
Resources			**−0.0862$^+$** (0.0511)		−0.0852 (0.0522)	**−0.0798** (0.0515)
Dependence				−0.0193 (0.0176)		
AutDensity# Homogeneity					0.0104 (0.0135)	
Average Density						−0.0290 (0.0533)
Homogeneity (all)						0.160 (0.159)
N	4882	4882	3165	2951	3165	3165

Stratified Cox proportional hazard models with robust standard errors in parentheses and coefficients reported. Bold entries indicate statistically significant values. $^+ p < 0.1$, $^* p < 0.05$, $^{**} p < 0.01$, $^{***} p < 0.001$

In contrast, another international-level variable is significantly related to the hazard of regime failure. Contagion significantly predicts autocratic replacements, but in a surprising way. Previous experiences of autocratic replacements in regionally proximate states actually decrease the hazard of experiencing a similar event over time. This might point to learning effects stressed by the recent literature on authoritarian collaboration, whereby late-risers during waves of instability might learn from earlier examples and adapt their strategies accordingly to prevent takeovers by rivaling elites (Ambrosio 2010; Bank and Edel 2015; Vanderhill 2012).

Domestic variables again conform mostly to previous scholarship. Personalist (omitted variable) and military regimes are the most stable vis-à-vis elite challengers. Economic growth protects from autocratic regime failure, just as it protected from democratization. Resource wealth only has a very weak effect but positive effect on regime survival, slightly decreasing the hazard of failure (but only at a 10 percent significance level). As previously argued, resource wealth can help to protect regimes from autocratic challengers because oil wealth increases security spending and can thus shield regimes more effectively from military coups (Wright et al. 2015).

This third major finding that membership in an autocrat club only helps to prevent democratic regime change but does not protect from autocratic replacements needs some further discussion. First, it suggests that we should rather talk about a system-boosting effect of RO membership instead of regime-boosting regionalism. Incumbents hoping for help to avert autocratic challenges from inside the ruling coalition such as military coups are less likely to benefit from their RO membership. Only when the status quo of autocratic rule within a regime is at stake and by extension the risk of democratization for the larger region increases does RO membership provide protection for autocratic incumbents.

This might be for two reasons. First, ROs view internal intra-elite struggles as a matter of sovereignty that falls under RO non-interference norms. Therefore, they are unlikely to offer support to safeguard an incumbent regime when it is threatened by other elites. Second, democratic regime change is more likely to cause a ripple effect in the region, thereby also affecting other RO members. Democratic regime change is a threat that is shared by all autocratic regimes independent of autocratic regime type, and tends to diffuse quickly within regions (Brinks and Coppedge 2006). Autocratic challenges, however, differ profoundly from one type of autocratic regime to the next. While monarchies are, for instance, volatile to palace revolts from within a royal family, dominant-party and personalist regimes are more often threatened by rival political leaders that instigate revolutions (Geddes

2003). Military regimes, in contrast, mostly end due to internal elite splits, as has been evidenced by the transition literature focusing on Latin America (O'Donnell et al. 1986). Thus, perceptions of similarity might filter to what extent regimes consider domestic challenges to potentially affect regime stability at home. This explanation also speaks to the literature on the role of threat perception to explain the spread of revolutionary movements (Weyland 2012), as well as the literature on foreign policy choice during times of uncertainty (Odinius and Kuntz 2015).

The findings became particularly pronounced during the 2017 military coup in Zimbabwe, as we will further see in Chapter 6. While the SADC supported Mugabe's dominant-party regime during the large-scale election crisis in 2008, the RO remained relatively uninvolved during the disempowerment of Mugabe by his own ZANU-PF cronies in November 2017. The election crisis in 2008 revolved around state–society relations, and would very likely have resulted in a turnover of government to the opposition party, thereby causing potential ripple effects across Southern Africa. The 2017 military coup, in contrast, involved intra-party elites aiming to replace Mugabe with another loyal party member. In fact, Emmerson Mnangagwa, Zimbabwe's vice president and long-time ally of Mugabe, was quickly sworn in as new president on November 24, 2017, ensuring the continuation of the autocratic rule of the ZANU-PF regime. Once it became clear that the coup would not lead to the establishment of a transitional regime with the inclusion of the opposition party, the SADC supported the coup and critical voices criticizing the Zimbabwean military quickly died down.

Robustness Tests

To test the robustness of results, several follow-up tests were performed that can all be found in the Online Appendix. First, I varied model specifications to check if results hold when changing the composition of risk sets with each failure event. Table A2 reports results from a conditional risk-set approach that stratifies on number of failure events, but resets time at every failure. Table A3 reports results from a simple counting approach, whereby failure events are essentially treated as equal, so the risk-set under analysis for a breakdown event k are all subjects under analysis at time t. In both cases, most results are not altered significantly. The only difference is that the Cold War becomes significant for both democratization and autocratic replacements, but in opposite directions. While the hazard of democratization increases significantly with the end of the Cold War, the risk of autocratic replacements decreases. The first result makes sense given that the third wave of democratization was initiated with the end of the Cold War. The increased stability of autocratic incumbents vis-á-vis autocratic challengers might be due to the fact that many autocratic regimes have transformed toward electoral party-based regimes under the rise of democratic elections as an international norm. Party-based regimes remain among the most stable regime category, while the numbers of military regimes—and with it the most important category of autocratic replacements in the form of coups—have decreased since 1990.

Second, I control for region-specific effects to ensure that results are not driven by significant differences between regions (Table A4). Including regional dummies does not alter the results in significant ways and suggests that estimates are not affected by homogeneity between regions. Third, I control if results hold when employing alternative measurements to the Polity variable. I construct the density variable based on the *v2x_polyarchy* variable in the Varieties of Democracy dataset (Coppedge et al. 2020) and find that the results remain robust to this alternative variable measurement (Table A7). Fourth, I exchange the main predictor variable Autocratic Density with an alternative variable measuring the number of autocratic RO memberships of a regime (*overlap*). The comparative regionalism literature has argued that many ROs are essentially dysfunctional paper tigers that are only set up to prevent pressure for policy implementation in favor of purely rhetorical forms of regionalism (Allison 2008; Söderbaum 2004a, 2004b). By creating competing and overlapping regional agendas, regimes hope to appease national constituencies and reinforce national sovereignty over external agendas of democracy promotion. However, if my theory is correct, membership in one RO that actively supplies support should produce the desired results. Neither exchanging Overlap for Autocratic Density nor adding it to the model changes the results significantly (see Table A5), which suggests that it is important to be a member of a highly autocratic RO instead of a mix of paper tigers.

Finally, I check if the results change when weighing ROs according to their aggregate GDP to control for variation in the economic power of institutions. While two ROs such as the Shanghai Cooperation Organization (SCO) and the Economic Community of the Great Lakes Countries (CEPGL) have similar autocratic density levels over time, the SCO with the economically powerful member states Russia and China should be able to provide more financial resources and assurances compared to CEPGL's small membership. Including a logged variable that measures the yearly aggregate total per capita GDP of all members divided by the number of RO member states does not achieve significance (see Table A8). This could indicate that financial redistributions are not necessarily the most important causal factor explaining survival, but that regimes might rather profit from non-material resources such as diplomatic support and legitimation. This also ties to previous literature that shows the importance of regionally supplemented legitimation strategies as an important benefit of RO membership (Debre 2021; Libman and Obydenkova 2018).

Conclusion

This chapter has provided evidence on the macro-dynamics between RO membership and authoritarian regime survival. The chapter has produced three important insights. First, autocracies sort into distinct organizations with similar membership. Simultaneous membership in very autocratic and very democratic organizations is rare. Instead, autocracies cluster in dictator clubs that help to reinforce their continued rule. Second, membership in dictator clubs systematically protects against democratization, significantly reducing the hazard of experiencing failure events across time and regions. Membership in ROs remains the most important international-level predictor over explanations from power-based or diffusion approaches. Third, membership protects against democratic regime failure but not against challengers from within elites that aim to replace the current leader with a different type of autocratic system. RO membership can thus be thought of as a systemic boost stabilizing authoritarianism as a form of rule, but not particular types of autocratic regimes and their leaders.

These results speak to the important effects of institutional factors in explaining domestic regime developments in the Global South. ROs also matter for the domestic politics of non-democratic regimes, and they might be more important than regional hegemons in our understanding of regime dynamics. These results speak to research highlighting the potential dark sides of international cooperation (Ferry et al. 2020; Hafner-Burton and Schneider 2019). By explicitly testing the reverse or unintended effects that ROs can have on domestic politics outside of Europe and the democratization paradigm, this chapter elucidates the conditions under which international institutions can produce democracy or strengthen authoritarian rule.

The results presented in this chapter provide macro evidence on the effects that dictator clubs have across regions of the Global South. Further exploration of these results and the underlying mechanisms producing the established patterns will form part and parcel of the qualitative analysis in the following three chapters. The chapters will discuss how RO membership helps to protect incumbents from challengers that threaten democratic regime change, why RO membership protects from democratic regime change but not from military coups, and how ROs can shield members from foreign interferences and influence international politics. In combination, the nested analysis can tell a fuller story about cause–effect relationships and confirm the plausibility of macro patterns by ruling out possible spurious relationships and omitted variable bias.

5
How Dictator Clubs Empower Autocratic Incumbents

The following chapters turn to analyze the theorized *mechanisms of regime-boosting*. In Chapter 2, we have theorized that regional organizations (ROs) can support authoritarian regime stabilization and thereby increase survival chances through three distinct mechanisms: *resource redistribution*, *regional relationship management*, and *international shielding*. Each of the following three chapters deals with one of the mechanisms to establish that the statistical relationship between membership in a dictator club and lower risk of democratization is not a spurious correlation.

In this chapter, we start with the redistributive effect of ROs that help autocratic incumbents to mitigate domestic challengers through material and immaterial resources. The chapter focuses on three cases to show how ROs help to legitimize regimes, co-opt political elites, and repress dissidents and public protest. Each case identifies a specific threat and corresponding survival strategy (see overview in Table 5.1). The first case deals with the co-optation (and repression) strategy of the Bahraini regime to deal with challenges from political activists and key elites from within the royal family during the Arab Spring uprisings in 2011 through financial (and military) aid received by the Gulf Cooperation Council (GCC). The second case shows how the Chinese Communist Party has been able to benefit from Shanghai Cooperation Organization (SCO) membership to strengthen the repression of Muslim Uighur minority groups in Xinjiang after the Urumqi riots in 2009. The third case focuses on the role of the Southern African Development Community (SADC) during the presidential election crisis in Zimbabwe in 2002 and follows the efforts of long-term leader Mugabe to remain in power by signaling democratic legitimacy to domestic audiences.

The cases are chosen for three distinct reasons. First, the models presented in the previous chapter revealed that more autocratic ROs are associated with lower likelihoods of democratization, while not having a systematic effect on changes between different types of autocratic regimes. Therefore, the three chosen cases focus on well-predicted cases; that is, cases with autocratic RO

How Regional Organizations Sustain Authoritarian Rule. Maria J. Debre, Oxford University Press.
© Maria J. Debre (2025). DOI: 10.1093/9780198903635.003.0005

involvement and the absence of democratization (Lieberman 2005b). While Bahrain, China, and Zimbabwe have faced major threats to their systems, all three regimes have never experienced moments of democratization in their countries' histories.

Second, since the argument is based on presenting evidence on survival—that is, non-change in the dependent variable—all three cases deal with crisis moments that make survival strategies and RO involvement more visible. Each case therefore focuses on a distinct threat and corresponding survival strategy employed by a member state to trace how the regimes managed to ensure their hold on power, and what role the RO played to solve the crisis moment.

Third, to increase the representativeness and external validity of findings, the case selection follows a most-different method (Gerring 2007) whereby cases are similar with regard to the dependent variable (survival) and the main independent variable (RO membership) but vary on other alternative explanatory variables that have been shown by the literature to be important domestic and international drivers of regime survival. Zimbabwe is an electoral autocracy in Sub-Saharan Africa, with poor economic and military capacity which has been highly isolated internationally due to European Union (EU) and United Nations (UN) sanctions put on the Mugabe regime in the 2000s. Bahrain is an absolute monarchy in the Middle East, with medium economic capacity that has strong ties to the United States due to multiple military bases stationed on their territory. Finally, China as a dominant party regime under the rule of the Chinese Communist Party (CCP) dominates regional relations due to its high economic performance and is one of the main emerging powers in global politics.

While the cases differ with regard to these major alternative explanations, all three are similar in that ROs were involved during a major moment of political instability, and all regimes managed to successfully survive the challenge in question. To establish that the relationship is not a spurious correlation, the chapter builds on official documents provided by regimes and ROs, secondary literature, and reporting by national and international media outlets collected from the Lexis-Nexis database to build a timeline of events that can trace when, how, and through which means ROs were involved in the successful solution of the crisis in a member regime.

Of course, by stressing similarities, I do not intend to deny that there are major differences in how events and RO involvement unfolded in each case, or that other factors might not play a causal role in explaining survival. Autocratic powerhouse Saudi Arabia has heavily dominated decisions in the GCC and seems to have played a big part in supporting the Bahraini regime to hold on to power (Zumbrägel 2020). However, as the following analysis shows, this does not preclude the GCC as an institution to also affect the successful resolution of the Arab Spring crisis substantively in Bahrain. The Xinjiang case, in contrast, deals with China as a regional power that has far more resources at its disposal to deal with domestic threats to begin with compared to Bahrain and Zimbabwe. As the analysis shows, the SCO, however, has become a major instrument in the Chinese toolbox of survival politics, and has been exploited in a similar manner by the other Central Asian member states to stabilize their rule. Finally, Zimbabwe has to deal with South Africa as a democratic regional power within the SADC. However, the SADC and the South African-led mediation process supported the aging dictator despite these inimical conditions.

Choosing a limited number of cases for within-case analysis allows for enough flexibility to study how other decisive factors have played a role in the survival of the regimes in each instance. As Beach and Pedersen (2013, 2016) convincingly argue, rigidly controlling for alternative explanations is only relevant for variance-based case studies that examine the effect of an x on the outcome y. In within-case analysis, we are interested in how a certain x (in this case an autocratic RO) is related to y (in this case system survival) through distinct causal processes. However, since every x can only explain some variance of y, several causal factors may explain all of the variance of y, as established in preceding cross-case analysis. Thus, several causal processes from different causal factors may conjointly produce survival, which can be accounted for during the in-depth within-case analysis.

Finally, one could argue that the Chinese case does not fall in the same category of potential system breakdown due to a threat of democratic challengers as the cases of Bahrain and Zimbabwe. After all, the Chinese case deals with territorial integrity, not calls for liberalization and democratic reform. However, I would argue that maintaining territorial integrity has become one of the fundamental grounds of legitimacy and identity of the CCP (see also Shambaugh 2013a, p. 56). Consequently, any threat of increased autonomy or even secession of any part of China can be considered a serious threat not only to Chinese territorial integrity but also to the political survival of the CCP as such.

The "One China Principle" has, for instance, become one of the main building blocks of Chinese foreign policy, with diplomatic relations between China and any other country premised on the recognition of Chinese claims over Taiwan. Territorial integrity has even been codified by law in 2005, whereby any CCP leader who allowed for the secession of any part of China could face criminal charges for this decision (Ricks 2017). More substantially, the CCP obtains its major source of legitimacy from the historical narrative that they liberated the nation from international plunderers, thereby restoring its former territorial integrity and sovereignty (Shambaugh 2013a, p. 56).

Table 5.1 Overview of cases

	Bahrain	China	Zimbabwe
Case	Arab Spring uprisings 2011	Urumqi riots 2009	Election crisis 2002
Challenge	Demand for political reform by opposition groups and elites	Civic unrest of Muslim minority population	Decreasing electoral support
Survival Strategy	Co-optation	Repression	Legitimation
RO Support	- Financial transfers from GCC Development Fund - Coordination of anti-Shia propaganda and "national dialogue" - GCC military intervention	- "Three evils" doctrine to criminalize activists - Intelligence sharing: blacklisting, denial of asylum, extradition - Joint military missions	- Favorable election monitoring - Support of anti-colonial legitimation strategy
Outcome	- Successful co-optation of Sunni population & de-legitimation of Shia opposition - Weakening of reform demands through mock "national dialogue"	- Successful criminalization of Muslim population as terrorists - Extradition, prosecution, and detention of Muslims across borders	- Legitimation of flawed elections as free and fair - Legitimation of Mugabe as post-colonial liberation hero

Thus, even though the Chinese case does not directly involve calls for democratic system change, the threat of secession does indirectly constitute a major threat to the regime and system survival of the CCP, and can thus serve as a fitting comparison. Given that there are sufficient and important similarities between all three cases, there is a lot to be gained from exploring these cases as one common pattern of regime-boosting regionalism.

The GCC and Co-optation: The 2011 Arab Spring Uprisings in Bahrain

Attempts at cooperation between the regimes on the Arabian Peninsula date back to before the formation of the GCC. With the withdrawal of British forces from the newly independent Gulf monarchies in 1971, Saudi Arabia pushed for closer cooperation of interior ministers on trans-border security matters in 1976 to fill the security vacuum and close ranks against potential external interference from Iran and Iraq (Partrick 2011). In the wake of the Iran–Iraq war in 1981, Saudi Arabia finally managed to push toward the formation of the GCC and unite only the Gulf monarchies by excluding Iraq, Iran, and Yemen from the organization. In its charter, the GCC sets out to achieve "coordination, cooperation, and integration on the path to unity," particularly stressing the "ties of special relations, common characteristics and similar systems founded on the creed of Islam which bind them" (GCC 1981). The GCC can thus be considered mainly as a bulwark to protect the internationally unique brand of Sunni-led dynastic monarchies both against Iran's Shia Islamist regime and revived Arab nationalism in Hussein's Iraq (Barnett and Gause III 1998; Holthaus 2010).

The GCC has repeatedly been characterized as a "gentlemen's club" (Bishara in Legrenzi 2011, p. 154). Decisions are taken unanimously by the six rulers according to the informal "rules of shaikhly exchange" (Legrenzi 2011, p. 150) during closed-door sessions at the biannual meetings of the Supreme Council. The Ministerial Council of Foreign Ministers negotiates and consults on recommendations submitted to the Supreme Council beforehand. The Secretariat of the GCC and its Secretary General mostly implement decisions, but don't have any enforcement capacity at their disposal (Barnett and Gause III 1998).

This mirrors the backroom style of decision-making practiced in the Gulf regimes. The six member states of the GCC are run as dynastic monarchies with vast oil reserves that base their legitimacy on traditional Sunni-monarchical identity and the provision of public goods. As "family businesses" (Herb 1999), the regimes decree over some of the largest natural oil and gas reserves in the world, forming the base of a rentier social contract that allows them to create the image of acting as benevolent patrons for their populations. In place of taxation, the regimes can instead provide for their citizens' every need (i.e. free healthcare, education, infrastructure, and monthly basic incomes). Of course, much of this money also finances co-optation of royal and tribal elites with well-paid government jobs and financial handouts as well as a vast repression machinery (Ross 2001b).

The Gulf regimes have mostly been challenged by in-fighting between warring family factions over the years, but they have rarely been subjected to pressure for democratization from below. Instead, external challenges such as the spread of Arab nationalism and interference by Shiite Iran posed the more prominent danger to the regimes' political systems based squarely on Sunni Islam and absolute monarchism. The Shi'a question is particularly troublesome for the smaller kingdom of Bahrain, where the minority Sunni royal family rule over a majority of Shi'a, and Shiite populations have increasingly been marginalized since the Iranian revolution (Abdo 2017). Although public protest has been a constant feature of Bahraini politics, where political opposition has increasingly been defined through Shiite Islamism (ICG 2005), previous demands during the "Bahraini Intifada" in the 1990s were mostly directed at improving the economic situation of Shi'a Bahrainis, but never really questioned the power of the monarchy.

The 2011 Arab Spring in Bahrain

This changed with the Arab Spring uprisings in 2011, which also swept across the Gulf. To the Gulf regimes, the Arab Spring uprisings represented a new type of substantial threat emanating from within their societies. Calls for constitutional monarchy that would severely limit or even remove the power of the ruling families only surfaced during the 2011 uprisings and played out especially strong in Bahrain's highly polarized society, where the Shiite population has increasingly been marginalized by the ruling Sunni royal family. Protestors in Manama's Pearl Roundabout kept chanting "the regime must fall, they will kill us all" and "down, down with the Khalifas" (Chulov et al. 2011, par. 14). Similar calls, albeit with much less severe protests, were issued in Oman and the eastern provinces of Saudi Arabia, posing a hitherto unknown threat to the survival of the Gulf regimes (Colombo 2012).

But the regime was also threatened from within the ruling family. Moderate reform sections around Crown Prince Salman were open to reform, and responded favorably to calls from the protestors to talk about the previously taboo subject of establishing a constitutional monarchy with more rights for Shiite citizens (ICG 2011). By reaching out to leading political societies, Crown Prince Salman hoped to secure a position for himself and his family faction in a future monarchical system. But the moved threatened the hard-liner faction headed by powerful Prime Minister Khalifa who preferred a security solution to the crisis that would allow secure the absolute power position of the Al-Khalifa family in the future.

Large-scale protests in Bahrain first broke out on February 14, 2011 when human rights activists called for a "Day of Rage" (Aljazeera 2011). Although initial protests at the Pearl Roundabout in Bahrain's capital Manama seemed to emulate the peaceful protests on Egypt's Tahrir square, they were met with a harsh response by security forces during the early days (Chulov et al. 2011). However, the Bahraini regime surprisingly withdrew its troops after these initial protests on February 19, and initiated a "national dialogue" headed by

Crown Prince Salman to calm the situation (Bahrain News Agency 2011a). But demonstrations still spread throughout the country as February wore on and demands turned more radical (Bahrain News Agency 2011d). As the protests extended into early March, leaders from the largest opposition groups started to call for more fundamental reforms of the political system into a democratic republic that would allow the prime minister and cabinet to be selected by a fully elected parliament (Katzman 2017, p. 5).

During this time, the GCC emerged as a critical actor in support of the Bahraini regime by providing an institutional forum to coordinate material support aimed at co-opting both reform-oriented factions within the royal family and pro-regime Sunni minority groups, as well as political activists and societies. In a first step, the Bahraini regime recurred to familiar ways of co-optation through large-scale investment projects and financial handouts. The regime announced that it would recruit up to 20,000 new people into all ministry departments and planned to invest 2.5 billion dollars into new housing projects across the country (Bahrain News Agency 2011b, 2011c). While bureaucratic jobs are well paid, secure, and highly attractive positions in the Gulf monarchies, they are effectively not available to the Shiite population that has been marginalized from public service (Abdo 2017). Instead, the regime intended to mainly co-opt Sunni citizens, the traditional support base of the regime. To finance this co-optation strategy, Bahrain was able to draw on the "Gulf Development Program," a 10 billion USD Marshall Plan-like package of support by the resource-rich GCC members to poorer Bahrain and Oman that was announced during the 118th session of GCC foreign ministers in March (Washington Post 2011).

The GCC also proved to be a valuable forum to coordinate these co-optation strategies from day one. Mere days after violent responses to initial protests, the extra-ordinary session of GCC foreign ministers marked a remarkable turn toward an initially peaceful handling of the crisis. Crown Prince Salman, head of the reform section within the Bahraini royal family, was tasked with initiating a national dialogue with protestors and political societies to carve out ways of reforming the kingdom. The dialogue was announced to table issues such as establishing a fully elected parliament with enhanced authority, redrawing voting districts to allow a fairer representation of Shiite population, and addressing sectarian polarization that were previously on the blacklist of topics to discuss. Many of the demands may have been a way to appease leading political societies via promises of institutionalized political dialogue without actual intentions to initiate wide-ranging reforms (Louër 2011). But the reform faction among the ruling family seemed to have won over the hard-liner security faction in terms of initial response with the help of the GCC: subsequent large-scale demonstrations until mid-March were staged without any violent responses from the regime (ICG 2011, p. 2). The strategy was a wise choice as it prevented further violent radicalization of protestors in comparison to developments in some of the neighboring Arab Republics (Yom 2014).

Co-optation of Sunni groups was additionally supported by a joint GCC propaganda campaign rolled out at the extra-ordinary meeting of GCC foreign ministers on February 17 that framed protestors as Iranian-led insurgencies. The summitry statement was the first time that references to alleged external interferences by Iran were made during the crisis. In the GCC summit statement, the RO rejects "any external interference in the internal affairs of the Kingdom of Bahrain" (Bahrain News Agency 2011a), and during the later regular summit Iran's alleged meddling was even reprimanded as "flagrant intervention" and a "violation of their sovereignty, independence and principles of good-neighborliness" (Gulf News (United Arab Emirates) 2011). Instead, the future of Gulf as a region of prosperity and wealth was tied to continued rule of the Bahraini Sunni family by the GCC: in "a world where winds of change are blowing," unity and continuity are "the solid shield in the face of these changes" (KUNA 2011, par. 7). A later report of the Bahraini Independent commission found that there was no evidence of Iranian involvement in the crisis (Bassiouni et al. 2011).

The co-optation strategy, however, seemed to take effect: while early protestors wore badges reading "No Sunni, No Shi'a, Just Bahraini," more and more Sunni Bahrainis started to support the regime as the protest movement wore on (Abdo 2017). Counter-demonstrations by leading Sunni religious scholars, a country-wide Sunni-led boycott against Shi'a-owned business by the so-called "National Unity Gathering"—a pan-Sunni bloc supporting the ruling family—and growing vandalism in Shi'a shrines and mosques are all evidence of the increasing resentment against Shi'a in response to the regime propaganda (ICG 2011). As Gulf scholar Valeri describes in a first-hand account of the developments: "As these rumors of Iranian involvement spread, more and more Sunnis distanced themselves from the movement" (France 24 2016). Even the leading political society Al-Wifaq decided to abandon harsher calls for democratic reform and agreed to engage in informal negotiations with the crown prince (ICG 2011).

But Crown Prince Salman still saw his reform-oriented solutions lose traction among the ruling GCC families. With increasingly harsher demands from the protest camps to abolish the monarchy altogether in early March, the hard-liner faction around the prime minister prepared for a security solution to the crisis. To the hard-liner faction around the prime minister, Crown

Prince Salman's negotiation strategy seemed to pose too big a threat for limited liberalization. Together with the military chief, Prime Minister Khalifa therefore initiated his preferred security solutions. On March 13, King Hamad asked for the support of GCC military troops under the joint "Peninsula Shield Force" command to squash protestors (Katzman 2017). Salman was sacked from his role as leader of the national dialogue and replaced by the Speaker of Parliament, who wields no executive and political power, and was thus the perfect decoy to continue a façade co-optation strategy with political opposition.

GCC Involvement since 2011

In the months following the uprisings, GCC security cooperation was updated to realize more effective cross-border persecution of critical actors, which allowed the Bahraini regime to severely clamp down on opposition groups, particularly those with a Shiite background (Katzman 2017). The Comprehensive Security Agreement agreed upon at the GCC Manama summit of 2012 allows for additional large-scale cross-border policing and legal action against dissidents by sharing information and personal data (Gulf News 2011). The Bahraini regime has managed to arrest and prosecute many of the demonstrators that took part in the public protest, and expatriate and thereby further marginalize the Shiite population in the years following the uprisings due to the agreement (The Economist 2017).

The importance of the updated agreement of 2012 lies in the possibility for regimes to prosecute critics of any other GCC regime, not just those criticizing their own monarchy. Since 2012, there have been a number of cases of cross-policing (Yom 2016). One more prominent example is the imprisonment of Kuwaiti member of parliament Dashti for his critique of Saudi Arabia and Bahrain by the Kuwaiti regime (Gulf News 2016). Furthermore, article 10 of the treaty allows for "support or aid on request to any state party ... to counter security unrest and disasters" (Human Rights Watch 2014, par. 15), which effectively institutionalizes the possibility for future military interventions to deal with protestors under the GCC framework.

The GCC has not only enlarged its cooperation in the realm of security but also extended aid programs to Bahrain in the last decade to further stabilize the regime. The GCC development fund had continuously dispersed grants to Bahrain in the years following the Arab Spring uprisings. In 2018, a capital injection of 10 billion US dollars was announced to help the Bahraini regime deal with a budget deficit due to declining oil prices and thereby soften the negative impact of its austerity program (Mogielnicki 2018). The five-year phased disbursement was used strategically by the regime, for instance, to support government employees put into early retirement (Mogielnicki 2018). However, the financial aid for the Bahraini regime was also a means to ensure foreign investors of continued support from richer Gulf allies, particularly during the Covid-19 crisis, which delayed Bahrain's fiscal balance program (Asharq Al-Awsat 2021).

The case highlights how the GCC has helped to redistribute material and immaterial resources to allow for the successful resolution of the crisis and keep the ruling Al-Khalifa family in power in Bahrain. The RO offered the regimes an established venue for the coordination and exchange of strategies. The fact that relevant actors met within the GCC framework only three days after the start of the crisis, that Bahrain made a 180-degree turn in crisis response right after the initial GCC emergency meeting, and that the ministers kept negotiating and announcing decisions within the RO framework attest to the importance of the institution as an instrument for autocratic regime survival. While reliance on bilateral relations and Saudi Arabia's status as regional power might have helped to resolve the crisis as well, the fact that all actors were able to channel and coordinate their efforts through an established institution was certainly a decisive asset to legitimize chosen actions.

As will be discussed in Chapter 6, the role of ROs as constraints to autocratic power politics becomes particularly important when members disagree about the solution to a political crisis. In 2011, all GCC regimes seemed to be aligned regarding the co-optation and repression strategies taken against protestors, or at least happy to follow along the path laid out by Saudi Arabia. In contrast, during the diplomatic crisis between Qatar and Saudi Arabia over Qatar's alleged involvement in financing terrorism in later years, Saudi Arabia and its allies reacted far more hesitantly toward Qatar. This is because diverging preferences among GCC members forced Saudi Arabia to build an ad hoc coalition of states outside the institutionalized context. It thus also remains questionable if Saudi Arabia would have agreed to send their troops to a neighboring country without the legitimacy of an institutionalized military framework protecting their intervention in 2011.

The SCO and Repression: The 2009 Urumqi Riots in China

Originally initiated as the "Shanghai Five" to resolve border issues and enhance mutual trust between Russia, the newly established Central Asian states, and China after the fall of the Soviet Union, the SCO was formally institutionalized in 2001.[1] In its founding document, the SCO is mainly depicted as a regional security institution that is aimed at combating non-traditional security threats common to Eurasia, particularly religious extremism, separatism, and terrorism (SCO 2001, 2002). These three threats have been coined the so-called "three evils," and have become one of the main pillars of cooperation within the SCO, institutionalized through the SCO Regional Antiterrorism Structure (RATS) (Ambrosio 2008; Aris 2009). SCO member states have also actively stylized the organization as "a new type of international order" that furthers the democratization of international relations by rejecting unipolarity and interference in sovereign matters (Cooley 2012; Facon 2013). This "Shanghai Spirit" is embodied through statements and practice and institutionalized in the founding treaties to advance consensus-based cooperation and respect for sovereignty and non-interference among member states (Ambrosio 2008).

The SCO's focus on separatism and terrorism is particularly important for China and the Central Asian regimes that have had to deal with porous border regions and repeated border conflicts since the end of the Soviet Union. To the CCP, upholding territorial integrity is of particular importance due to increasing political engagement by ethnic minority groups that are clustered in the Western border provinces Xinjiang and Tibet and demanding more autonomy (Clarke 2013). The CCP's central legitimation narrative has been built on the notion of a united China encompassing all border regions (most importantly Taiwan) and is both codified in domestic law and enacted internationally through the "One China Principle" (Shambaugh 2013b). The "centrality and intermediate position in Eurasia between the great sedentary homelands of Europe, Iran, India and China" (Millward 2007, p. 1) has historically presented China with the challenge of isolating and integrating the frontier region.

Xinjiang is one of China's so-called "autonomous regions" with a predominantly Muslim population of Turk ethnicity. The region was incorporated into the Chinese state with the CCP's accession to power in 1949 but had previously experienced short episodes of independence under the Qing Dynasty. In 1933 and between 1944 and 1949, Turkic-Muslims had proclaimed an independent "East Turkestan Republic" that still fuels claims to independence today (Clarke 2013). Large groups of Uyghurs also reside within the Central Asian states of Kazakhstan, Uzbekistan, and Kyrgyzstan,

---

[1] The current members include China, Kazakhstan, Kyrgyzstan, Russia, Tajikistan, and Uzbekistan, as well as India and Pakistan who joined in 2017.

with China being afraid of trans-border organization of Uyghur activities. However, Uyghur separatist movements follow different visions for an independent East Turkistan within the borders of Xinjiang, and are thus highly fragmented. In fact, there seems to be no single Uyghur agenda, with some groups advocating for a separate state and some for cultural distinction within China, while others support full integration into China (van wie Davis 2008, p. 16).

Notwithstanding this, China has designated many of the Uyghur groups as terrorist organizations, including the East Turkistan Islamic Party, the East Turkistan Liberation Organization (ETLO), the World Uyghur Congress (WUC) headquartered in Germany, and the East Turkistan Islamic Movement (ETIM) (van wie Davis 2008, p. 21). While the extent of Uyghur-institutionalized opposition and its ability to enact organized terrorist attacks on China have been seriously questioned (e.g. Kan 2010a),[2] the Communist Party has intensified their practice of treating Xinjiang as a second Chechnya, and fueled perceptions of Uyghur groups as terrorist suicide bombers (Millward 2007, p. 348). By linking Uyghur groups to international terrorism in the wake of the war on terror after 9/11, China has been able to intensify its repression strategy with decreased risk of international backlash (Amnesty International 2002a, 2002b; Clarke 2010). Only with the publication of a string of leaked documents in the "Xinjiang Papers," the "Xinjiang Cables," and the "Xinjiang Police Files" by a consortium of journalists did China have to face more serious pressure over accusations of Muslim Uighurs being detained in "re-education camps," especially if they have family outside of China (*China Cables Exposes Chilling Details of Mass Detention in Xinjiang* 2019; Ramzy and Buckley 2019; Sudworth and The V. J. Team 2022).

The Urumqi Riots of 2009

The Uighur issue first surfaced in the international media in July 2009, when demonstrations broke out in Xinjiang's capital city Urumqi and soon radicalized after clashes with police in the days after (New York Times 2009). According to Chinese official figures, 197 people were killed, over 1,700 were injured, and hundreds of shops and thousands of vehicles were destroyed,

---

[2] In fact, the US Congressional Research Service has argued that there was not enough evidence to corroborate that websites allegedly belonging to ETIM had not been set up by third parties, such as the People's Republic of China itself (Kan 2010b, p. 7). Furthermore, the report details that a US Court of Appeals had released Uyghur ETIM members held in Guantanamo in 2009, since the prosecution couldn't produce sufficient evidence of a connection between ETIM and al-Qaeda or the Taliban (Kan 2010b, p. 10).

with Han being the overwhelmingly injured party (HRIC 2011a, section VII). However, the WUC—an organization of exiled Uyghurs—has disputed these statements, claiming that 90 percent of the dead were in fact Uyghurs (BBC News 2009a). Similarly, the US state department had voiced reservations about the Chinese victimization of Han in terms of casualty numbers that could not be independently verified (Kan 2010b).

While the sources of unrest remain contested with both Uighurs and the CCP claiming that the other attacked first, the CPP reacted with a complete lock-down and communications blackout in Xinjiang, large-scale arrests of more than 1,400 Uighurs in the subsequent weeks, and a fervent public relations campaign against Uighur groups that framed riots as Islamic terrorism (New York Times 2009). Xinjiang Governor Nur Bekri blamed the exiled dissident leader of WUC, Rebiya Kadeer, for orchestrating the protests, citing evidence of phone conversations between her and people in China placed on July 5 (BBC News 2009c). Pieces in the state-led newspaper China Daily on July 16 and 18 accuse WUC of coordinating with the terrorist organization ETIM and receiving training from al-Qaeda in Pakistan, quoting Bo Xiao, director of the Commission for Legislative Affairs of the Standing Committee of Xinjiang regional People's Congress, who states that "the nature of the riot has the major characteristics of a typical terrorist attack" (China Daily 2009).

The SCO played a decisive role in the CCP repressing rioters more effectively both by helping to frame and criminalize protestors as Islamic terrorists based on the SCO "three evils" doctrine and by exploiting joint intelligence and military command structures to pursue, deter, and threaten Uighurs across borders in subsequent months. When riots first broke out on July 5, the CCP was intent on reporting the incident in the Chinese state media and framing rioting Uighurs as illegitimate terrorists that had to be pursued and prosecuted. To this end, the CCP relied heavily on the "three evils doctrine," which refers to the main objective of the SCO, the fight against religious extremism, terrorism, and separatism. The CCP deployed loudspeaker trucks and red banners warning against the "three evils" all over Xinjiang, security forces carried banners reading "we must defeat the terrorists" and "oppose ethnic separatism and hatred" (BBC News 2009b), and Han Chinese interviewed on TV kept stating that they would not let the "three evils" destroy social harmony and economic progress (NBC News 2009). The SCO Secretary General further lent support to the framing, announcing tightened SCO cooperation in the face of the "three evils": "The fight against the 'East Turkestan' forces has been the top priority of the SCO since it was established, and we are confident that we will emerge the winner" (China Daily 2009).

While the riots had been largely squashed by July 8, Uighur mobilization remained an immediate danger to the CCP and the authorities therefore proceeded to employ a number of measures in the following days, weeks, and months to repress and prosecute Uighurs and deter future actions. In a first step, the CCP began to arrest large numbers of Uighurs based on accusations tied to the three evils, particularly terrorism and separatism. Based on estimations by non-governmental organizations (NGOs), up to 1,400 Uighurs were arrested, with more than 200 prosecutions tied to terrorism charges and at least 30 death sentences issued by the end of 2009 (Amnesty International 2010; Human Rights Watch 2009a, 2009b). In a second step, joint intelligence structures allowed the CCP to pursue and prosecute Uighurs across borders through blacklisting, extradition, and denial of asylum organized within RATS (Cooley and Heathershaw 2017). Based on these blacklists, the CCP had previously already framed the World Uighur Congress as a terrorist organization, and now moved to accuse its exiled Uighur dissident leader Rebiya Kadeer for orchestrating the Urumqi riots from abroad as early as July 6 (BBC News 2009c). The accusation was widely broadcast on national TV to further soothe enraged Han Chinese and legitimize the repression of Uighur groups.

Additionally, an updated SCO Counter-Terrorism Convention signed earlier in 2009 had established jurisdiction over individuals and groups accused of terrorism in any of the SCO member states (SCO 2009, art. 5). The NGO Human Rights in China (HRIC) documented more than 70 cases of forcible returns between SCO members, among them several that had fled Xinjiang after having been targeted by Chinese authorities for alleged connections to terrorist groups (HRIC 2011b). In a prominent case, Kazakhstan repatriated Uyghur refugee, Ershidin Israil, who had fled Xinjiang following the 2009 riots, although he had already been granted refugee status by the UN High Commissioner for Refugees (UNHCR). On Chinese request, Israil was detained, refused departure to Scandinavia, and transferred to China in May 2011 (Reuters 2011). UNHCR even transferred the power to decide upon the refugee status of Chinese Uighurs to the Kazakh authorities, giving them more power to enact the joint SCO extradition agreements (US Department of State 2012).

In the wake of the 2009 unrests, China has also invoked the extradition of 20 Uyghurs from the SCO partner state Cambodia (Wong 2010). Although the group had already applied to the UNHCR for refugee status, China claimed it had evidence of suspected connections between members of the group and ETIM, and influenced Cambodia to extradite the whole group despite official protests from the US and UN. In 2010, the Ministry of Public Security in China announced that it had uncovered a "terrorist

106   How Regional Organizations Sustain Authoritarian Rule

cell" that had planned terrorist attacks among "a group of 20 deported from a neighboring country" (Kan 2010b, p. 13), thereby supposedly aiming to retroactively justify the extradition.

Third, the CCP moved to enshrine the "three evils" doctrine into regional law immediately after the end of the riots through the 2009 amendment to the XUAR Regulation on the Comprehensive Management of Social Order in order to establish a legal basis for future prosecution of Uighurs as terrorists, a move that has been mirrored in other SCO member states (HRIC 2011b). In a final step, joint SCO military training missions were employed to warn future dissidents against challenging the regime. The 2010 SCO "Peace Mission" following the Urumqi riots staged the largest counter-terrorism drill to date in Kazakhstan, with over 5,000 troops from most SCO member states participating to showcase "a 'timely' demonstration of the SCO's contribution to combat terrorism, separatism and extremism" (Weitz 2010, p. 9).

SCO Involvement since 2009

In the years immediately after the Urumqi riots, it seemed like the Xinjiang situation had ebbed away. But a stabbing of around 150 people at a Chinese train station by Uighur militants as well as a suicide bombing at an Urumqi train station marked a turning point. In a speech delivered to party officials during Xi's only trip to Xinjiang in 2014, Xi called for an all-out "struggle against terrorism, infiltration and separatism" using the "organs of dictatorship," showing "absolutely no mercy" (Ramzy and Buckley 2019). The CCP has erected large-scale internment camps for Uighurs branded as "Vocational Education and Training Centers" since 2017 as evidenced by a number of leaked documents (*China Cables Exposes Chilling Details of Mass Detention in Xinjiang* 2019; Ramzy and Buckley 2019; Sudworth and The V. J. Team 2022). Conservative estimations, for instance by the Xinjiang Victims Database (Benuin 2022), attest to more than 48,000 forced imprisonments, mostly of Uighurs and other Muslim minority groups from China and abroad. According to the CCP, however, this strategy is a necessary step in the fight against terrorism:

> Xinjiang is a beautiful, peaceful and prosperous region in China. Three years ago, this was not the case. It had become a battle ground—thousands of terrorist incidents happened in Xinjiang between 1990s and 2016, and thousands of innocent people got killed. So there's an enormous uproar among the Xinjiang people for the government to take resolute measures to tackle this issue. Since the measures

> have been taken, there's no single terrorist incident in the past three years. Xinjiang again turns into a prosperous, beautiful and peaceful region. (Allen-Ebrahimian 2019)

The SCO has repeatedly played an important role in supporting the CCP's vast repression regime erected in Xinjiang. Most prominently, the SCO has helped to locate and extradite many Uighur nationals abroad over the years. Part of the CCP's actions consists of forcible returns of Uighurs with foreign passports by way of extradition. In the Authoritarian Actions Abroad Database (AAAD), which collects instances of extraterritorial repression by authoritarian regimes, China ranks as number two among the most serious offenders together with Uzbekistan and Russia (Dukalskis 2021). The repressive actions abroad by China, including extraditions, abductions, and threats against individuals and their families, span 167 cases involving more than 700 people. Interestingly, these types of actions mostly extend to members and associated states to the SCO, while actions against Muslims in non-aligned states such as Australia or Canada usually rather included informal attempts of threats to individuals and their families. Out of 22 cases with Australia as a target country, 21 included threats, while only 1 was an abduction. In contrast, among the SCO member states, out of 11 reported cases, 10 included extraditions while only 1 was a threat.

The practice of extraditions also extends to observers and associated states who have ratified treaties with the SCO. Turkey, for instance, has been an officially associated "dialogue partner" of the SCO since 2013 and declared its intention to become a full member in 2022. With many Muslim minorities residing in Turkey, China has been able to secure or attempt extraditions in 18 cases and threatened individuals in 6. The same goes for Egypt, where 8 out of 10 individuals were extradited or arrested by the Egyptian state. As Dukalskis declares himself, these recorded cases are probably only the tip of the iceberg, with many more cases of forced returns never being reported by the media or NGOs (Dukalskis 2021, p. 75).[3]

Similar instances of extradition and denial of asylum based on the SCO agreement have been documented all over Central Asia (Cooley and Heathershaw 2017; Kan 2010b). While SCO-RATS blacklists are not made public, in 2010, RATS Director Dzhumanbekov stated that the RATS database already lists 42 organizations and over 1,100 individuals related to "terrorism, separatism, and extremism" that can now be prosecuted across

---

[3] The database does not discern if some of these cases might also include legitimate requests to return criminals to China.

all SCO member states (SCO 2010). In the wake of the US withdrawal from Afghanistan, the SCO states including new members India and Pakistan have also declared their intention to step up their joint fight against the "three evils" and the establishment of a single joint list (The Hindu 2022). While the threat of terrorist groups extending into South Asia is not unfounded, past listing practices of RATS have shown that much of the activities are rather directed against domestic opposition instead of genuine counter-terrorism coordination.

Human rights groups such as HRIC have long voiced concerns that the expansion of blacklists is a result of "logrolling"; that is, each authoritarian regime listing their respective oppositional groups and dissidents in addition to genuine terrorist threats in exchange for the acceptance of the targets by the other SCO members (HRIC 2011a). According to HRIC (2011a), the potential scope of information that could be shared within SCO is vast, judging from domestic surveillance capabilities. In the aftermath of the Urumqi riots, China has installed more than 47,000 surveillance cameras in Urumqi alone, particularly inside and around mosques, monasteries, and hotels (Wines 2010). Every SCO member state could thus potentially tap into an extensive set of information on the activities of dissidents and opposition groups across the SCO, with only minimal requirements for requesting information.

In light of these circumstances, the UN Special Rapporteur on counter-terrorism had already voiced serious concerns about the cooperation of intelligence agencies of SCO member states over 10 years ago: "This sharing of data and information is not subject to any meaningful form of oversight and there are no human rights safeguards attached to data and information sharing" (United Nations General Assembly 2009, p. 10). These warnings turned into hard reality 12 years later given the vast expansion of the repression machinery in Xinjiang. In a 2022 assessment of the United Nations Human Rights Office, the High Commissioner accused China, stating that many members of the Uighur community have been "forcibly returned, or being placed at risk of forcible return to China, in breach of the prohibition under international law of refoulement" (OHCHR 2022, p. 42, par. 139).

The SADC and Legitimation: The 2002 Presidential Elections in Zimbabwe

Regionalism in Southern Africa was initiated under the Southern African Development Coordination Conference (SADCC) in 1980 by the so-called "Frontline States" (FLS)—a coalition of actors that fought to advance anti-apartheid struggle and economic independence from South Africa.

SADCC was transformed into the SADC in 1992 with the inclusion of newly independent Namibia and post-apartheid South Africa. In contrast to the GCC and SCO, the SADC is characterized by lower levels of autocratic homogeneity. While some of the states, most prominently South Africa, democratized within the last two decades, in others, prominent autocrats such as Zimbabwe's Robert Mugabe hung on to power for years, supported by dominant parties.

These dominant party systems had been particularly challenged by the rise of election monitoring as an international norm because the influence of pronouncements by election monitoring missions (EOMs) on domestic politics has sharply increased (Fawn 2013; Hyde 2011; Kelley 2012). Particularly authoritarian regimes have been faced with a double dilemma: either conform to international standards of democratic elections and risk losing power, or defy standards and risk losing legitimacy and international recognition in the process (Hyde 2011). This dilemma has given rise to a "shadow market" of election groups under the umbrella of autocratic ROs, offering relatively uncritical international validation of flawed elections, and thus leverage for autocratic regimes to signal democratic legitimacy at home and abroad (Fawn 2006; Hyde and Marinov 2014). These shadow election groups usually involve lenient monitors from friendly countries or authoritarian ROs that feign monitoring to quickly legitimize flawed elections as democratic, free, and fair immediately after the end of electoral proceedings (Debre and Morgenbesser 2017).

SADC is an active election monitor in Southern Africa but remains among the least critical ROs globally (Kelley 2009). At the same time, many of the elections in Southern Africa have been ranked as highly flawed by independent academic evaluations such as the Integrity of Elections Project (Norris et al. 2014). The SADC only adopted the SADC Principles and Guidelines Governing Democratic Elections in 2004 following the Organization of African Unity (OAU) Declaration on the Principles Governing Democratic Elections in Africa of 2002. While it has also been formally empowered to promote democracy in its charter (art. 5), and theoretically even has the competence to intervene in case of a military coup or threat to the legitimate authority of the state based on the "Protocol on Politics, Defense and Security Cooperation" (art. 11), it rarely makes use of its powers, instead usually opting to support incumbent regimes.

Presidential Elections in 2002

The trend of international election monitoring has particularly affected the Zimbabwean regime under the rule of long-time President Robert Mugabe.

Mugabe and his ZANU-PF party had been in power since the foundation of independent Zimbabwe in 1980. While regularly holding elections, there had never been a serious challenge to its rule for almost 20 years and successfully contesting elections was thus considered as a given by the Mugabe regime. This changed during the presidential elections in 2002. The election was contested by several parties, among them the newly created opposition party MDC under the leadership of Morgan Tsvangirai. Although only established toward the end of 1999, the MDC had already amassed a large number of followers and its first surprising successes during the parliamentary elections in 2001. While Mugabe eventually emerged victorious, winning 56 percent of the votes over 41 percent for Tsvangirai, the presidential elections were the closest in Zimbabwe history to date. The SADC's support emerged as a crucial element of the regime's efforts to legitimize the electoral outcome and Mugabe's continued rule.

Elections were held between March 9 and 11 under difficult circumstances. Following violent farm seizures as part of the fast-track land reform program in 2000, the country was in upheaval. The issue of redistribution of land from white farmers to black communities had been on the agenda since the Lancaster House agreement of 1979 in which the British had offered to pay for the redistribution of land should white farmers willingly decide to sell it. By the mid-1990s, a policy change allowed the Mugabe regime to expropriate white farmers in exchange for compensation, which led to significant numbers of commercial farms being taken over by party elites (Dowden 2008, p. 144ff). Enraged war veterans who felt cheated out of their share of the pie started to move against the remaining white farm workers and often violently forced them and their black workforce off their estates (Human Rights Watch 2002a). They were soon joined by state security forces that hoped to use the seizures to move against MDC support bases (ibid.).

Zimbabwe's land reform program, its primary drivers as well as the long-term consequences, are still a topic of debate years after its enactment (Laurie 2017; Scoones et al. 2010). While the land reforms caused widespread economic, social, and political upheavals, they were also a way for the liberation party ZANU-PF to deal with the very real racialized ownership patterns left from decades of colonial rule. However, given that the country's economy largely ran on agricultural production and food exports, the land reforms in combination with international sanctions caused a macroeconomic meltdown including soaring unemployment, increased poverty rates, and hyperinflation in the years following the redistributions due to instability, uncertainty over property rights, and displaced workforces (Laurie 2017, p. 13ff).

Shortly before violent land seizures began, the government had already tried to expand its powers in a new constitution in 2000 to legalize compulsory land seizures without compensation. To their own surprise, they lost the popular vote. Only six months earlier, the MDC had formed as the first credible opposition party, representing mostly black urban constituencies, as well as white farmers and their black farm workers; ZANU-PF in contrast classically represented war veterans and black rural citizens. The surprising success of the MDC "no" campaign against the 2000 constitutional vote meant that ZANU-PF and Mugabe faced, for the first time in their 20-year rule, a credible challenge going into the 2002 elections. Winning the 2002 elections was thus crucial to ZANU-PF because they would determine the future direction of the land redistribution program and thus also their ability to remain in power long term.

The elections were hotly contested, and ZANU-PF recurred to familiar patterns of intimidation and repression to deal with challengers. The run-up to the elections was characterized by widespread violence against opposition members—and those that the government thought were party support bases. Reports by Amnesty International and Human Rights Watch detail arrests, attacks, and even killings of MDC politicians, as well as arbitrary detentions, threats, and torture of journalists and members of the judiciary (Amnesty International 2002c; Human Rights Watch 2002b). Many of the victims were black farmworkers that were swept up and targeted during the land seizure campaign because they were thought to support the MDC (Human Rights Watch 2002a; Laurie 2017).

Many election observers therefore wanted to be present to evaluate the proceedings. More than 40,000 local observers applied, but only 400 were eventually accredited by the regime (Baker 2002). International observers faced similar restrictions. The head of the EU mission had been denied accreditation by the Zimbabwe election commission, after which the complete EU observation mission was withdrawn and a round of sanctions targeting political leaders for Mugabe's ZANU-PF party enacted as response (The Guardian 2002). Similarly, US observers from the Carter Institute and the National Democratic Institute (NDI) did not receive accreditation (Carter Center 2002).

However, a host of friendly ROs sent missions that received accreditation, including the African, Caribbean, and Pacific (ACP) group of nations, the Common Market for East and Southern Africa (COMESA), the Economic Community of West African States (ECOWAS), the Non-Aligned Movement (NAM), the OAU, and the SADC. The regime also tried to ensure that things went their way during the polling days. Stations in urban areas with more

MDC-leaning voter bases were reportedly reduced, while polling stations in rural areas that were ZANU-PF land were increased (BBC News 2003). Voters were also more stringently vetted in rural areas where they had to produce passports, mail-in ballots were restricted to government workers living abroad, and voters with dual citizenship were not allowed to vote according to a new law passed shortly before elections (ibid.). All measures seemed to be directed at limiting cosmopolitan, internationally oriented, and younger voters that were more likely supporters of the MDC.

Despite these hostile conditions, most African ROs found little to complain about concerning the elections. COMESA, the OAU, and the SADC ministerial support team all called the elections credible, free, and fair. SADC's mission, for instance, declared that "despite reported incidents of pre-election violence and some logistical shortcomings during voting, it is the considered opinion of the SADC Ministerial Task Force that the elections were substantially free and fair, and were a true reflection of the will of the people of Zimbabwe" (EISA 2002). Gertrude Mongella, the head of the OAU Observer Mission, likewise stated in a press conference for journalists in Harare that "on the basis of observations made during the voting, verification and counting process on the ground and the objective realities, the OAU Observer team wishes to state that in general the election was transparent, credible, free and fair" (ibid.).

In contrast, the few international observers that were allowed into the country made starkly different comments. The United States Assistant Secretary of State for African Affairs, Walter Kansteiner, said in a statement in Johannesburg that "Zimbabwe's presidential elections of 9–11 March were fundamentally flawed … ignoring the norms and standards which govern elections throughout the Southern African Development Community and to which Zimbabwe had committed" (US Department of State 2002). The Norwegian team added that "Campaigning was overshadowed by political violence. Although there were incidents on both sides, in some cases one can see a clear strategy of violence by government forces against the opposition" (DW 2002). The Zimbabwe Election Support Network (ZESN), a local NGO that had been collecting information since the parliamentary elections in 2000, also concluded that the elections "violated almost all of the SADC Parliamentary Forum Norms and Standards. … In summary, there is no way these elections could be described as substantially free and fair" (ZESN 2002).

The regime, however, made clever use of these conflicting statements. Instead of suppressing critical reports, negative statements from Western observers were printed openly but dismissed as post-colonial imperialism with reference to very real double standards and racist policies employed by Western countries and organizations. Critical regional and Zimbabwean voices were furthermore accused of collusion with Western powers, thereby undermining the black liberation struggle. At the same time, electoral outcomes were legitimized by reference to the judgments rendered by fellow African ROs.

In the run-up to the elections, Mugabe already used international sanctions to his advantage. During large rallies such as that in Domboramwari in late February, he accused the British and US of double standards. Referring to the contested Florida recount during the US presidential elections in 2001, Mugabe stated: "Have they forgotten Florida? Who won in Florida? Was it Bush or Al Gore? They must answer that question. ... Did we interfere? No, we didn't, because it was an American affair" (The Herald 2002a). Referring to an alleged assassination plot planned by Tsvangirai, Mugabe also called out racist reporting on international terrorism, saying that "terrorism is only when Bin Laden causes terror to the United States. When terror is planned against blacks, it is not terrorism?" (ibid.). Likewise, he equated voting for the MDC with supporting white imperialism during the same rally, saying that "the land issue was the unfinished business of the liberation struggle and that voting for the MDC would mean that the land would forever remain in the hands of the white colonisers" (ibid.).

SADC further strengthened this de-legitimation strategy by repeatedly calling out foreign powers for criticizing Zimbabwe based on perceived "imperialist" interference in African affairs. In response to the contested Zimbabwe land reform project, the SADC implored the international community to stop the "projection of a negative image of Zimbabwe which has had adverse effects on the economy of Zimbabwe" (SADC 2001, p. 141), and further reiterated that "some Western countries have authorized the broadcasting from their territories by their nationals of hostile and inciting propaganda against the Government of the Republic of Zimbabwe" (SADC 2002, p. 146). In later years, the SADC still called for all sanctions to be lifted, and particularly appealed to Britain to "honour its compensation obligations with regards to land reform" (SADC 2007) despite a rapidly deteriorating economic and human rights situation. While these statements on Western interferences on the African continent and adverse effects of sanctions call out important problems found in the highly politicized and racialized international sanction practices, they also help to legitimize an autocratic leader who violently moves against opposition and their supporters to remain in power.

Two days after Mugabe was declared a winner in the elections, the leading Zimbabwean newspaper *The Herald* published a major article under the headline "Sharp Divisions between Western Countries, Africa Emerge over Poll Result" (The Herald 2002b). The newspaper is state-run and faces little opposition due to stringent accreditation rules. In the piece, a number of African observer missions and their mission statements legitimizing the elections as free and fair are reported, urging Zimbabweans to accept the electoral results because of the support offered by "black African nations" (ibid.). Zimbabwean experts are quoted, discrediting Western reports as prejudiced: "Our interests have nothing to do with how people report about us. The West is our enemy and it would be surprising if they gave any favourable comment about us" (ibid.) reads a statement from a political scientist from the University of Zimbabwe.

In the weeks after the elections, further reports in *The Herald* emerged that intended to boost Mugabe as the liberation hero while further discrediting critical statements. The SADC Parliamentary Forum, for instance, which had been one of the few regional institutions in Southern Africa to criticize the elections, as well as ZESN, were accused of being EU puppets as they were largely financed by EU funds (The Herald 2002c). The MDC was likewise portrayed as a foreign asset by ZANU-PF: "The MDC is foreign directed and is drunk with foreign undemocratic, unAfrican and unZimbabwean ideas. That's why they say we should have an election run by foreigners ... they say we should have the Commonwealth or the UN to run our election," said ZANU-PF's information and publicity deputy national secretary (The Herald 2002g). At the same time, *The Herald* reported on congratulatory messages received by President Mugabe from regional and local groups that enjoy good standing within Zimbabwean society such as the Indigenous Business Women's Organization or Faith for the Nation (The Herald 2002f).

It is difficult to render a final judgment as to the extent to which the legitimation campaign and the SADC's support actually helped the regime to stay in power. But it is clear that the support from African ROs formed a major building block of the legitimation strategy employed by Mugabe and ZANU-PF throughout the election cycle. In the absence of regional support, the opposition's claim to electoral fraud and victories in their legal and public battles against the regime might have borne fruit. Instead, the SADC extended a protective hand over Africa's "liberation hero."

Mugabe himself attested to this fact. In his commencement speech, he explicitly thanked his fellow SADC members, foreshadowing the mutual support that he and other Southern African leaders extend to each other to remain in power: "I thank you for your brotherhood and solidarity. May we continue together, moving together, rendering advice and counsel to each other, even correcting each other where mistakes are being made" (The Herald 2002e). International observers, in contrast, are slammed:

> They want to choose who shall rule Zimbabwe, and if the person they have chosen does not win, and another wins as has happened in this particular case, no, the election has not been free and fair. It's only free and fair when we, the powers that be, we who count much more than you, say you have won (ibid.).

Attending the inauguration, current head of the SADC, Malawi President Muluzu, had previously rendered the final SADC judgment, thereby closing the lid on any further challenges: "SADC endorses the position taken by the SADC ministerial task force on Zimbabwe that the elections were substantially free and fair" (The Herald 2002d).

SADC Involvement since 2002

The SADC's support has helped to keep Mugabe and his party in power for years despite growing challenges in subsequent elections. When Mugabe came under increasing pressure to step down after violently moving against any opposition and grossly manipulating electoral results during the 2008 general elections (International Crisis Group 2008), the SADC again stepped in to support his standing as Africa's liberation hero. SADC reports continuously minimized the violence that Mugabe's ZANU-PF security forces inflicted on opposition supporters. The final SADC statement on the elections even commended the government for holding peaceful elections, and only called for a speedy announcement and broad acceptance of results (SADC 2008a). Mugabe was invited to attend the African Union (AU) summitry meeting in full standing only a week after his ostensible loss (African Union 2008; SADC 2008b) and South Africa intervened at the United Nations Security Council to lobby against resolutions calling for additional sanctions (United Nations 2008).

But in contrast to 2002, the MDC did not give in but demanded executive control. The SADC launched a mediation mission to negotiate a power-sharing arrangement in the months following the election. The mission helped to keep Mugabe and his loyal party cadres in executive control. The final agreement signed September 15 grants Mugabe full executive power, with oppositional candidate Tsvangirai as head of a toothless second cabinet and loyal Mugabe party cadres in charge of key Ministries (NBC News 2008a). In spite of rigged elections, the SADC's continued diplomatic support thus enabled Mugabe to refuse exit by claiming that he was the legitimately elected leader of Zimbabwe, with the opposition party and regional critics unable to initiate SADC action to intervene in their favor.

Mugabe was again able to exploit the SADC-coined discourse on pan-African solidarity and renaissance to boost his status as liberation hero domestically. This rhetoric particularly surfaced before and after important SADC meetings to prevent critics from successfully demanding institutional intervention against the regime. Oppositional candidate Tsvangirai was asked to "deliberately engage in reversing the gains of our liberation" (BBC News 2008a) to discredit his accusations of vote rigging before the SADC emergency meeting in April, with Southern African President Mbeki strengthening Mugabe's propaganda by calling Tsvangirai "a militant critic" instead of "taking responsibility for the future of Zimbabwe" (News24 2008b). In the wake of the SADC summitry meeting in August, Mugabe furthermore accused regional critic Botswana of deliberately destabilizing Zimbabwe as a "surrogate" of Western imperial power interference (Mail & Guardian 2008), thereby paving the way for a successful SADC mediation mission.

By the time of the next general elections in 2013, the regime had managed to return to business as usual with both Mugabe and ZANU-PF gaining absolute majorities. The SADC continued to support the regime along this road, rendering quick endorsements of the election to avoid another violent turn. Two days after the elections, which took place on July 31, 2013, both the AU and SADC EOMs held press conferences and published preliminary reports. The head of the AU mission, former Nigerian President Obasanjo, already called the elections free and fair, stating that observed irregularities did not impinge on the overall outcome of the polls (BBC News 2013). The SADC preliminary statement further notes that the elections were "characterized by an atmosphere of peace and political tolerance," that "political parties and candidates were able to freely undertake their political activities unhindered," and that the elections constitute "a new chapter in the process of consolidation of democracy" in Zimbabwe (SADC 2013, p. 17). The Integrity of Elections Project in contrast ranks the overall quality of the 2013 general elections as very low (Norris et al. 2016).

The story of regional support for ZANU-PF and Mugabe also foreshadows how old alliances and institutionalized rules of cooperation can help protect leaders from external interference. As we will further see in Chapter 6, neighboring states had called for interference in Zimbabwe to protect citizens from violence and remove Mugabe from power in 2008, the SADC Tribunal issued a landmark ruling against the regime, and dissenting regional voices from South Africa questioned the legitimacy of the 2002 election results. But the SADC has held a protective hand over the long-term leader to prevent regional critics successfully challenging his rule. This helped to suppress the publication of the "Khampepe report" for 12 years, a damning report on the 2002 Zimbabwe elections detailing the failings of the Mugabe regime drawn up by South African judges; it prevented Botswana and Zambia from moving against Mugabe unilaterally after the 2008 post-election violence; it supported the abolishment of the SADC Tribunal when it rendered judgments against the Zimbabwe regime; and it remained on the side-lines when ZANU-PF finally replaced the aging dictator with his second-in-command in a contested coup in 2017 to ensure the future rule of the dominant party. Even though Mugabe was not very well liked, he enjoyed a status as anti-apartheid hero who liberated Zimbabwe and tried to give back land to black communities, and his efforts to push back against international Western powers were valued among fellow SADC members. This status in combination with the SADC's preference for non-interference on the side of oppositional actors is the glue that repeatedly protected Mugabe from losing power.

6
How Dictator Clubs Constrain Regional Challengers

In this chapter, we turn to investigate the second theorized mechanism, *regional relationship management*. We analyze how dictator clubs establish formal and informal principles for multilateral cooperation through regional organizations (ROs) and thereby force critical regional challengers to conform to these agreed-upon rules. Membership in a dictator club thereby constrains dissenting actors from across the region. These types of regional challenges can stem from the governments and leaders of other RO member states, but also from civil society actors or RO bureaucracies from the region. Importantly, these types of challenges do not originate from within national borders of the regime in question and are therefore not open to the same types of survival strategies that autocratic regimes usually employ to deal with internal challengers.

The chapter further follows the Mugabe regime in Zimbabwe to investigate how the RO dealt with three distinct regional challengers: critical election reports from Southern African judges of the 2002 elections, challenges from fellow Southern African Development Community (SADC) members to remove Mugabe from power after the 2008 election crisis, and a landmark court ruling against the regime from the newly established SADC tribunal in 2008. The SADC was instrumental in dealing with these challenges in all three instances. Due to consensual decision-making procedures in the main SADC bodies and long-standing alliances between liberation movement parties, challenging actors had little room to maneuver against the Mugabe regime and in favor of the opposition. Despite formal authority of the RO to promote and protect democracy and human rights, norms of solidarity and stability define relationships within the SADC. In combination with the requirement for consensual decision-making, these rules of engagement in the SADC thereby ensure the protection of regimes in power from dissenting challengers.

The chapter then turns to investigate the military coup in 2017 that removed Mugabe from power in a within-case design. Similar dynamics that

How Regional Organizations Sustain Authoritarian Rule. Maria J. Debre, Oxford University Press.
© Maria J. Debre (2025). DOI: 10.1093/9780198903635.003.0006

explain how Mugabe survived during previous crises now account for his removal and can explain why the SADC did not come to Mugabe's rescue in 2017. After a long-term internal struggle for Mugabe's succession within the dominant party, the military was intent on putting his former second-in command in the presidential office. However, Mugabe was set on promoting is wife to the position. Finally, the military opted to forcibly remove him from power. This time around, critical voices that were wary of the military coup due to considerations for democratic principles were constrained. Instead, the SADC opted for a hands-off stance that allowed for the transition toward the new leader who would carry on the rule of the dominant party regime.

We have already seen the differential impact of membership in a dictator club that stabilizes autocratic members by preventing democratization but not autocratic replacements in the statistical analysis in Chapter 4. The SADC case exemplifies why dictator clubs often opt for interference only in support of the ruling elite to safeguard stability in the face of a potentially tumultuous democratic transition. In contrast, when only the leaders at the top of a regime are exchanged, stability of authoritarian rule is usually guaranteed. Additionally, relationships between members of the dictator clubs are often not only garnered between the leaders themselves but rather represent broad ties between the many members of the ruling coalition. Thus, alliances within dictator clubs usually protect whole regimes, not the individual leader.

Regional challenges are particularly likely in a more heterogenous region where membership in the dictator club is characterized by different types of regimes (democratic/autocratic) or other types of differences such as ideologies or types of autocracies (monarchy, personalist, ruling party, or military). In these cases, making sure that varying preferences between members will not endanger the elites in power by institutionalizing rules of regional cooperation is essential.

The SADC is a representative case to probe the role of an RO in a more heterogenous region due to coexisting democratic and autocratic regimes within one organization. While some of the states, most prominently South Africa, democratized within the last two decades, in others prominent autocrats hang on to power. However, since the foundation of the SADC, there has been little change to the overall status quo of rule in member states. Only Mozambique and Zambia have, according to some measurements such as Polity IV, improved their democratic quality over the last few years, although they still fall short of passing a threshold to genuine democracy. The status of other member states is contested. While Polity IV ranks Botswana and Namibia as democracies since 1992, Geddes et al. (2014, 2018) code both countries as autocratic party-based regimes for the same period. They argue that despite largely free and fair elections, both regimes exhibit extensive limitations to competition and power is too centralized on the ruling elite. These differences, however, often lead to dissenting preferences on the proper course of action when regimes and leaders are faced with difficult domestic political circumstances.

However, old bilateral ties of solidarity between liberation movements are still strong and form the basis for negotiations during the SADC summits of heads of states. The SADC's roots as an anti-apartheid movement live on and form the basis for strong norms of solidarity between ruling parties that have developed out of the liberation struggle (see also Nathan 2012 on this argument). In fact, Tanzanian president at the time, Mpaka, characterized SADC as "rooted in struggle; from which we have much to learn ... the first lesson is unity. ... And today, as we wage the struggle to carve for ourselves a place at the table of a global economy, we must remain united. There is no alternative to unity" (quoted in van der Vleuten and Hulse 2013, p. 15). This unity particularly applies to several core countries of the liberation movement, namely Angola, Botswana, Mozambique, Namibia, South Africa, Tanzania, Zambia, and Zimbabwe, although changing governments have had different effects on this coalition over time, as we will see throughout the chapter.

These norms of solidarity combine with the consensual decision-making structure of the SADC that require unanimity for all decisions of the heads of states and governments as well as the executive committees. Negotiation outcomes therefore usually favor old elites in power and constrain critical voices or interference outside of the SADC framework. While the SADC has been formally empowered to promote democracy in its charter (art. 5), and theoretically even has the competence to intervene in case of a military coup or threat to the legitimate authority of the state based on the Protocol on Politics, Defense and Security Cooperation (art. 11), this objective rather seems symbolic. In practice, the SADC protects its members irrespective of violations of human rights or democratic standards, opting for stability and the status quo instead of interference in favor of democracy. This does not mean that the SADC rejects interference in domestic affairs to stay on the side-lines of political events. As we will see, the organization is more than willing to intervene on the side of ruling parties, but usually refrains from supporting the side of the opposition and thereby constrains and suppresses critical voices from within their ranks.

The chapter shows how the SADC and Zimbabwe exemplify this dynamic. It is divided into four sections. First, it shows how the SADC's heads of states decided to suppress the publication of the so-called "Khampepe report" for 12 years, a damning report on the 2002 Zimbabwe elections detailing the failings of the Mugabe regime. The report was drawn up by two South African judges. But instead of supporting critical voices during the 2002 elections, South Africa fought a lengthy legal battle to keep the report under wraps. As the new African Union (AU) chairperson at the time, South African President Mbeki was intent on showcasing the commitment of African ROs to democracy and preventing dissenting actors from voicing criticism of fellow members.

Second, it highlights how both Botswana and Zambia had called for interference in Zimbabwe to protect citizens from violence and remove Mugabe from power in 2008. However, both had to negotiate a joint African response within the RO and were not able to act on their calls to bring down Robert Mugabe's government. Due to the alliance between South Africa, Angola, the Democratic Republic of the Congo (DRC), Mozambique, and Namibia, the SADC instead extended democratic legitimacy to the Zimbabwe regime, supported Mugabe's refusal to relinquish executive power, and strengthened his re-legitimation campaign as the true leader of the anti-colonial liberation struggle fighting against imperialist powers. Third, the chapter traces how the SADC decided to abolish its own tribunal when it rendered judgments against the Zimbabwe regime, realizing the dangers of an interventionist court for the sovereignty of all members. Fourth, the chapter shows how the RO remained on the side-lines when ZANU-PF replaced the aging and increasingly unable dictator with his second-in-command in a coup in 2017 to ensure the future rule of the dominant party.

The "Khampepe Report": Challenges from Southern African Judges

Picking up where we left off in the previous chapter, ZANU-PF and Mugabe successfully dealt with a highly popular oppositional challenge from the MDC party during the 2002 elections. A mix of targeted violence against MDC supporters and validation by regional SADC election monitors helped the regime to deal with the crisis. In fact, the SADC election mission had declared the presidential run-off as legitimate shortly after the vote. But crisis was not completely averted yet. In fact, South Africa had commissioned an independent report by two prominent judges, Sisi Khampepe and Dikgang Moseneke, who traveled to Zimbabwe on an independent mission. The subsequent "Khampepe report," as it became known in the press, created a legal minefield for the SADC and South Africa in the coming years, as it contradicted the main findings from the SADC mission on important points.

The report only became public after a lengthy legal battle by a leading South African newspaper, *Mail & Guardian* (*M&G*), which had requested access to the report under the information access law and finally won the legal battle in 2014 to have the document declassified (Mail & Guardian 2024). South Africa and the SADC, in turn, did everything in their power to keep the report under wraps, and for good reason. In contrast to the SADC election mission, Khampepe and Moseneke came to starkly different conclusions:

> However, having regard to all the circumstances, and in particular the cumulative substantial departures from international standards of free and fair elections found in Zimbabwe during the pre-election period, these elections, in our view, cannot be considered to be free and fair. (Khampepe and Moseneke 2002, p. 26)

Why exactly Southern African then-President Mbeki commissioned an independent legal report on the Zimbabwean elections is unclear. Maybe he hoped to get additional ammunition to discredit international observers and to support Mugabe and ZANU-PF. But when the results of the report became known to Mbeki and other SADC leaders shortly after the elections, they needed to act. While Mugabe is skilled at using inconsistencies between international and regional verdicts to his advantage, a damning report by a prominent and powerful neighbor would have shot the carefully crafted legitimation strategy to pieces.

South Africa was therefore in a difficult position in 2002. As first chairperson of the newly founded African Union, South African President Mbeki was intent on showing a changing face of democratic, stable, and economically viable Sub-Saharan Africa, branded as "African renaissance" to the world. Mbeki imprinted his vision of "African renaissance" in the New Partnership for Africa's Development (NEPAD), lobbied for the establishment of a Pan-African Parliament (PAP), and oversaw the drafting of the Protocol establishing the African Court on Human and Peoples Rights. Simultaneously, the SADC's institutional structure saw reform as well, with the Protocol on Politics, Defense, and Security Cooperation passed in 2001 introducing closer cooperation and more possibilities for intervention in domestic politics of member states. The Zimbabwe situation was clearly a critical case for the new institutional set-up and vision for the continent. Neither Mbeki nor other SADC members wanted to mess with the newly minted picture of a democratically engaged Sub-Saharan Africa, but at the same time new institutional arrangements empowered critical actors to move against ruling elites.

The SADC heads therefore opted to bury the report, with Mbeki classifying it to prevent the document from becoming part of the public record (Mail & Guardian 2008). Their strategy seemed to have worked in the first instance, given that the report was only published in 2014 after a long court battle—by which time the Mugabe regime was again firmly in the saddle. Even in the regional press, there was no mention of the report in the immediate aftermath of the 2002 elections. However, *M&G* started to lobby the government for its release in 2007, the year leading up to Zimbabwe's next presidential elections. When the South African government did not comply, *M&G* finally filed a lawsuit to gain access to the report under the Protection of Access to Information Act of 2002 (PAIA) (Ngcobo 2011). The matter went through the courts, with the South African government arguing the report was a record of cabinet and therefor exempt from the PAIA Act (ibid., p. 2). Finally, *M&G* managed to obtain a victory in the Constitutional Court on November 14, 2014, after having gone through lengthy appeals in front of every South African court (Benjamin 2014).

The hard fight against the report's publication exemplifies the stakes that critical challenges from within the region pose for the SADC's ability to keep supporting their own. Constraining these critical voices was particularly pertinent for South Africa's and Zimbabwe's strategy to continuously employ a consistent legitimation narrative of democratic elections as validated by regional monitors. The *M&G* lawsuit came at the heels of Zimbabwe's 2008 election crisis. This was a time when much depended on the SADC's credibility both as election monitor and perception as objective and legitimate mediator during the contentious power-sharing negotiations that followed ZANU-PF's defeat at the polls. As we will see in the next section, the SADC was instrumental in constraining critical SADC members during the 2008 crisis to keep Mugabe in office. It was therefore vital to keep the damning Khampepe report, a critical voice from the SADC, under wraps for as long as possible.

The potentially damning effect the report would have had on the SADC's and South Africa's reputation if released is exemplified in the harsh accusations and debates even after the publication of the report in 2014—almost 12 years after the contentious elections took place. *M&G* accused Mbeki and subsequent governments of a betrayal of democracy: "by trying to play God, he undermined the democratic will of Zimbabweans and helped to entrench a pattern of electoral violence and intimidation in subsequent polls" (Mail & Guardian 2014b). Likewise, Tsvangirai accused South Africa of "wittingly or unwittingly aid[ing] the subversion of democratic processes in Zimbabwe" (Mail & Guardian 2014a). Mbeki tried to defend the SADC's

2002 decision to support the legitimacy of election results and to suppress the report on procedural matters. He noted that the Khampepe report was based on the narrow findings by two judges, who "had neither the capacity nor the mandate to carry out the observation work done by the SAPOM [South African Parliamentary Observer Mission] and the SAOM [South African Observer Mission], and it exceeded both its capacity and its mandate" (Mbeki 2014). Luckily for the SADC, by 2014 Mugabe had already regained full power of office and the report was not able to do any more damage to his rule.

The Zimbabwe Election Crisis of 2008: Challenges from Critical SADC Members

The support Mugabe received from the SADC in 2002 set the scene for the second major election crisis of the decade in 2008. The clash between international observers and the Mugabe regime escalated during the 2002 elections. The head of the European Union (EU) mission had been denied accreditation by the Zimbabwe election commission after critical comments. In consequence, the complete EU observation mission was withdrawn, leading to a round of EU sanctions targeting political leaders from Mugabe's ZANU-PF party (The Guardian 2002). Similarly, US observers from the Carter Institute and the National Democratic Institute (NDI) did not receive accreditation (Carter Center 2002). Only a few international observers, for instance from the Commonwealth and Norway, were left on the ground, all denouncing the elections as non-free and fair (e.g. NORDEM 2002). While the regime skillfully de-legitimized these critical reports in 2002, the regime tried to prepare for the 2008 elections by banning international missions from monitoring its election completely, thereby also hoping to avoid international challenges completely. Thus, in 2008, only regional monitoring missions from friendly neighbors and ROs were allowed into the country by stressing the importance of recognition by African partners in the spirit of African renaissance.

But the general elections including votes both for parliament and the presidential office still turned out to be highly contested and almost cost the Mugabe regime their grip on power, not only because of intensified domestic opposition but also because of powerful regional critics from within the SADC. The first round of the 2008 elections was set for March 29, with incumbent Mugabe running for the dominant ZANU-PF party and oppositional candidate Tsvangirai for the MDC. Vote counting turned into a lengthy and contentious process, as the MDC candidate was projected to win by several estimates, and ZANU-PF candidates lodged complaints for a recount of votes.

While the Zimbabwe Electoral Commission (ZEC) held off on an announcement of official results for five weeks, the party elites seemed intent on finding a solution to the regime's electoral defeat. They settled on announcing results that would necessitate a second round of presidential run-off elections, being unable to pressure the ZEC into manipulating results in favor of a Mugabe win (International Crisis Group 2008, p. 5). Finally, after over a month, the ZEC announced the official results with 47.9 percent of votes for Tsvangirai and 43.2 percent for Mugabe, necessitating a second run-off election round. MDC leaders accused Mugabe and the ZANU-PF of blatant vote rigging during the recount, and called for a national unity government of all parties without Mugabe's involvement (BBC News 2008b). However, ZANU-PF refused to negotiate Mugabe's exit and instead insisted on a second round of voting (International Crisis Group 2008).

After the announcement of a second round of voting, large-scale state-sponsored violence gripped the country. According to reports, ZANU-PF-related security forces targeted members of the opposition party MDC and areas where support for the party had been strongest, while the government moved against civil society organizations and electoral officials (Human Rights Watch 2008a; International Crisis Group 2008). While state-sponsored violence had been a constant during Zimbabwean elections since the rise of a coherent opposition in 1999, the extent and numbers after the first round of voting in 2008 surpassed all previous experiences. The violence made it almost impossible for MDC leaders to campaign during the run-up to the second round of voting, and finally led to Tsvangirai's withdrawal from the race on June 23 (Dugger and Bearak 2008). Although Tsvangirai's name remained on the ballot during the vote on June 27 for technical reasons, the final tally showed Mugabe officially winning with 85.5 percent, and the incumbent was immediately sworn in after the victory announcement on June 29.

However, since the MDC had also won a majority of seats in the parliamentary elections, Mugabe was forced to open up to negotiations of a national unity government, mediated by South African President Mbeki under the auspices of the SADC. On September 15, a power-sharing agreement (PSA) was signed between Mugabe and Tsvangirai, which allowed Mugabe to remain president while Tsvangirai would become prime minister (NBC News 2008b). After further lengthy and mediated negotiations about the allocation of ministries between the two parties, Tsvangirai was finally sworn in as prime minister in February 2009 with Mugabe remaining in the presidential office.

Compared to 2002, the handling of the crisis did increasingly divide the SADC over the course of events and led to significant critical calls for a removal of Mugabe as president from a number of regional players. Prominent former allies of Mugabe—among them the African National Congress (ANC) in South Africa, the Tanzania African National Union, the Botswana Democratic Party, and the Movement for Multiparty Democracy in Zambia—openly denounced the violence (Borger and Rice 2008), and the presidents of Botswana and Kenia even called for the suspension of Zimbabwe from further SADC and AU meetings (BBC News 2008c). Furthermore, Mbeki's role as SADC mediator turned into a highly contested issue (ICG 2008), with Zambian president Mwanawasa even accusing him of acting as "Mugabe's messenger" (Nathan 2012, p. 72).

Regional election monitoring officials also eventually turned their back on the regime and voiced reservations about the quality of the second round of run-off elections. During the first round, the SADC was one of the main Election Observation Missions (EOMs) evaluating electoral proceedings due to the banishment of international observers, and had no issue with fully supporting the quality of the elections. Its first preliminary report on March 30 validated the elections as a peaceful and credible expression of the will of the people (Nyamanhindi 2008). However, this stance changed in the wake of the first election round. Both SADC special envoy Mamabolo and SADC executive secretary Salomao conveyed their concerns that the political environment in Zimbabwe was not suited for free and fair elections during the pre-electoral phase (Zimbabwe Independent 2008). The final report of the SADC EOM to the second round of voting consequently is very clear in its conclusion that the elections could not be characterized as democratic:

> The process leading up to the presidential run-off elections held on 27 June 2008 did not conform to SADC Principles and Guidelines Governing Democratic Elections. ... The Mission is of the view that the prevailing environment impinged on the credibility of the electoral process. The elections did not represent the will of the people of Zimbabwe. (SADC 2008c, p. 6)

Particularly noteworthy also is the vocal critical stance of Botswana's government under the relatively young President Khama, whose father had been a loyal ally to Mugabe and ZANU-PF. When violence flared up after the first election round, Botswana granted exile to opposition candidate Tsvangirai, who found refuge in a secret location in Gaborone (Dugger 2008). Khama went even further, deploying military contingents along the 600-kilometer Botswana–Zimbabwe border and announcing a possible military intervention in Zimbabwe if Mugabe did not step down (Sunday Standard 2008). According to Wikileaks cables, Khama even sent his general to request military assistance from the US, where General Tlkokwane met with US defense cooperation officials from the US Embassy in July due to the heightened tensions with Zimbabwe (Wikileaks 2008).

Given these outspoken critical regional challengers, why was the opposition not able to move more forcefully against Mugabe with the help of regional pressure? Why has Mugabe and the ZANU-PF regime managed to survive in power despite their ostentatious election loss, large-scale violence against opposition candidates, and mounting regional pressure, and even managed to win back an absolute majority for ZANU-PF during the following presidential elections in 2013? One explanation is the role that the SADC played in constraining critical neighbors in this very heterogeneous region. While some SADC members were increasingly concerned over the Zimbabwe question and ready to move against the former "liberation hero," overall the RO remained highly divided on how to handle the situation. Refraining from outright endorsement of the elections and Mugabe's actions, a divided body of heads of states was only able to issue vague statements in the months following the elections. This, in turn, protected the regime's strategy of repression and deferral, and made it impossible for critical RO members to successfully lobby for a removal or even reprimand of Mugabe's regime in a multilateral setting.

This dynamic started with the first election round in March 2008. Due to the long delay in announcing electoral results, the SADC convened an emergency meeting called by Zambian President Mwanawasa on April 12. However, both the official SADC statement and remarks by Southern African president Mbeki, who had met with both candidates before the summit, remained free of open criticism of Mugabe and his ZANU-PF party, although the extent of the state-led violence and the possibility of election tampering during the recount was already a matter of international concern (Human Rights Watch 2008b). While Zambia's president and summitry convener Mwanawasa had opened the meeting by stating that "standing by and doing nothing was no longer an option" (The Star 2008, par. 5), Mbeki insisted that the issue was a matter of domestic affairs. Mbeki even announced that "there is no crisis in Zimbabwe" (The Telegraph 2008, par. 1) and that the elections represented "a normal electoral process" (ibid., par. 4). His position is mirrored in the final SADC statement, which did not contain any harsh language,

128 How Regional Organizations Sustain Authoritarian Rule

but only called for a speedy announcement and broad acceptance of results without any reference to Mugabe or ZANU-PF (News24 2008a).

Two main reasons explain the SADC's inaction in the case of Zimbabwe during this first summitry meeting. First, the SADC's main body has to decide on matters according to unanimity rules, which often lead to minimal statements in contested matters. In essence, only 3 out of 15 SADC members were firmly on the side of the MDC opposition: Zambia, Botswana, and Tanzania.[1] On the other side, powerful members such as South Africa, Angola, Namibia, the DRC, and Malawi remained loyal to Mugabe. Importantly, also Mozambique and Swaziland, who were both members of the troika leading the important Organ on Politics, Defense, and Security (OPDS) at the time, were rather loyal supporters of ZANU-PF. Under these circumstances, members calling for suspension or even critical language regarding the conduct of the regime simply did not have enough negotiating power during the emergency summit in April. Importantly, however, Mugabe supporters were also not able to press for more open support of the ruling regime, given internal critics. This led to a minimal vague statement that satisfied both sides.

Second, many of the SADC regimes were also afraid of setting a negative precedent, whereby more intrusive measures could also be taken against them in cases of future domestic misconduct. Informed by past negative experiences when South African President Mandela called for sanctions against the Nigerian regime and was subsequently isolated within the SADC for acting as a bully, many SADC members rather opted to refrain from intervention in favor of democracy and human rights out of fear of similar isolation (Nathan 2012, p. 78; van der Vleuten 2007, p. 162). After the official announcement of election results on May 2, this pattern of inaction regarding Mugabe therefore continued. Communiqués released by SADC summits and extra-ordinary meetings of the OPDS Troika during the following year remain largely free of criticism or condemnation of Mugabe and his ZANU-PF party regime. Instead, statements are clouded in non-committal language that obscures the extent of the crisis and refrain from taking a stance.

The SADC's division became further evident during the lengthy negotiations of the PSA, during which Southern African President Mbeki in his capacity as official SADC envoy repeatedly threw his weight behind Mugabe. The negotiations of the PSA started under the auspices of the SADC on July 21, 2008, but were not off to a good start. Mbeki refused to meet with the opposition candidate at first, and instead favored "quiet diplomacy" with Mugabe in the hopes of reaching a quick agreement with his long-term

---

[1] While Kenia was an outspoken critic, it is not an SADC member.

How Dictator Clubs Constrain Regional Challengers **129**

political ally. Instead, the negotiation process turned into a protracted affair and faced numerous obstacles, including disagreements over the distribution of key ministerial portfolios, concerns about the military's role, and Mugabe's refusal to concede his position as ruling president and to allot much executive power to Tsvangirai. Eventually, in September 2008, the parties reached an official agreement that saw the creation of a unity government. Tsvangirai became the prime minister, while Mugabe retained the presidency. But strife was not over; it continued during the implementation phase, with Tsvangirai only being sworn in as prime minister in February 2009.

Due to the many deadlocks along the road of negotiation and implementation, several SADC emergency meetings and special sessions were called by both sides to rule on contentious issues. At each meeting, Mugabe was, however, able to mobilize his coalition of supportive regional allies. In consequence, the SADC failed to take a clear stance on contested issue, or to confront Mugabe in a meaningful way. The first regular summitry meeting after the elections in August 2008 intensified the deep divisions among SADC members on the Zimbabwe question that had already become apparent during the emergency summit in April. Botswana's head of state Seretse Ian Khama, Zambia's Mwanawasa, and Tanzanian President Jakaya Kikwete who was also chair of the AU were the most outspoken critics of the Mugabe regime. Mwanawasa, however, was unwell during the summit and not able to attend,[2] with Foreign Affairs Minister Pande attending on his behalf. Khama boycotted the meeting to protest Mugabe's inclusion. In a statement released before the summit, he declared:

> Botswana does not accept the results of the June 27th run-off election in Zimbabwe as it violated the core principles of SADC, the African Union and United Nations. (The Irish Times 2008)

> The authorities in Harare under the present circumstances should not be represented at the political level at any SADC Summit as that would be equal to giving them legitimacy. (Aljazeera 2008)

However, the trio stood little chance. Majorities hadn't changed since April, and the main summitry meeting did not contain a substantive conclusion on how to deal with the negotiation deadlocks, only including a non-committal sentence on Zimbabwe in its final communiqué. Specifically, the communiqué notes that "the region remains relatively stable and peaceful

---

[2] In fact, Mwanawasa died only days after the summit, on August 19, 2008. The MDC opposition thereby lost a critical and powerful supporter during an essential moment.

with challenges in ... Zimbabwe, which unless addressed, could negatively affect the pace of implementation of the regional integration agenda" (SADC 2008d, p. 2). The summitry meeting then tasked the OPDS troika to further handle specifics in the Zimbabwe question. The troika at the time consisted of Mugabe allies King Mswati III of Swaziland, President Guebuza (Mozambique), and dos Sontos (Angola) who were united in their support for Mugabe and ZANU-PF. Their conclusions therefore remained completely uncritical, encouraging parties of the negotiation process to "sign any outstanding agreements and conclude the negotiations as a matter of urgency, to restore political stability in Zimbabwe," and to "convene Parliament to give effect to the will of the people as expressed in the Parliamentary elections held on 29 March 2008" (SADC 2008b).

Even after the PSA was signed in September 2008, implementation again stalled over the allocation of government ministries, making further SADC meetings necessary. In October 2008, the SADC OPDS Troika met several times in Mbabane and Harare to discuss the political situation in Zimbabwe. Tsvangirai managed to gain a small victory, convincing the troika members to call for a full SADC emergency summit to decide on the contentious allocation process, thereby removing the decision from Mugabe's immediate allies in the troika. During the emergency summit in November 2008 in Johannesburg, the deadlock about the allocation of the ministry of Home Affairs, which Tsvangirai claimed for the MDC, was put on the agenda. Although South Africa's support for Mugabe was slightly waning due to domestic turmoil after Mbeki's resignation as president and ANC party leader in September 2008, Mugabe still had enough supporters on his side. During the meeting, the body decided on a co-sharing of the contested position by both parties (McGreal 2008). This result can again be seen against the backdrop of unanimity requirements in the body, with neither the pro-Mugabe nor the pro-Tsvangirai side being able to convince the body of their position.

Another extra-ordinary SADC summit was convened in January 2009 in Pretoria, South Africa. At this point, negotiations about the allocation of cabinet positions had further dragged on, with Mugabe and ZANU-PF repeatedly backtracking on settled matters and stalling the inauguration of government. Two main points were on the agenda this time: the positions of the Reserve Bank governor and that of the Attorney-General. While the MDC demanded the removal of the current position holders, both long-term loyal Mugabe officials, Mugabe refused to concede on all points. Again, regional allies of Tsvangirai stood little chance. Essentially, the final SADC communiqué postponed most of the decisions: it decided that "the appointments of the Reserve

Bank Governor and the Attorney General will be dealt with by the inclusive government after its formation" and that "the allocation of ministerial portfolios endorsed by the SADC Extraordinary Summit held on 9 November 2008 shall be reviewed six months after the inauguration of the Inclusive Government" (SADC 2009a, p. 3).

However, the body did manage to convince Tsvangirai and Mugabe to finally agree on an inauguration date in February, where Mugabe would be allowed to remain in the presidential office, and Tsvangirai would become prime minister. Mugabe thus retained full executive power, presiding over the cabinet that he filled with old and loyal party elites, while Tsvangirai became prime minister and presided over a second cabinet, the newly created Council of Ministers (SADC 2008e). After the cabinet was finally sworn in in February and was able to start its work, the MDC increasingly saw their power dwindle. Mugabe refused to replace the Reserve Bank Governor and Attorney-General as called for in the SADC communiqué and to appoint MDC provincial governors according to the agreed-upon distribution. Tsvangirai therefore went on a final campaign tour ahead of the 29th Ordinary Summit of Heads of State and Government held on September 7–8, 2009 in Kinshasa to advocate for a more critical position of the SADC on ZANU-PF's repeated breach of the PSA and SADC decisions. Tsvangirai hoped that his efforts would get the 2009 Summit to issue a critical reprimand of ZANU-PF and Mugabe.

Instead, he had to realize his growing isolation at the regional level. The situation in Zimbabwe was taken off the agenda prior to the meeting because South African former President Mbeki as head of the Zimbabwe negotiation team refrained from attending to present a progress report. Instead, newly elected SADC chairperson Joseph Kaliba from the DRC promised a possible SADC extra-ordinary meeting on Zimbabwe—which, however, never materialized. Without a clear basis for decision, the heads of states only issued a diplomatic statement commending the "progress made in the implementation of the Global Political Agreement" and calling on "the international community to remove all forms of sanctions against Zimbabwe" (SADC 2009b).

Additionally, Mugabe was also able to count on his network of allies for support within the AU. During the 2008 AU summitry meeting in Sharm El-Sheik, the AU took a similar stance on the Zimbabwe crisis as the SADC, although the Tanzanian president and critic of Mugabe acted as chair of the summit at the time. Still, the final resolution on Zimbabwe only expressed deep concern "with the prevailing situation in Zimbabwe" and "the violence and loss of life that has occurred" (African Union 2008, p. 1), and refrained from openly condemning Mugabe and his regime for any wrongdoing. On the contrary, during the 11th Ordinary Session of the AU Assembly of Heads of States, Mugabe was in attendance and there was no mention of Zimbabwe as a case for concern during opening statements (Badza 2009). By treating him like the legitimate representative instead of criticizing him for his violent reaction to oppositional protest, these invitations passively endorsed and validated his status as legitimately elected head of state representing Zimbabwe on the international stage. Regional critics had little stand in both ROs, and were constrained to move against Mugabe by his network of allies and consensual decision-making procedures that favor the status quo of regimes over transitional pro-democracy actors.

The SADC Tribunal: Challenges from a Regional Court

While trying to navigate the election crises and regional challengers from other SADC heads of states, the Mugabe regime was simultaneously faced with a major regional threat in the form of the landmark case of *Mike Campbell (Pvt) Ltd and Others v Republic of Zimbabwe*, tried in front of the SADC tribunal. In 2007, Mike Campbell, a white farmer threatened with eviction from his land in the course of the contentious ZANU-PF land reform program, filed an application with the SADC tribunal to challenge the eviction by the Mugabe regime (Southern African Legal Information Institute (SAFLII) 2008). More than 70 individuals joined the lawsuit, making the case one of the major challenges to a central policy program of the regime. In 2008, the SADC tribunal made a landmark ruling against the government of Zimbabwe, stating that the country's land reform policies were racially discriminatory and violated international law (ibid.).

Formally agreed upon during the negotiations for the establishment of the SADC in 1992, the SADC tribunal was officially institutionalized with sitting judges in 2005. Its main objectives were to ensure adherence to SADC Treaty provisions by all SADC members. While it did not have a direct human rights mandate according to the founding Protocol, the Court considered the protection of human rights, democracy, and the rule of law as one of its core functions to protect Article 4 of the SADC Treaty (Southern African Legal Information Institute (SAFLII) 2008). The tribunal was a progressive legal achievement in the landscape of regional dispute settlement, particularly among dictator clubs. The original mandate of the 1992 Protocol on the SADC tribunal granted it jurisdiction over disputes between SADC member states, including cases involving the interpretation and application of the SADC Treaty and subsidiary instruments (art. 15). However, one of the groundbreaking aspects of the SADC tribunal's jurisdiction was its openness to individuals and non-state entities. This meant that not only member states but also individuals and institutions could bring cases before the tribunal related to human rights violations within the SADC region.

The case against Zimbabwe was brought before the SADC tribunal by a group of dispossessed white Zimbabwean farmers who had been forced off their land without any form of compensation as a result of the government's land reform program. These farmers sought legal recourse, arguing that the land seizures were racially discriminatory, violated property rights, and contravened international law (Southern African Legal Information Institute (SAFLII) 2008, par. I). The farmers had previously tried to avert the seizure of their land in front of the Supreme Court of Zimbabwe (ibid., par. II). The Mugabe regime had changed the constitution to allow for land expropriation by the Zimbabwean government without financial compensation or the possibility to challenge the expropriation in front of a court through amendment 17 in 2005. In 2006, the Gazetted Land (Consequential Provisions) Act came into effect, requiring all farmers to vacate homes acquired by the Zimbabwean government through amendment 17 within 90 days. Finally, in 2008, the Zimbabwean Supreme Court ruled against Campbell, dismissing all challenges (The Zimbabwean 2008). To achieve temporary relief, Campbell had already appealed to the SADC tribunal in 2007. The tribunal issued an emergency decision and ruled that the eviction should be temporarily put on hold until a final verdict was reached (Southern African Legal Information Institute (SAFLII) 2007).

However, the final verdict in the SADC case was further postponed to November 2008, both because more farmers joined the Campbell case to fight their evictions and resettled farmers wanted to intervene on the side of the Zimbabwean government. Despite the tribunal's orders to postpone any eviction until it had reached a verdict, Campbell's farm was invaded by ZANU-PF militias in 2008, threatening workers, destroying crops, and finally chasing the family off their land (Dugger 2008). Finally, in November 2008, the tribunal held that the forced displacement of white farmers without adequate compensation constituted a breach of human rights and property rights protections, thereby finding for the plaintiffs in all matters (Southern African Legal Information Institute (SAFLII) 2008, par. VIII (c)).

Despite the politically sensitive topic concerning re-distribution of land toward black farmers to deal with the issue of property rights and the legacy of apartheid rule, the tribunal's decision was hailed by most African human rights advocates and legal experts in the region as a success for human rights

134 How Regional Organizations Sustain Authoritarian Rule

protection (e.g. Southern Africa Litigation Centre 2010). Given that the farmers had received no compensation for their evictions and many farms were redistributed to loyal Mugabe cadres, the already contentious land reform program was placed on even shakier legal ground. Indeed, the tribunal itself argued in its judgment that:

> (b) had fair compensation [been] paid in respect of the expropriated lands, and (c) the lands expropriated were indeed distributed to poor, landless and other disadvantaged and marginalized individuals or groups, rendering the purpose of the programme legitimate, the differential treatment afforded to the Applicants would not constitute racial discrimination. (Southern African Legal Information Institute (SAFLII) 2008, par. V)

But the tribunal faced immediate resistance, not only from the Zimbabwean government but also from other SADC member states. President Mugabe's administration, critical of the tribunal's authority, initially dismissed the ruling as an "exercise in futility" (New Zimbabwe 2008). Interestingly, the government never tried to challenge the ruling on substantive grounds. The Zimbabwean government made a formal argument to contest the ruling, claiming that the tribunal was illegal because its founding treaty had never been ratified by two thirds of the members of the bloc (Sasa 2009). After a judgment to grant temporary relief, the state-owned Zimbabwean newspaper *The Herald* reported an Attorney-General's official stating that the government had "no choice now but to point out that the creation of the Tribunal was an administrative blunder that cannot be allowed to continue to subsist" (ibid.). The Zimbabwean Justice Minister Chinamasa then expressed in a letter to the tribunal that Zimbabwe would therefore withdraw from the court and that the government would continue to evict and prosecute farmers in spite of the tribunal's ruling to comply with the principles in the Zimbabwean constitution (ibid.).

The debate essentially revolved around the question of primacy of international versus domestic law. In a High Court decision in 2010, Zimbabwean sitting judge Patel argued that the tribunal's rulings directly contradict Zimbabwean constitutional law, which remains the supreme law of the state, and would therefore not be enforced in the country (Oxford Public International Law 2010). In contrast, the SADC Court ruled in a follow-up decision in 2009 that the Zimbabwean government was in contempt of the court and that its ruling should take precedent, and thus referred the case to the SADC summit for action, hoping for support in the matter (Southern African Legal Information Institute (SAFLII) 2009).

However, the debate on primacy of international versus domestic law also alerted other SADC members to the dangers of an interventionist regional court that could potentially cause serious reputational damages when deciding in favor of individual petitioners and against ruling regimes and parties. Lesotho, for instance, was facing a costly lawsuit for breach of contract from a diamond mining company, Botswana was challenged by a potential trial for the forcible removal of indigenous groups from their lands in the Kalahari Desert, and Tanzania narrowly avoided a ruling in a case of alleged torture in 2009. South Africa's negative experience with previous efforts to move more forcefully against human rights violations in neighboring states has likewise incentivized the state to remain cautious of supporting a more authoritative regional human rights institution. While South Africa supported the legality of the tribunal in general, it refrained from lobbying for measures to force Zimbabwe to comply with the ruling. In an interview, deputy director general of the South African department of international relations in fact stated that:

> There is a broad consensus in the region to have a tribunal. However, there has to be a broad understanding of the legal framework establishing it and it is also critical to understand that the implementation of the aims and objectives of SADC does not depend on the tribunal. (Christie 2011b)

During the SADC summit in 2010, the heads of states decided to order a review of the "functions and ... terms of reference of the SADC Tribunal" (SADC 2010), which was undertaken by an independent law consultancy. But the SADC summit seemed to have already settled on curtailing the rights of the Court before the independent evaluation was even finalized. During the same session, it failed to renew and appoint new judges to the tribunal during the summit, thereby leaving the Court powerless with only 4 out of 10 judges remaining. A report submitted by a number of legal organizations across Southern Africa urged the SADC to reconsider its decision, accusing the summit of essentially "sabotag[ing]" the tribunal (Southern Africa Litigation Centre 2010). Likewise, the commissioned report later found that the tribunal was, in fact, properly constituted and competent to rule in all matters pertaining to the SADC Treaty, including human rights complaints (Bell 2011).

But the heads of states were startled, and the Zimbabwe regime employed its usual rhetoric to lobby for the Zimbabwe position to curtail the court. *The Herald*, for instance, stated in a scandalizing 2011 article that "if [the tribunal's] programmes are funded by donors, who tend to be Western donors, then SADC remains open to manipulation. ... He who pays the piper calls the tune" (The Herald 2011). The rhetoric worked. SADC members decided during their 2012 summit to limit the tribunal's jurisdiction to "disputes between member states" (SADC 2012, par. 24) and removed the right to petition by individuals and non-state entities, going explicitly against the review report. Given that no SADC member had ever taken another state to court since the establishment of the tribunal, regional jurisdiction was essentially abolished. The remaining judges wrote a letter of protest, calling the move illegal according to international law (Pillay et al. 2011). In an interview with *M&G*, former tribunal President Pillay said that the members felt they had

> created a monster that would devour us all ... until that point the tribunal had been a gambit to get funds from the European Union and others ... It gave off all the right buzz words, you know, "democracy, rule of law, human rights ..." and then they got the shock of their lives when we said these principles are not only aspirational but also justiciable and enforceable and we showed that we meant what we said. (Christie 2011a)

The demise of the SADC tribunal highlights the challenges faced by regional judicial bodies in balancing legal principles with political dynamics. Being dependent on the willingness of the SADC to enforce rulings and supply the court with the necessary authority, the tribunal not only faced significant constraints but was even abolished when it moved too forcefully against the ruling regime of SADC members. Intended more as a signaling device in an era of expanding human rights when established in the 1990s, the region had reached a sobering decade with many of the former hopefuls of democratization clinging successfully to power and moving more openly against domestic and regional opposition.

Campbell died in 2011, likely because of injuries sustained during the violent removal from his farm. In his stead, his son-in-law in cooperation with the Zimbabwean Human Rights NGO Forum and another plaintiff attempted a last resort: they filed a case in front of the African Court on Human and People's Rights against the SADC heads of states. This was a first, with individuals taking not only a single state but essentially a whole RO to court for violation of the African Human Rights Charter. The plaintiffs argued that the African Charter granted individuals access to courts in their territories. But the case was unsuccessful. After lengthy deliberations, the Commission ruled in 2014 that it had no jurisdiction over the establishment and mandate of the tribunal, but only over access to national courts (The Zimbabwe Situation 2014). Thus, the matter was closed. Mugabe took over the AU presidency in 2015.

The 2017 Zimbabwe Coup: Challenges from within the Zimbabwean Elite

By constraining both domestic and regional challengers, the SADC had enabled the Mugabe regime to remain in power in the face of two highly tumultuous election crises and his contentious land reform program. In 2013, Mugabe and ZANU-PF even managed to return to absolute power by winning the general elections in a sweeping victory. The MDC opposition was ousted from executive control, in no small part due to the support of the SADC for the established political elite over the last decade. However, by 2017, the ruling party was increasingly divided, particularly over the question of succession of 93-year-old Mugabe, with factions supporting different individuals within the party. The dissatisfaction finally led to a military coup that removed Mugabe from power and installed his former second-in-command in the presidential office.

Why did the SADC not come to Mugabe's rescue this time around? At the outset of the coup, several SADC members condemned it, calling either for a reinstatement of Mugabe or the installment of a transitional unity government. But as events progressed, the SADC's executive organs decided to remain on the side-lines this time around. One way to explain this inaction is certainly SADC's dislike for domestic interference in favor of oppositional movements and challenging actors and a rhetorical commitment to sovereignty and solidarity that we have seen in previous events. Out of fear of future reprisals, autocratic and democratic leaders alike often err on the side of caution to defend human rights and democracy beyond declaratory statements. Similarly, the consensual decision-making procedure in the troika and summit added to slow decision-taking, with SADC openly supporting neither the ousted dictator nor the military.

But there is a further facet that might have played a role in this case: the coup was a matter of intra-elite fighting, not a potential case of democratization. While SADC members initially disapproved of the coup when a potential hand-over to an inclusive government led by opposition leader Tsvangirai was an option, the RO later returned to its uncritical stance when it became clear that the ruling party would stay in power under its long-term party cadre Mnangagwa.

One of the key catalysts for increasing mobilization against Mugabe was indeed the dismissal of Vice President Emmerson Mnangagwa in early November 2017. Mnangagwa, a veteran of the liberation war and a key figure within ZANU-PF, was seen as a potential successor to Mugabe and his long-term right hand, who kept the regime going and could guarantee the stability of the country. However, his dismissal, which came amid accusations of

138 How Regional Organizations Sustain Authoritarian Rule

disloyalty and plotting to seize power, intensified the factionalism within the party. In July 2016, the powerful Zimbabwe National Liberation War Veterans Association (ZNLWVA), previously a key ally of Mugabe, had already publicly withdrawn its support (Dzirutwe 2016). Additionally, rumors about the ascension of Grace Mugabe, the First Lady and a controversial figure in ZANU-PF, to the presidency further intensified worries and fighting about Mugabe's succession (BBC News 2017).

On the night of November 14, 2017, the military moved decisively against Mugabe, deploying troops and tanks to the streets of the capital, Harare. Major General Sibusiso Moyo appeared on national television, announcing that the military was targeting "criminals" around Mugabe and that it was not a coup but a "bloodless correction" (France 24 2017a). The military's intervention marked a departure from the constitutional order and raised concerns about the potential for violence and instability. In the following days, Mugabe was placed under house arrest and negotiations between the military and political leaders took place. The military's intervention had significant support from within ZANU-PF, including members who had been purged by Mugabe in the preceding years (ibid.). While the military had a prominent role in the events, the coup also saw popular demonstrations, with thousands of Zimbabweans taking to the streets in support of the military action because of growing discontent due to economic hardships and frustration with the political status quo (France 24 2017b).

As the political crisis unfolded, ZANU-PF issued an ultimatum to Mugabe, demanding his resignation as the party's leader. On November 21, 2017, facing increasing pressure from the military, ZANU-PF, and the public, Robert Mugabe resigned as president of Zimbabwe after 37 years in power. Following his resignation, celebrations erupted across the country, with citizens expressing a mix of relief and hope for a new democratic political chapter (RTE News 2017). Mnangagwa himself painted the coup as a democratic restart of the country (ibid.), with former Kenyan President Odinga congratulating the country, saying it had "succeeded in peacefully overthrowing tyranny and dictatorship and created for [itself] the promise of a prosperous future that only democracy can provide" (Asamba 2017).

Emmerson Mnangagwa returned to Zimbabwe following a brief exile during the military coup, and was inaugurated as the new president on November 24, 2017. Mnangagwa, known as the "Crocodile" due to his political cunning, had a long history within ZANU-PF and had served in various capacities, including as a security chief, before he was sacked by Mugabe only days before the coup (Pelz 2017). Hopes of democratization among the public were therefore misplaced: Mnangagwa continued the authoritarian

ZANU-PF rule of Zimbabwe without much change to electoral proceedings or concerns for human rights. While Freedom House shortly upgraded Zimbabwe in its ranking to *partly free* due to the quality of elections for a new government held in 2018, the country quickly plummeted again to *not free* by 2020 (Freedom House 2021). Likewise, there was a very slight increase in the Varieties of Democracy Measure for Zimbabwe in 2018, but overall the country remains firmly in the autocratic camp today (Coppedge et al. 2023).

Initially, several SADC members were unhappy about the way the military tried to force out Mugabe. Namibia's foreign minister Nandi-Ndaitwah expressed concern over instability in the region and urged all actors to abide by the SADC Treaty provisions (Nandi-Ndaitwah 2017). There were even rumors reported by Sky News that Grace Mugabe found refuge in Namibia, although this was denied by the Namibian government (Sky News 2017). Zambian president Lungu likewise criticized the military, calling it an illegal takeover "out of tune with modern politics" (Lusaka Times 2017). While Zambia had previously been a harsh critic of Mugabe under President Mwanawasa, Lungu had come to power in 2015 in highly contested elections—and was subsequently afraid of a similar collusion between the powerful opposition and military in his own country to remove him from his office. Even Alpha Conde, president of Guinea and AU leader at the time, initially condemned the actions as a coup, stating that it was "clearly soldiers trying to take power by force" (Sky News 2017).

A day after the military detained Mugabe and put the leader under house arrest, the SADC troika—now made up of Zambia, Angola, and Tanzania—met for an emergency session. However, the meeting ended without a clear statement on the matter, instead calling for an emergency session of the full SADC assembly (SADC Troika 2017). Apparently, the troika was unable to decide on the proper way to handle the events, divided between trying to preserve stability in the region by supporting Mugabe or getting rid of the increasingly unpopular "liberation hero." Given that this first emergency session was held while the outcome was still up in the air, it was at this point unclear who would take over if Mugabe did actually step down. While the return of Mnangagwa seemed to be in the works, during these early days rumors also circulated that the military might favor the installment of a transitional government including ZANU-PF and the oppositional MDC party of Tsvangirai (Sky News 2017).

However, critical voices faded as the coup went on and it became clear that Mugabe would be replaced by his former second-in-command who would bring stability without the need for a transitional government or participation of oppositional actors. While the SADC acknowledged the crisis, it stopped short of labeling the events as a coup. The organization opted for a common diplomatic stance, urging all parties to exercise restraint and calling for a peaceful resolution within the framework of Zimbabwe's constitution (SADC Troika 2017). Likewise, the AU later refrained from characterizing the events in Zimbabwe as a coup, but rather framed it as a legitimate expression of the will of the people. In a statement in immediate reaction to the political developments, the AU chairperson stated, the AU "recognizes that the Zimbabwean people have expressed their will that there should be a peaceful transfer of power in a manner that secures the democratic future of their country" (RTE News 2017).

The Zimbabwean coup was not a reaction by the military to an unconstitutional takeover of power by an oppositional actor in a supposed effort to restore democratic governance. Rather, it represented an attempt to remove the current autocratic leader from power by an intra-elite faction, and to replace him with another long-term member of that same political elite. In this vein, the coup was a means to safeguard the ruling regime in the face of an aging and increasingly unable dictator who wanted to pass on the office to his politically inexperienced wife. As events unfolded, Mugabe's fellow club members learned that they did not have to fear instability or the potential for a democratic takeover by oppositional actors. Thus, the reaction of the dictator club in this instance was non-interference because there was essentially no regime to safeguard. This conforms to findings from the statistical analysis in Chapter 4: all else equal, dictator clubs do not intervene in support of a regime in matters of intra-elite fighting because this is usually not a matter of potential democratization and thus is not necessarily perceived as a threat to the stability of other RO member regimes.

The SADC has very limited experience with military interventions or even sanctions and suspensions against member states. When it did intervene, it was usually to safeguard one of their own or to punish an oppositional actor—not to oust a sitting autocratic president. In 1998, an SADC military mission mostly consisting of troops from Zimbabwe, Namibia, and Angola supported the troubled regime of Laurent Kabila in the DRC in his fight against rebel forces. SADC troops were part of the ensuing five-year civil war. The SADC later negotiated the Lusaka Ceasefire Agreement and sent large observer missions to the first ever elections in 2006. Until 2019, Kabila's son remained in power as president of the DRC.

Similarly, Lesotho's ruling party found itself faced with successful mobilization of the opposition claiming electoral fraud of the 1998 presidential elections. The SADC not only commissioned a report freeing the ruling party of any malpractice accusations during the elections but also sent a military mission under the lead of South Africa in support of the ruling party. In 2009, the president of Madagascar was forced to cede power to the oppositional party leader due to public protest. The SADC troika swiftly responded with a threat of sanctions, and during an extra-ordinary meeting, the SADC summit decided to suspend Madagascar. While the SADC's suspension did not help the ousted president to ever regain his office, the suspension was clearly a means to punish the opposition for moving against a sitting president, and the swift reply played out very differently from the situation in Zimbabwe in 2017.

These findings also speak to the wider literature on coup-proofing—a strategy whereby leaders that face a risk of military coups cooperate through regional institutions to protect each other from forcible removal by the military through mutual defense pacts (Boutton 2019; Cottiero 2023; Hohlstein 2022). In several cases, joint militaries have likewise been deployed in member states on behalf of troubled incumbents across the globe. As we have seen in Chapter 5, the Gulf Cooperation Council (GCC) deployed a military mission under the Peninsular Shield Force to suppress demonstrations calling for the end of the absolutist monarchy in Bahrain in 2011. In 2022, Russian-led troops entered Kazakhstan under a joint mission of the Collective Security Treaty Organization (CSTO) to aid the troubled Tokayev regime repress pro-democratic protestors (Satubaldina 2022). In 2007, the Economic Community of Central African States (ECCAS) essentially served as presidential guard to Central African Republic President Bozizé under the MICOPAX mission, while the Economic Community of West African States (ECOWAS) had repeatedly intervened in favor of sitting incumbents in Sierra Leone, the Gambia, and Liberia.

However, the SADC case also shows the limits of this reciprocal mechanism. Where leaders have grown too unpopular, the RO may rather opt to save the regime instead of intervening in favor of an ousted leader. While Mugabe had previously supported fellow liberation movement presidents, even by sending military personnel as in the case of the DRC, the aging president had offended many former regional supporters by supporting his young and inexperienced wife over a seasoned and well-connected party cadre. Thus, unity was extended to the regime, not the specific leader in question.

Summary and Conclusion

The chapter showed how membership in a dictator club can help to constrain regional challengers during contentious political moments, thereby helping autocratic regimes avert additional pressure and support for dissenting actors through *regional relationship management*. The example of the SADC, a highly heterogenous organization, showed that three reasons were particularly important to constrain challengers. First, the RO had established strong norms of solidarity stemming from its roots as a Southern African liberation movement in the 1980s. While democracy and human rights had been adopted on paper to signal compliance with international demands for political liberalization in the 1990s, solidarity remains the defining norm that guides practical relationships in the region today.

Second, ties between the former liberation movements in SADC member states now define the relationships between ruling parties, constituting powerful informal alliances within the organization. Regional challengers that want to move against ruling autocratic regimes thus have a hard time to lobby for interference on the side of democratic opposition or human rights protection. But even party leaders have to be careful—once they become too controversial and costly, support can wane. When Robert Mugabe increasingly turned into a nuisance for regional cooperation, his standing as the "liberation hero" no longer trumped considerations for continued stability and solidarity with his party under new leadership. This has also happened to other leaders like Libya's Gaddafi who was sanctioned and targeted by the Arab League once he created too much cost for the region during the Arab Spring (Debre 2021; Odinius and Kuntz 2015). Third, the consensual style of decision-making in the main SADC executive bodies and assembly makes it even harder for challengers to gain ground. While they could, in principle, hold autocratic majorities hostage by refusing to join in on consensual decisions, in practice challengers usually fall behind majority lines and merely manage to water down more open support for autocratic members. In combination, SADC decisions usually favor ruling autocratic elites that receive continued support from loyal allies while critics are constrained during negotiations.

The SADC is a particularly interesting case because it is a dictator club with a democratic hegemon—South Africa. However, South Africa has usually been considered a reluctant hegemon with regard to supporting democratization on the continent due to the support the ANC—the main opposition movement during South African apartheid rule—received from other SADC members over the years in their long struggle against the apartheid government, particularly from Zimbabwe, Namibia, Angola, and Mozambique (e.g. Clark 2016). Thus, South Africa usually refrains from criticizing other SADC members where prominent liberation figures and their parties are still in power, particularly because of norms of solidarity enshrined by the SADC (see also Levitsky and Way 2013; Nathan 2012; van der Vleuten and Hulse 2013 for more on the history of liberation movements in Southern Africa). Thus, by managing their relationships through institutionalized cooperation, autocrats can avert interference and pressure from regional challengers, even in heterogenous settings with powerful democratic members.

7
How Dictator Clubs Shield from External Pressure

In this last empirical chapter, we turn to investigate the third theorized mechanism: the role that regional organizations (ROs) can play to *shield autocratic regimes from the negative externalities* resulting from different forms of international pressure in a most-similar system design. The chapter focuses on the diverging trajectories of two neighboring Central American countries, Nicaragua and Honduras. Both countries share a number of similarities, including their size and geographical location, as well as instable political histories, low economic growth, and high corruption and poverty rates. Central America is also a good case to investigate external pressure with the US playing a major role both as a member of the Organization of American States (OAS) and a significant aid donor to the region.

However, both countries also exhibit divergent trajectories with regard to autocratization and democratization over the last decade, as can be seen in Figure 7.1. While Nicaragua has descended into full authoritarian rule since 2006, with scores at their lowest around 0.2 on the 0–1 Varieties of Democracy scale in 2023, Honduras has managed to remain at the margins of autocracy and regain democratic governance by 2023. As we will see in this chapter, one important explanation to understand these divergent trajectories is membership in a dictator club. Nicaragua under the Ortega rule joined the Bolivarian Alliance for the Peoples of our Americas (ALBA) in 2007 and remains a member to this day. Honduras initially joined the RO in 2008 but left shortly after a coup in 2009, thereby being much more sensitive to outside pressure due to high dependency on international funding.

This chapter traces how Nicaraguan President Ortega was able to employ costly survival strategies ranging from electoral manipulation to protest repression through the help of ALBA. By subsidizing ALBA member states with cheap oil and easy finances, ALBA managed to remove pressure from Nicaragua associated with international development aid from multilateral donor institutions during the consolidation of Ortega's rule. It also initiated a campaign to challenge the legitimacy of the OAS and its human

How Regional Organizations Sustain Authoritarian Rule. Maria J. Debre, Oxford University Press.
© Maria J. Debre (2025). DOI: 10.1093/9780198903635.003.0007

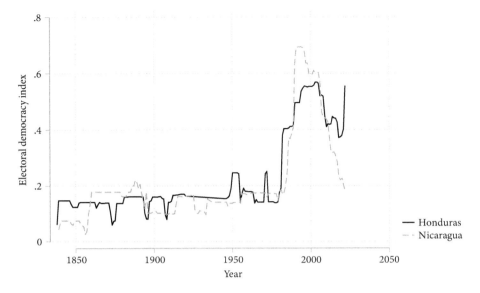

Figure 7.1 Development of electoral democracy index for Nicaragua and Honduras, 1900–2023 (own depiction based on Varieties of Democracy (Coppedge et al. 2023)).
Note: Data from Varieties of Democracy instead of Polity was used here due to the more recent coverage that dates up to 2022 instead of only to 2018.

rights mechanism, involving the organization in a lengthy reform process that averted attention from election manipulation and reduced the willingness of the OAS to deal more firmly with discretions of ALBA members. Finally, ALBA members also became active on behalf of the Ortega regime in international fora, managing to prevent the issue being tabled by the United Nations Security Council (UNSC) with the help of Russia and China. Only their interventions on behalf of Nicaragua in the UN Human Rights Council (UNHRC) remained unsuccessful. But the HRC resolutions did little harm to the regime so far. With ALBA's declining geopolitical importance due to falling oil prices and political turmoil in key members, Nicaragua was left to fend for itself without the help of the dictator club. However, the regime managed to find new allies. The Central American Development Bank (CABEI) offset costs when the US and European Union (EU) enacted economic sanctions, and China and Russia started to engage with the regime when CABEI finally removed Ortega's ally, CABEI's President Mossi, in 2023.

In contrast, neighboring Honduras quickly faced regional and international condemnation and sanctions during a 2009 coup. But more importantly, Honduras's dependency on international aid put the country under heavy pressure in the following years when the conservative National Party abolished presidential term limits in 2015 and manipulated the 2017 presidential elections, resulting in a continuation of President Hernández's administration. Under the auspices first of the United Nations (UN) and later the OAS, the electoral law of Honduras and its central Electoral Council were reformed. The reform culminated in higher-quality elections in 2021, with the opposition taking over the presidential office. Additionally, the OAS established the Mission to Support the Fight against Corruption and Impunity in Honduras (MACCIH), an international body to investigate charges of corruption. With pressure mounting on the Hernández government due to multiple corruption charges leveled against members of his National Party by MACCIH, the former president eventually lost the popular vote under reformed election laws and was even extradited to the US to face prosecution for drug trafficking.

Through this comparison, the chapter highlights how membership in a dictator club can help to ease and prevent international pressure put on an autocratic regime involved in repression and election manipulation. Nicaraguan president Ortega was able to freely expand his autocratic rule and even remain firmly in place when faced with international sanctions due in no small part to the support from ALBA and other autocratic partners. In contrast, the Honduran National Party under Hernández was heavily constrained by international pressure and had to conform to reform concessions under UN and OAS umbrellas that ultimately led to the end of the autocratization period. This chapter details ALBA's role as financier of autocratic consolidation and its efforts to challenge regional democratic ROs, particularly the OAS, to prevent external pressure from its human rights and democracy mechanisms and to intervene on the side of Nicaragua in international fora. The chapter also highlights some of the limits that ALBA members faced in their efforts to prevent international sanctions and alternative strategies of the Ortega regime after the decline in ALBA's geopolitical importance. The chapter finishes with a comparison with the Honduran case, where regional and international organizations have eventually managed to keep democratic decline in check.

Regionalism in Latin America

While Pan-America as an idea can be traced back to the times of Simón Bolívar, institutionalized cooperation was mainly driven by the United States with the establishment of the OAS as an instrument to unite the Americas against rising Communist threats after the Second World War (Bianculli 2016). Today, a number of overlapping regional initiatives characterize the different visions for a united Latin America: on the one hand, trade blocs like the Latin American Free Trade Association (LAFTA), which later transformed into the Latin American Integration Association (ALADI), founded in 1960, show early attempts to establish market-driven forms of economic cooperation similar to initiatives on the European continent. These free trade blocs finally culminated in the establishment of MERCOSUR in 1991, also known as the Common Market of the South, as an attempt to foster deeper economic integration on the South American continent. In contrast, left and socialist leaders were trying to establish a political union in South America that would serve as a counterweight to American influence and neo-liberal economic policy, which was finalized in 2004 with UNASUR's foundation (Kellogg 2007; Pia Riggirozzi and Tussie 2012).

Similar tensions are visible in Central America. The Central American Integration System (SICA) and CABEI represent early and market-driven forms of economic integration. In contrast, ALBA embodies a political integration initiative set up by the late Venezuelan president Hugo Chávez and then-Cuban president Fidel Castro in response to the perceived failures of neo-liberal economic policies and the dominance of the United States in the region in 2004. The alliance was named after two of the most iconic figures in Latin American history: Simón Bolívar, the Venezuelan military and political leader who played a key role in the region's struggle for independence from Spanish colonial rule, and José Martí, the Cuban writer and revolutionary who advocated for Latin American unity. Since its inception, ALBA has expanded to include a number of leftist governments beyond its founding members, Venezuela and Cuba. These include Bolivia, Nicaragua, and Ecuador, as well as Caribbean members Saint Vincent and the Grenadines, Antigua and Barbuda, Dominica, Saint Lucia, and Grenada.

ALBA is guided by the pursuit of an alternative to US-led market-driven regional integration initiative, with mutual cooperation, respect for sovereignty, and social development at its central founding principles (Bianculli 2016)—similar to other autocratic organizations presented in this book. At its core is what has been termed "petro-diplomacy," the establishment of the regional energy initiative Petrocaribe that provides subsidized Venezuelan oil to ALBA members to allow for state-driven investments in social welfare and economic programs (Girvan 2011). With the rise of oil prices in the 2000s, Petrocaribe led to unprecedented economic growth in many ALBA members, and established the club as a geopolitical force to counter US power in the region. However, with falling oil prices by the mid-2010s, oil diplomacy and with it ALBA's golden time started to fade, leaving central member states in political crisis.

Nicaragua's Descent into Authoritarian Rule

Hailed as a success story of Latin American civil war reconciliation and transformation, Nicaragua has turned into one of the most repressive regimes on the continent in the last decade (Papada et al. 2023). Notably, this process of autocratization was led by Daniel Ortega, once the poster child of democratization and leader of the Sandinista National Liberation Front (FSLN) in its fight against the Somoza dictatorship. The period following the Second World War in Nicaragua was dominated by the Somoza dynasty. Anastasio Somoza García, who first came to power in 1937, established a repressive authoritarian regime that controlled the country for several decades. Somoza García was assassinated in 1956, but his family's grip on power remained unbroken. His two sons, Luis Somoza Debayle and Anastasio Somoza Debayle, successively held the presidency, maintaining the family's control over the country. Due to its anti-communist stance, the Somoza regime enjoyed the support of the US who saw the country as a strategic bulwark against Communist Cuba in the region.

When popular discontent with the dictatorship increased dramatically during the 1970s, the left-wing revolutionary FSLN Sandinista movement, with Daniel Ortega as one of the main leaders, managed to successfully seize power in 1979, ending the Somoza rule. Although Ortega's FSLN received widespread support for their social and economic reforms, including land reforms and expanded access to education and healthcare, they faced significant opposition from the US, which viewed the revolution as a threat to its anti-Communist partnerships in the region.

To counter the Sandinista success in Nicaragua, the US under President Ronald Reagan initiated a covert operation to support anti-Sandinista rebels, the Contras, leading to the infamous Contra Wars. Ten years of civil war with significant civilian casualties and widespread human rights abuses on both sides left the country and region with a high distaste for any type of foreign interference until this day. The US, which provided funding, training, and weapons to the Contras to undermine the Sandinista government, had later been found guilty by the International Court of Justice to have committed serious breaches of international law (World Legal Information Institute (WorldLII) 1986). But without ratification of these international treaties on the side of the US, the rulings remained toothless.

Finally, in 1990, Violeta Chamorro surprisingly won the presidential elections backed by a coalition of anti-Sandinista parties, and the FSLN peacefully transferred power, thereby initiating a period of democratization and post-war reconciliation. The experience of dictatorship and civil war, however, still influences Nicaraguan politics today, and importantly introduced strict presidential term limits in the constitution of 1987: a president can only serve for a single five-year term and return for one additional non-consecutive term after leaving office for five years (Constitución Política De La República De Nicaragua 1987, par. 147).

Having served one presidential term in the 1980s, Daniel Ortega was therefore eligible to attempt re-election with a renewed and moderated FSLN. After several unsuccessful tries, Ortega finally managed his political comeback by winning the 2006 presidential election in a highly contested and close result, returning to the presidency after a 16-year absence. However, Ortega soon turned into the dictator he once fought hard to dismiss. While his re-election in 2006 was marred by some irregularities but overall constituted relatively free and fair proceedings (EU Election Observation Mission 2006), the real power struggle started when he attempted to run for a second consecutive term five years later. By stacking the Supreme Court with loyal Sandinista judges, Ortega managed to gain a ruling to take out the prohibition of non-consecutive terms from the constitution (BBC News 2009d; Schmidt 2009; *Sentencia [S.] No. 504, de las 5:00 p.m.* 2009, pp. 17–18). Ortega then won the re-election in 2011 with a resounding victory that put the FSLN in control of the National Assembly in 2014, and subsequently administered a constitutional amendment that scrapped term limits altogether, thereby clearing the way for his continued rule in the future (Gibney 2014).

Ortega's authoritarian tendencies have become more pronounced over time. He has used the judicial system to persecute political opponents, passed laws restricting the activities of civil society organizations, and manipulated electoral rules to his advantage (Freedom House 2023). The 2011 elections where already highly contested and criticized for irregularities (e.g. European Union Election Observation Mission Nicaragua 2011), but the regime abolished all external monitoring in 2016 with the last 2021 elections no longer conforming to any international standards. The EU Council stated that "not only has the Nicaraguan Government deprived the people of Nicaragua of the civil and political right to vote in a credible, inclusive, fair and transparent election, it has also fallen short of its own commitments on human rights and fundamental freedoms" (Council of the EU 2021).

Since 2011, Ortega and his government have increasingly tightened their control over state institutions, including the Supreme Court and the electoral authority, effectively eliminating most checks and balances (UN Human Rights Council 2023). Ortega's authoritarian rule has also extended to media control. His government has cracked down on independent media outlets, limiting the freedom of the press and stifling dissenting voices (ibid.). This control over the media has made it increasingly difficult for opposition voices to reach the public. The Ortega regime has exiled important opposition actors from the church and human rights organizations, expelled UN officials after critical reports, and seen a resignation of central political figures from the Central Bank and Supreme Court (BBC News 2018; Dell'orto 2023; UN News 2018).

At the same time, Ortega and the FSLN have enjoyed widespread support among Nicaraguans, at least in the first decade of his rule. The regime introduced a number of social and economic programs that have boosted the economy and contributed to improvements in human development indicators and poverty reduction (The World Bank 2024). As we will shortly see, many of these programs to finance autocratization have been pay-rolled by ALBA and other regional institutions. Ortega's return to power can be seen as a characteristic case of executive aggrandizement (Bermeo 2016), with a slow but steady decrease of political checks and balances and co-optation and infiltration of political institutions with loyal Sandinista party cadres. The extended Ortega family runs important businesses and, most importantly, Ortega's wife has been put up as vice president and hopeful successor to the regime.

Only in the last five years has the regime been forced to turn to more outright repressive tactics. When economic redistribution from ALBA slowly dried up and criticism from domestic opposition grew louder, the regime took the costly decision to move against dissidents and demonstrators more forcefully. In April 2018, a series of protests erupted in Nicaragua in response to social security reforms and Ortega's authoritarian rule. The protests quickly evolved into a broader movement against the government. After a particularly large protest rally on Mother's day in May 2018, Sandinista paramilitaries violently attacked protestors and pursued demonstration leaders. The "Mother's Day massacre," as the day became coined by the opposition, and ensuing violence left around 450 dead, with 600 disappearances recorded by Nicaraguan non-governmental organizations (NGOs) and an OAS fact-finding mission (Partlow 2018a, 2018b). This moment put the regime more firmly on the international agenda, although international criticism, pressure, and threats of sanctions had been issued by multilateral institutions and Western states before—but without real consequences until the violent escalations of 2018.

External Pressure on the Ortega Regime

Trouble for Ortega started with his attempt at re-election in 2011 and the necessary changes to term limits decided in 2009. Several international actors had already voiced criticism with regard to the decision of the Supreme Court in 2009 to scrap the term limit only for Sandinista candidates. The European Parliament, for instance, stated that the necessary process to change the constitution should have been legitimized through a National Assembly vote following the Court's ruling and condemned the decision to change term limits as illegal (European Parliament 2009). The EU-Canada Budget support group explicitly warned Ortega in a letter that the court decision "represents a reduction of democratic spaces [that reduces] citizens' civil and political rights" (The Tico Times 2008a). Several EU member states had already started to cut funding to the government in 2008 in response to irregularities during the municipal elections, with the EU finally deciding to also cut 32 million USD from its budgetary support to Nicaragua during the same year (The Tico Times 2008b). While Ortega attempted a constitutional referendum after the Court's decision, the project was dropped eventually.

External pressure on the regime increased after the polls closed in 2011. The OAS observer mission stated that they were denied access in 10 out of 52 polling stations (Al Jazeera 2011). The EU mission called the elections "a deterioration in the democratic quality of Nicaraguan electoral processes, due to the lack of transparency and neutrality with which they were administered by the Supreme Electoral Council" (European Union Election Observation Mission Nicaragua 2011). However, both institutions abstained from taking any further measures.

In the US, calls from Republican lawmakers to take stronger actions against the Ortega regime also grew louder. The leader of the foreign affairs committee, Ros-Lehtinen, demanded that the US administration put pressure on Ortega to administer new elections, and Marco Rubio and colleagues introduced a bipartisan resolution condemning the democratic deterioration in Nicaragua (Tamayo 2011). Although the Obama administration refrained from supporting stronger measures under the Nicaraguan Investment Conditionality Act (NICA), the US quietly cut down big chunks of foreign aid to Nicaragua in the following years due to its democratic erosion (Meyer and Sullivan 2012, p. 12). Ironically, however, the US still considered the Nicaraguan military an independent actor, and continued its funding as a counter-narcotic partner up until 2018.

Stronger measures were only used for Nicaragua after more severe human rights violations committed in 2018 and the following years. The US issued

152 How Regional Organizations Sustain Authoritarian Rule

sanctions against the immediate Ortega family and party cadre based on NICA starting with Executive Order 13,851 in November 2018. Several expansions of the US sanction regime followed with a sanction list including more than 500 individuals, their family members, and key industries by 2023. Importantly, the RENACER Act of 2021 empowered the US government to veto loans to Nicaragua by multilateral banks and to move for suspension of Nicaragua from the Dominican Republic-Central America Free Trade Agreement (CAFTA-DR) (US Senate 2021). Likewise, the EU, UK, Canada, and Switzerland followed suit, putting in place several sanction regimes to target political elites and Ortega allies.[1]

The OAS had remained relatively inactive with regard to Nicaragua overall. While it had been quite critical about irregularities in the 2008 municipal elections (OAS 2009b), there were no immediate reactions to the alleged election manipulation in 2011 and 2016, or the decision to scrap term limits in 2009 and 2014. The OAS Permanent Council only started to call attention to the situation in Nicaragua starting in 2018 with a number of resolutions calling for continued dialogue and improvement of democratic governance. However, no hard measures, particularly a suspension, were taken or even suggested during the council meetings. While the OAS usually only issues suspensions as a response to unconstitutional changes of government such as coups (e.g. Palestini 2021), the organization had at least issued much stronger criticisms in similar situations such as the contentious Bolivarian elections in 2020 (Kurmanaev and Trigo 2020), as well as Honduras during the 2010s, as we will later see in the last section of this chapter.

Apart from suspension, the OAS's strongest set of mechanisms consists of measures taken by the Inter-American Commission on Human Rights (IACHR), including individual petitions, reports, and precautionary measures. While individual petitions allow victims, their representatives, or NGOs to submit complaints regarding alleged human rights abuses committed by member states, reports usually focus on a specific issue or country to raise awareness, encourage dialogue, and provide recommendations for improving human rights practices, while precautionary measures aim to prevent irreparable harm to individuals or groups facing imminent threats by directly urging member states to take immediate action to safeguard individuals at risk.

In 2018, the IACHR finally initiated a special monitoring mission in response to alleged human rights violations committed by the Ortega regime after the number of individual petitions received by the IACHR skyrocketed

---

[1] A detailed list of international sanctions against Nicaragua can be found in the Online Appendix.

from 11 in 2017 to 294 in 2018 (Inter-American Commission on Human Rights 2023). Several reports were published as response between 2018 and 2023 condemning the escalation of state-perpetrated violence (Special Monitoring Mission for Nicaragua 2023). However, none of the mechanisms available to the IACHR include hard measures such as financial or diplomatic sanctions and none of the petitions so far have been referred to the Inter-American Court of Human Rights that could try human rights violations of the Ortega regime in individual cases.

International institutions faced similar hurdles. The UN Security Council, the only organ that can initiate a biding far-reaching multilateral sanction regime of international scale, put the situation in Nicaragua on the agenda in 2018, but did not manage to even debate a draft resolution or statement (United Nations Security Council 2018). The UNHRC passed a number of resolutions on Nicaragua since 2018 including the establishment of a group of experts to evaluate the human rights situation in Nicaragua which is, however, not allowed access on the ground (UNHRC 2022, 2023). But just like the IACHR, the council has no ability to issue harder sanctions apart from trying to increase reputational costs for the Ortega regime.

Importantly, the International Monetary Fund (IMF) and World Bank even continued increasing their lending budget for Nicaragua between 2018 and 2021 due to a humanitarian assistance exemption from the US NICA Act in response to disaster relief for hurricane flooding and Covid-19 measures (Robinson 2022). Only in 2022, after the US tightened measures through RENACER, did the US use its influence in these funding institutions to cut loans directly disbursed to the Nicaraguan government.

ROs as Financiers of Dictators

ALBA and Autocratic Consolidation

How did Ortega and his regime manage to expand their power over 10 years without facing harsher international measures and remain firmly in the saddle even when confronted with a wide-ranging sanction regime put in place by international actors since 2018? Usually, only powerful countries of geopolitical importance and those who are members of international organizations (IOs) with hard voting rules are likely to be spared as sanction targets (Donno 2010; von Borzyskowski and Vabulas 2019b). Neither explanation applies to Nicaragua. One piece of the puzzle is the role ROs play as financiers of dictators. In the first 10 years of autocratic consolidation, Ortega profited immensely from financial redistribution through ALBA that helped to boost the popularity both domestically and internationally and eased pressure put on other regimes like Honduras in similar circumstances.

Ortega joined ALBA shortly after his election victory in 2007, aligning with several other leftist governments that had come to power on the mainland during the same time, including Ecuador, Bolivia, and Venezuela. United by a strong stance against neo-liberal economic policy and American interventionism in the region, these new ALBA members decided to join forces to support each other along the road of autocratization. A central tenet in their joint quest was the Petrocaribe agreement, a regional energy cooperation initiative set up in 2005 to provide ALBA members with favorable energy terms that would underwrite economic growth and remove pressure to seek international aid from Western donors.

As one of the world's major oil-producing nations, Venezuela offered member countries discounted oil prices and favorable financing terms for oil purchases. In the case of Nicaragua, the Ortega regime was able to purchase oil at 50 percent the cost of shipments, with the remainder only due over the next 23 years at 2 percent interest (Waddell 2018). In a first step, this allowed Ortega to redirect funds that would have been spent on high oil prices toward critical social programs, infrastructure development, and poverty alleviation initiatives. The Petrocaribe agreement spurred unusual economic growth in Nicaragua, with a peak of 6.4 percent GDP growth in 2012 and an average of 4.1 percent between 2007 and 2017.

However, the scheme was much broader, not only financing a healthy economic growth and thereby buying the Ortega regime popular support but also protecting the regime from international pressure by providing large budgets free of international conditionality. As a consortium of transnational journalists uncovered under the hashtag #Petrofraud, the Petrocaribe agreement was, in fact, a large money-laundering scheme profiting ALBA governments with large uncontrolled budgets (Connectas 2019). The import and export of oil between Venezuela and Nicaragua was managed by Alba de Nicaragua S.A., also known as Albanisa, a joint venture between the Venezuelan state-owned oil company Petróleos de Venezuela, S.A. (PDVSA) and Nicaraguan Petronic established in 2007, and set up under the ALBA framework. Through privatizing the management of oil shipments from the Petrocaribe agreement, both regimes managed to divert the billion-dollar Albanisa fund from parliamentary oversight directly into personal budgets. As later asserted by the US government and the Connectas investigative reports, Albanisa mainly served the Ortega regime to siphon off money from oil portfolios to support loyal Sandinista regime supporters and finance its repressive police apparatus (US Department of the Treasury 2023a).

To achieve this, the extended Ortega family bought or set up a number of companies related to Albanisa, including wind energy parks (Alba Generación) and a forestry unit (Alba Forestal), but also an oil refinery, an airline, a cellphone company, a hotel, luxury apartment buildings, a tilapia fish farm, a cotton and rice business, a pig farm, and even a silkworm business (Sáenz 2019). The most prominent and important enterprises of them all, Distribuidora Nicaraguense de Petróleos (DNP), Zanzibar Investment, and El Goliat, were run directly by Ortega's son (ibid.). The regime even transformed a small cooperative Sandinista bank, Caruna, into the internationally operative bank Banco Corporativo (BanCorp) that would handle the roughly 2.5 billion USD Albanisa fund (ibid.).

An investigative report by the Nicaraguan newspaper *El Confidential* found that most of these companies only existed on paper (Chamorro 2016). This was done for two reasons. First, subsidized oil received by Venezuela was sold at market prices through DNP gas stations run by Ortega's son, and allowed cash flow to be laundered through BanCorp and later poured into family-owned front companies to directly profit Ortega (Confidencial 2021). Second, a lot of oil allegedly never even arrived in Nicaragua in the first place, but was only registered on paper with front companies creating necessary paper trails to move PDVSA and Albanisa funds into regime hands (Connectas 2019; Farah and Yates 2019).

In an interview with the newspaper *Univision*, former Ortega ally and Albanisa deputy manager Obregón recounts his unease with a mega-project to build an oil refinery worth 6.6 billion USD called "The supreme dream of Bolivar" (Adams and Aburto 2018). The project never materialized, also because Nicaragua did not produce any oil in the first place. But it allowed the regime to move money from Albanisa through the infrastructure projects to fund payments of non-existent work and materials of Ortega front companies and then launder the clean money into BanCorp (Farah and Yates 2019).

The corruption network set up through ALBA had an important effect on the Ortega regime. When international governments first started to cut aid programs with Nicaragua or attempted to pressure the regime due to its increasing autocratization, the regime did not have to rely on highly conditional aid programs from the World Bank, IMF, or the EU. As early as 2009, the US Millenium Challenge Corporation (MCC), a bilateral foreign aid agency of the US government, cut its funding program over 175 million USD to Nicaragua as a response to irregularities in the municipal elections of 2008 (Millennium Challenge Corporation 2009) while the EU cut around

32 million USD in 2008 (The Tico Times 2008b). This was later followed by further restrictions of US funding after the 2011 elections. Several EU member states likewise started to cut bilateral support to the regime as early as 2007, including Sweden, Germany, and the UK (Niebel 2008). To the Ortega regime, this was no threat given that Albanisa promised safe and easy finances free of international constraints. Just on the contrary, the Ortega government decided to stop negotiations for a joint EU–Central American Free Trade agreement in 2009 when the EU Parliament and Commission started to be more openly critical of his government (Niebel 2009) and attacked the EU ambassador to Nicaragua, Francesca Mosca, and international donors as "flies that land in filth" (The Tico Times 2008a). But even without the support of donors from the Global North, the regime was able to boast an unprecedented economic growth in the following years, thereby mitigating any potential financial costs from international criticism of term limit extensions and election irregularities through membership in a dictator club.

New Partners and International Sanctions

However, crisis was looming. With the end of high oil prices in 2015 and political upheaval in two key ALBA members, Venezuela and Ecuador, a continuation of the Albanisa support network for Nicaragua became nearly impossible to retain by 2016. After Maduro succeeded Chávez as president of Venezuela in 2013, he faced immediate challenges including high inflation, a declining oil sector, and shortages of basic goods. With the opposition's victory in parliamentary elections in 2015, gridlock and political repression intensified. When Maduro was inaugurated for a second term in 2019 in widely criticized elections, opposition leader Guaidó declared himself interim president, essentially establishing an alternative government recognized by many regional and international actors as legitimate representative of Venezuela. Importantly, this included a reversal of the withdrawal declaration from the OAS made in 2017 by the Maduro government on behalf of Guidó, whose government acted as official representative of Venezuela in the OAS starting in 2019. Additionally, Ecuador declared its withdrawal from ALBA under newly elected President Moreno in 2018 in a surprise reversal of the leftist election platform he ran on. This meant that two key members of ALBA had essentially deserted the dictator club, leaving Nicaragua, Cuba, and Bolivia to fight on their own.

But the Ortega regime managed to acquire new regional support and financial backing in the form of CABEI. As a multilateral development bank,

CABEI plays a pivotal role in fostering economic integration and development in the form of infrastructure, energy, environmental sustainability, and social programs across the Central American region. The bank does not, however, count as a dictator club, having all Central American countries as well as several non-regional democratic members from South America, plus South Korea, Taiwan, and Spain as members.

Still, Ortega found a receptive partner in CABEI's President Mossi, a Honduran national who was elected president of the bank in 2017 with the help of votes from Nicaragua (Olivares 2022). Despite mounting international sanctions, CABEI had increased its funding portfolio for Nicaragua since 2017 with an estimated 3.5 billion USD worth of development projects undertaken until 2023 (Berg 2023b). Nicaragua thereby turned into the biggest debtor in CABEI's lending portfolio at almost 26 percent of the overall budget volume (Berg 2023a). One of the projects included financing the expansion of the Nicaraguan National Police, officially to strengthen regional security structures in the country (CABEI 2014). While the loan had already been subscribed in 2014, CABEI only canceled the disbursement of the last financing tranche in 2020 after the US had specifically put the Nicaraguan police on their sanctions list (CABEI 2020). However, until 2020, the national Nicaraguan budget for the police and security increased substantively, with the Nicaraguan police acting as the main arm of repression under the Ortega regime (US Department of the Treasury 2023b). Further projects, however, were continued even after the tightening of sanctions, with a peak in disbursements in 2021 (Organized Crime and Corruption Reporting Project (OCCRP) 2023). CABEI, for instance, went ahead with the finalization of a new headquarters building situated in the Nicaraguan capital Managua, with construction initiated in 2019 in a grand event including CABEI President Mossi and Ortega Treasury Chief Acosta shaking hands in front of friendly reporters (Robinson 2019).

While the inauguration was suspended several times after a vote of 10 board members including Taiwan against the finalization at the end of 2021, the official event went ahead in March 2022 with CABEI President Mossi in attendance, adding no doubt to further legitimization of the regime (CABEI 2022). Mossi's term as president of CABEI was not renewed in 2023 due in no small part to his close ties with the Ortega regime, which had earned him the title "banker to dictators" (Berg 2023b). But CABEI was not the only financier of the regime despite sanctions being in place. Due to a humanitarian disaster exemption clause in the US NICA Act, both the IMF and World Bank had continued to disperse loans to the Ortega regime until 2021 to aid with Covid-19 and two hurricane disasters.

Only after the RENACER Act in 2021 tightened these exemptions did the US use its influence in both institutions to stop disbursements. Similar influence was missing in CABEI, where the US was not a member. While Spain and Costa Rica openly voiced criticism of CABEI's actions, Nicaragua was still able to count on the support of enough board members, namely Honduras, El Salvador, and even Taiwan, to enable Mossi to follow his program of unconditional "policy-based loans" (Olivares 2022; Organized Crime and Corruption Reporting Project (OCCRP) 2023). Taiwan did eventually drop its support for the Nicaragua regime potentially because of pressure from the US and European partners over support against China by the end of 2021. Only days after, Nicaragua publicly denounced its support for Taiwan and announced the establishment of official relations with China (MercoPress 2021). By the end of 2023, Ortega officially signed a free trade agreement with China, calling it a "Christmas present ... that frees us from any sanctions" (Confidencial 2023). With the waning of regional support, first from its own dictator club ALBA, then from the co-opted institution CABEI, the Ortega regime seems set to find new potent financial backers to uphold its repressive apparatus in the face of continuing international sanctions.

RO Interventions in Regional and International Fora

Being able to finance the repressive apparatus has been immensely helpful for the Ortega regime to expand autocratization and stay in power even when hard sanction regimes were put in place. But financing is only one piece of the puzzle. Nicaragua's ALBA membership was also important to attempt to weaken the ability particularly of the OAS to take measures, and to intervene on behalf of the regime at UN institutions, albeit with mixed success across institutions.

After Ortega's return to the presidency in 2007, a first step in consolidating power was to ensure the victory of Sandinista candidates in municipal elections in 2008. Accusations of vote rigging and violent attacks on opposition candidates by armed Sandinista supporters soon surfaced (Carroll 2008). While the elections had not been observed by international monitors, OAS Secretary General Insulza voiced strong concerns over the conduct of the elections, fearing democratic erosions in the face of state-sponsored violence (OAS 2009b). This was one of the last official critical statements that the OAS made with regard to Nicaragua until 2018. Neither the expansion and ultimate abolishment of term limits in 2009 and 2014 nor troubled elections in 2016 elicited much official critical OAS reactions. No international observers, for instance, were allowed to enter Nicaragua in 2016 and 2021, and the main opposition candidate was forced to drop out of the race. Still, the OAS only released a press statement on continued dialogue between the organization and the regime, without any further critical statement from OAS officials (OAS 2016b). This stands in stark contrast to OAS reactions in neighboring Honduras during the same time and in similar circumstances, as the later comparison will show.

A central reason for its silence has certainly been the constant attacks and contestation that the OAS and particularly its human rights mechanism has seen from ALBA ever since the consolidation of the block in the late 2000s. This challenge of the OAS's legitimacy culminated in the so-called "strengthening process" of the human rights commission. The process, however, was indeed intended as the opposite of strengthening. Proposals by central ALBA members Nicaragua, Venezuela, Bolivia, and Ecuador included a number of changes to central features of the human rights mechanism that would have severely limited its functionality: a prohibition of earmarked funding, a reduction of the budget and autonomy of the special rapporteur on freedom of expression, limited ability to investigate and grant precautionary measures, and an abolishment of chapter IV of the commission's annual report, where countries with particularly troublesome human rights records are listed (IJRC 2012).

The strengthening process resulted in a contentious two-year consolidation procedure that was initiated in 2011 and saw numerous working groups, reports, and public consultations culminating in a lengthy special session of the OAS General Assembly in March 2013. ALBA members had several other member states on their side, particularly on the thorny issue of earmarked funding often used by the US to increase budgets of special rapporteurships while at the same time not being part of the inter-American human rights system themselves.

During the special session on March 22, 2013, two competing resolutions were on the table. The first was drafted by a general committee based on a previous summary report, the second a very short draft by the ALBA group containing only a single operative paragraph:

> Direct[ing] the Permanent Council to continue the dialogue on the functioning and strengthening of the Inter-American human rights system, in particular with regard to aspects of particular importance, such as precautionary measures, the headquarters of the Inter-American Commission on Human Rights (IACH), chapter IV, universality, indivisibility of human rights, rapporteurships and the autonomy and independence of the IACHR; and that it present the results of this dialogue at the XLIV Regular Session of General Assembly of the OAS [to take place in 2014]. (Quoted in IJRC 2013)

160 How Regional Organizations Sustain Authoritarian Rule

After a 13-hour marathon session, the OAS General Assembly finally managed to agree on a new consolidated draft (OAS 2013) based on the first resolution, but containing a new operative paragraph 2 directing the Permanent Council to continue its dialogue on the strengthening process. While the four ALBA members were still opposed, the draft garnered the support of 22 votes in favor (IJRC 2013). However, the new operative paragraph also left the door wide open for further challenges on the side of ALBA members in future years.

With the OAS human rights mechanism under attack, the ability and willingness to engage more critically with Nicaragua and other ALBA members on issues of election manipulation and executive corruption on the side of the OAS secretariate was likely limited. Instead of fueling further politicization from ALBA, the bureaucracy seems to have decided to only intervene where legal realities were more clear-cut or less push-back was expected. Only when human rights violations in Nicaragua, but also in Venezuela, became hard to ignore did the OAS take up more forceful action again. ALBA's attacks thus seem to have played out well to silence and avert criticism.

But engagement on the side of members did not stop at the regional level. ALBA also increasingly became active on the international scene, particularly in the UNHRC and the Security Council when member states' human rights issues were addressed. In 2018, the UN Security Council put the situation in Nicaragua on its agenda. Under the heading of discussing "Cooperation between the United Nations and Regional and Subregional Organizations in Maintaining International Peace and Security," the US had requested the special session on the situation in Nicaragua to be put on the agenda.

In addition to all regular members at the time, which included Bolivia, Venezuela and Nicaragua, as well as the secretary general of the OAS and a Nicaraguan civil society leader, were invited to join the meeting. The ALBA members intervened on the side of Nicaragua during the debate (United Nations Security Council 2018). Bolivia rejected the meeting's agenda, arguing that the situation in Nicaragua did not pose any threat to international peace and security, and accused the US of inciting instability in Nicaragua in accordance with their history of bloody interventionism in the country (ibid., p. 16f.). Venezuela, still represented by the Maduro government in global IOs, argued along similar lines, stating that it "reiterates its rejection of the manner in which some countries invoke the humanitarian pretext to use the Security Council as a tool to promote their policy of regime change that has caused so much damage to the peoples of Africa and the Middle East" (ibid., p. 22f.). Further important support came from Russia and China, who stressed the domestic nature of the situation. No draft resolution was introduced, and the meeting ended without a vote. The UNSC has not put Nicaragua on its agenda again since.

ALBA also regularly interfered on the side of members in the UNHRC when country-specific action was put on the agenda. Starting in 2015, for instance, Venezuela's human rights record was regularly part of the debate under item 2 with different members speaking out on behalf of ALBA against measures taken by the HRC in the case of Venezuela (ALBA 2019a; Permanent Representative of Cuba to the United Nations 2019; Plurinational State of Bolivia 2015). The same efforts were made with regard to Nicaragua when its human rights record was put on the agenda following the events in 2018.

During session 40 in 2019, the situation in Nicaragua was first discussed with draft resolution A/HRC/40/L.8 introduced by a number of OAS countries (UNHRC 2019). Bolivia made a strong intervention in favor of Nicaragua on behalf of ALBA members condemning any initiative that threatens the sovereignty of the country, with Cuba calling for a recorded vote on the draft (ALBA 2019b). However, their efforts failed, with only three votes against the resolution. In the next session in the summer of 2019, ALBA members seem to have decided to tackle the issue by making a high number of interventions. These were not only intended to defend Nicaragua (ALBA 2019d) but also tackled several general items to call out the politicized nature of human rights resolutions and to call for more respect for cooperation and dialogue in the decision-making of the HRC (ALBA 2019c, 2019d; Delegation of Venezuela 2019). In spite of their efforts, a resolution on the situation in Nicaragua was again tabled in session 42 in the fall of 2019. While this time, ALBA members garnered some more votes against the draft, although they still failed to prevent the resolution from passing.

However, with the decline of ALBA by the end of the 2010s, interventions on behalf of Nicaragua also become fewer and fewer, leading to repeated country-specific resolutions in the years until 2023. With governmental change in Bolivia in 2021, only Cuba and Venezuela were left as political allies. However, new international partners such as China and Russia tried to come to Ortega's rescue, slowly increasing the tally in the vote against resolutions. Still, the fight for Nicaragua in the HRC remained unsuccessful with a Group of Human Rights Experts established in session 49 in 2022 through resolution 49/3 to assess alleged human rights abuses committed in Nicaragua since 2018 more closely (UNHRC 2022). But given the mostly reputational costs of HRC action, few repercussions have since materialized for Ortega through the various HRC interventions, with the regime still firmly in the saddle in 2023.

Comparison: International Pressure and Democratic Renewal in Honduras

Honduras had come to renewed international attention with the political coup and subsequent suspension from the OAS in 2009. The Central American nation bordering Nicaragua to the north scores among the lowest on indicators of economic growth and human development on the Latin American continent. Political instability, coups, and corruption have run rampant in the country ever since its independence. Honduras is also highly dependent on foreign aid. It had signed an Enhanced Structural Adjustment Facility (ESAF) with the IMF in 1999, received significant debt relief including the suspension of bilateral debt service payments and bilateral debt reduction by the Paris Club in the 2000s, and qualified for the Heavily Indebted Poor Countries Initiative (HIPC). To increase economic growth, Honduras also signed CAFTA, a free trade agreement with the United States, in 2005.

Against this background, President Zelaya came into office on a liberal platform in 2006, but soon began to shift policies to the left. He joined ALBA in 2008, intent on becoming part of Petrocaribe to profit from the same favorable energy agreements to finance social spending and reduce international dependency (Honduran News 2008). However, Zelaya's move toward ALBA was abruptly ended with a military coup in 2009. When he proposed a nonbinding referendum to amend the constitution and scrap term limits, Zelaya faced united opposition from the legislature, the courts, and the public. Honduras featured an exceptionally strict term limits regulation, allowing only single four-year terms and no exceptions for re-runs. Fearing that Zelaya may try to extend his own tenure and attempt re-election (Cordoba 2009), the proposed referendum was declared illegal, impeachment proceedings were initiated, and finally Zelaya was forcibly removed from power and sent into exile by the military acting on a Supreme Court order (Lacey 2009).

Most of the international community was united in the view that the coup was illegal, denouncing the unconstitutional removal of a democratically elected leader. The OAS condemned the coup and suspended Honduras's membership (OAS 2009a). The United Nations General Assembly passed a resolution calling for the restoration of Zelaya (UN Press 2009). The EU also denounced the coup, as did numerous individual countries, including the United States (Reuters 2009). International aid institutions, from the World Bank to the Inter-American Development Bank, jointly decided to freeze loans worth more than 450 million USD in 2009, representing a big chunk of the Honduran annual budget (Reuters 2010). Although Zelaya returned to Honduras in 2010, he did not contest the 2009 elections, which initiated a 12-year rule by the conservative National Party.

While the strong international reaction to the coup is not necessarily surprising, the development of Honduras over the next 12 years shows how international dependency and pressure can help to keep a country on the democratic downwards trend on track. Honduras left ALBA in 2009 and was therefore not able to count on the same type of support that neighboring Ortega had in his efforts to expand rule. Honduras democratic decline continued particularly after a controversial Supreme Court decision to void Article 239 of the constitution and scrap term limits after all in 2015 (The Guardian 2015). While supporters of the conservative party had fiercely opposed the move under President Zelaya, they now supported President Hernández in his efforts to gain re-election.

In 2017, Hernández won the presidential re-elections on a narrow margin against his main challenger, Salvador Nasralla, a television host and opposition candidate running on the Alliance Against the Dictatorship coalition. As initial vote tallies favored Nasralla, a sudden suspension of the vote count raised suspicions of manipulation (Malkin 2017b). When the count resumed, Hernández began to close the gap and eventually surpassed Nasralla. In consequences, protests erupted across the country, with allegations of human rights abuses by security forces against demonstrators (teleSUR 2018). Despite the controversy, Hernández was declared the winner and thus was the first Honduran president to take the office for a second term.

The National Party's move to abolish term limits and manipulate elections came at a heavy price. While the OAS had remained silent in the face of similar events in 2014 and 2016 in Nicaragua, the OAS monitoring mission highlighted numerous issues with the election process in the case of Honduras. Particularly, they criticized the conduct of the Supreme Electoral Council in charge of electoral oversight, and called for a re-run of the proceedings based on an analysis of a Georgetown political scientist who detailed statistical irregularities in the distribution of counted votes after its suspension (Nooruddin 2017; OAS 2017). In the US, several politicians raised concerns over the election results, stating that "there were multiple opportunities for fraud in this election, and only a determination by impartial international observers that the vote tally was fair and transparent will provide the necessary credibility to the process" (Malkin 2017b). While the Trump administration officially wanted to release a 50 million USD aid package after the elections to retain Honduras as a central ally in their anti-narcotic fight, democratic Senator Leahy withheld the payout for a significant

164 How Regional Organizations Sustain Authoritarian Rule

amount of time, placing pressure on the Honduran regime to work with the OAS (Malkin 2017a).

While Hernández was eventually able to stay in the presidential office, the events led to two significant reform processes due to continued international pressure. First, a UN-sponsored national dialogue to negotiate an electoral reform was initiated, establishing two new electoral bodies to replace the old Electoral Council and to work on a new electoral law (UN Peacebuilding 2021). The process, however, was marred with setbacks, with Hernández's National Party initially boycotting large parts of the negotiations (teleSUR 2018). The dialogue ended without a binding agreement in 2018, but Congress still managed to pass an electoral reform bill in 2019 and a new electoral law in 2021 that addressed some of the main issues, including voter registration and institutional oversight (International Crisis Group 2019, 2021). Of particular importance was also the more critical tone of the US administration toward Honduras in 2018 to convince the National Party to undergo some of the suggested reform points. While the US had still released further aid to the country despite records of human rights abuses in 2017, Trump had threatened to cut aid to unnamed Latin American countries for "pouring drugs" into the US in 2018 (Voice of America 2018).[2] Still, when presidential elections took place under the new law in 2021, Hernández and the National Party lost the vote to the candidate on the left, Castro, wife of former President Zelaya. Her election victory was widely seen as a move toward democratic renewal, with democracy ratings on V-Dem increasing significantly from electoral autocracy to electoral democracy until 2023.

Second, Hernández's rule was constrained by pressure to establish the Mission to Support the Fight against Corruption and Impunity in Honduras (MACCIH), a body established in a 2015 agreement between the Honduran government and the OAS (OAS 2016a). Led by a group of international experts and supported by the OAS, MACCIH operated independently to investigate corruption cases, propose legislative reforms, and enhance the capacity of Honduran institutions in their anti-corruption efforts. The mission's mandate included supporting judicial processes, improving the efficiency of the public prosecutor's office, and fostering accountability in public administration (ibid.). Despite its initial promise, MACCIH faced challenges, including resistance from entrenched political interests and limited resources. But it also managed to build up significant pressure on

---

[2] Honduras had also voted with the US against a UN General Assembly resolution in December 2018 criticizing the US for moving the Israeli embassy to Jerusalem to soothe tensions.

the conservative government by investigating corruption charges involving ruling party elites, leading the administration to expire the Mission's mandate in 2020 (International Crisis Group 2021). Following his election loss, Hernández had to face severe charges of corruption surrounding drug trafficking, and was extradited to the US in November 2021 to be prosecuted for helping to smuggle drugs into the country during his time as elected official (Associated Press 2022). Castro, in contrast, had started to take up negotiations with the UN to establish an international anti-corruption mechanisms similar to the now defunct International Commission against Impunity in Guatemala (CICIG), signing a Memorandum of Understanding on the matter with Secretary General Guterres in 2022.

Conclusion

In this chapter, we have seen how membership in a dictators' club can help shield from international pressure put on autocratic regimes by providing unconditional financial support, contesting the legitimacy of international actors, and intervening on the side of the regime in question in international fora. The chapter has shown how Nicaraguan President Ortega, with the assistance of ALBA, employed extensive survival strategies, including electoral manipulation and protest repression. ALBA's support, offering cheap oil and financial aid, alleviated international pressure on Nicaragua during Ortega's consolidation of power. ALBA initiated a campaign challenging the OAS's legitimacy, leading to a reform process that diverted attention from election manipulation. ALBA members, aided by Russia and China, prevented the Nicaragua issue from reaching the United Nations Security Council, though UNHRC interventions were unsuccessful. Despite ALBA's waning influence due to falling oil prices, Nicaragua found new allies. The Central American Development Bank offset US and EU sanctions, and China and Russia engaged after CABEI removed Ortega's ally, President Mossi, in 2023.

In contrast, Honduras was heavily reliant on international aid after President Hernández quit ALBA membership in 2009. Despite the National Party's manipulation of the 2017 presidential elections, international efforts, initially under the UN and later the OAS, led to electoral and institutional reforms. These reforms culminated in improved 2021 elections, with the opposition assuming the presidency. The OAS's MACCIH investigated corruption charges, mounting pressure on the Hernández government. Under reformed election laws, Hernández lost the popular vote and was extradited to the US for drug trafficking prosecution, showcasing the significant impact of international scrutiny and reforms.

The chapter also highlights some of the limitations of dictator clubs. Where regimes are dependent on financial redistribution from club membership to sustain their rule, waning support due to economic changes can cause major trouble for regimes. While dictator clubs also offer important legitimacy boosts as we have seen in Chapter 5, sustaining the repressive apparatus is key to surviving in power. But as the example of Nicaragua shows, autocrats are skilled at acquiring new sources of funding. In this respect, China's role as international financial donor is becoming more and more important as highlighted by the development finance literature (Dreher et al. 2022). Dictator clubs are also limited in successfully lobbying in IOs. While ALBA members frequently intervened on behalf of their members, particularly in the UN, their success is rather limited. In the Security Council, they needed the support of Russia and China to veto resolutions. In the Human Rights Council, they failed to acquire necessary majorities. However, the reputational costs for Nicaragua from UNHRC action were, so far, relatively negligible. While membership in a dictator club can thus not necessarily prevent sanctions from being enacted, it can cushion the blow and offset some of the reputational and financial costs.

8
Conclusion

Why do autocrats decide to join formal organizations and bear the associated sovereignty costs? In what ways do autocratic regional organizations (ROs) differ from ROs with predominantly democratic membership? Does membership in ROs actually prolong the time in power for autocratic incumbents, and if so, does it help all incumbents equally? And how exactly can RO membership help incumbents increase their survival chances when faced with politically challenging situations? These have been the central questions guiding this book. By answering these questions, the book intended to shift attention away from a liberal paradigm and onto the role of international institutions in explaining domestic regime trajectories beyond democratic regime change. While much of the debates in international relations today surround the "crisis" or "end" of the liberal international order stemming from endogenous threats from within established democracies, this book highlights how outside challenges from dictator clubs normalize authoritarian practices and thereby stabilized authoritarian rule.

The book has sought to conceptualize, trace, and explore the development, functioning, and effects of dictator clubs over time and across regions in a comparative perspective to offer a broad and encompassing picture on this phenomenon in world politics. This final chapter will cover two last objectives. Firstly, I will draw out the main findings of the book and connections to other recent research conducted in this quickly developing research field. Secondly, I will ponder on the implications of the findings from this book for the state and development of democracy as well as global governance more broadly. In a time when the future of both is more unclear than it has been in decades, this last chapter intends to provide food for thought on democracy and autocracy in an internationally connected world.

Dictator Clubs across Space and Time

This book has uncovered how dictator clubs developed across regions from 1946 to 2020. Authoritarian and democratic ROs grew roughly at the same

How Regional Organizations Sustain Authoritarian Rule. Maria J. Debre, Oxford University Press.
© Maria J. Debre (2025). DOI: 10.1093/9780198903635.003.0008

speed until the early 1960s with the early foundations of continental ROs such as the Organization of American States (OAS) and the League of Arab States (LOAS), as well as the first initiatives of economic cooperation on the European continent. In post-Second World War Europe, regional integration was pursued as a peace project to contain nationalism and rebuild crippled economies. In the Global South, however, regionalism was intertwined with post-colonial nation building (Acharya 1992, 2016). Inspired by movements such as pan-Arabism and Pan-Africanism, regional projects reflected efforts by newly created states to protect their national sovereignty rather than build supranational institutions (Getachew 2019; Oloruntoba 2020). Accordingly, a host of newly founded ROs emerged between 1960 and 1990, signifying the second wave of regional institution building. With the third wave of democratization, democratic ROs gained ground in the 1990s, with both types of organizations growing at roughly the same speed since the 2000s.

The third wave of regionalism starting during the height of political democratization in the 1990s might suggest a decline of dictator clubs. However, a more nuanced view presented in Chapter 3 suggests that dictator clubs have become more heterogenous during this time, consisting of a range of anocracies or hybrid regimes as they have been described in the literature—but overall remaining firmly autocratic. During the same time, democratic clubs experienced a decline in their democratic character, attributed mainly to democratic backsliding and the rise of right-wing populism starting in the mid-2000s, and leading to a notable crisis for the foundational identity and functioning of democratic organizations worldwide by the end of the second decade of the 2000s.

The development of dictator clubs over time and across regions also suggests a sorting effect: democracies and autocracies tend to associate within institutions to align with their respective regime types at foundation—and this remains so until RO death, or at least until 2020, the end of the study period of this book. In fact, very few ROs covered in this book exhibit diverse membership, with many simultaneously highly democratic and highly autocratic members. The exceptions are a few institutions that were specifically founded with an objective of inter-regional cooperation in mind such as the Organization for Security and Cooperation in Europe (OSCE), the Union for the Mediterranean (UfM), and Southeast Asian Treaty Organization (SEATO). Democratic clubs often install entry requirements that force states to undergo significant reforms before being able to become members, explaining the homogeneity of democratic ROs (Schimmelfennig 2003; Schimmelfennig and Sedelmeier 2005; Schneider 2008). Dictator clubs do not usually impose similar membership criteria, explaining their somewhat lower homogeneity.

The Reinforcement Effect of RO Membership

One of the central findings of this book is a reinforcement effect of RO membership for regime type: newly democratic members gain support to consolidate their governments through membership in democratic clubs, while autocratic incumbents can count on institutional resources to prolong their time in office and retain authoritarian regional environments. In fact, membership in a highly autocratic dictator club substantially increases the likelihood of survival from 40 to 70 years compared to membership in less autocratic institutions. Thus, membership in a dictator club makes survival about six times more likely compared to regimes with a membership in less autocratic institutions. Chapter 5 highlighted how tangible and intangible support accorded to incumbent regimes by dictator clubs explains this effect: regimes as diverse as Bahrain, China, and Zimbabwe have been able to stay in power during political critical moments where democratic regime change was imminent due to diplomatic, financial, and technical resource redistribution from ROs. Chapter 7 further expanded on the role that dictator clubs can play to fend off international pressure for democratic regime change. While the Ortega regime was able to consolidate its power through the support of the Bolivarian Alliance for the Peoples of Our Americas (ALBA) and the Central American Development Bank (CABEI), autocratization was ended in neighboring Honduras due to international dependence.

The analysis also showed that this system-boosting effect of RO membership also holds for both more homogenous and more heterogenous dictator clubs: even when the membership of a dictator club has become more diverse during the third wave of democratization, these clubs still provide the necessary perks to deal with internal and external challengers. One explanation for this effect was laid out in Chapter 6: RO membership can constrain more democratic members and prevent them from successfully moving against autocratic incumbents during times of political upheaval. Neither democratic hegemon South Africa nor democratic Zambia or Botswana were willing or able to provide meaningful ways to support the Zimbabwean opposition party when they were harassed and manipulated out of several election wins. Instead, they accepted or even promoted a strategy of diplomatic support for the incumbent Mugabe regime. This shows how the commitment among like-minded regional allies within dictator clubs to support each other is a key factor influencing regime survival—even when ROs are formally equipped with democracy clauses or have democratic members.

The statistical analysis also revealed that empowered RO bureaucrats, most importantly RO courts and tribunals, cannot exert a constraining influence on members of dictator clubs. This might point to a patronage function: while authoritarian ROs may be equipped with standing courts and judges, there is a risk of them being co-opted to render judgments in favor of incumbents. Even when this is not the case, independently acting judges might be reined in or their rights might be curtailed, as happened with the Southern African Development Community (SADC) tribunal when it ruled against Zimbabwe's regime in 2008.

Finally, the identified reinforcement effect only holds for threats of democratic regime change. Autocrats are more inclined to pool resources and support incumbents when they perceive a threat affecting their own regimes. In these cases, dictator clubs offer tangible and intangible resources to be used against internal challengers, or to ease outside pressure that might force democratic reforms in a member state. In contrast, ROs often remain uninvolved in intra-elite power struggles. This finding is exemplified by the 2017 military coup in Zimbabwe, where the SADC remained uninvolved in the intra-party power shift, indicating that regional support or interference depends on the nature of the threat to autocratic stability.

These findings on the role of institutions are especially important in light of the prevailing view that has asserted that regional powers play a stabilizing role for neighboring autocracies, often working through ROs (Kneuer et al. 2018; Tansey 2016a). However, the mere presence of a regional power as a member in a dictator club does not have a systematic impact on regime survival, as is evident from the statistical analysis in Chapter 4. This also ties in with similar findings by other scholars who, for instance, find that despite China's significant global involvement, there is little effect on the long-term survival chances for dependent regimes (Bader 2015; Bader and Daxecker 2015). As shown in Chapters 5 and 6 of this book, regional powers such as Saudi Arabia are much more hesitant to intervene in neighboring states outside of institutionalized arrangements due to legitimacy concerns, while even democratic powers like South Africa feel compelled to abide by RO solidarity norms that prevent them from openly supporting pro-democracy actors. Dictator clubs thus offer constraints to regional powers, preventing both autocratic and democratic ones from exerting too much unwanted influence over other member states. In fact, studies have even argued that there might be unintended consequences similar to backlash effects from democracy promotion: autocratic powers could inadvertently steer liberal reform movements toward forming alliances with Western partners, thereby promoting democratization (Börzel 2015).

Resource Redistribution, Regional Relationship Management, and International Shielding

To better understand the reinforcement effect of membership in a dictator club, the book delves deeper into several case studies to highlight the underlying mechanisms. Three main processes come to light. First, dictator clubs are significant sites of *resource redistribution*. As the three cases in Chapter 5 show—Bahrain during the Arab Spring, China's repression of the Uighur minority in 2009, and Zimbabwe's presidential election crisis in 2002—ROs contribute to legitimizing regimes, co-opting elites, and suppressing dissent by offering both tangible and intangible forms of support. Second, dictator clubs are means of *regional relationship management*, and provide constraints on powerful and dissenting members or challenges from RO bureaucrats, as the case of the heterogenous SADC exemplifies in Chapter 6. Finally, dictator clubs are means to provide a *shield from international pressure*. Chapter 7 shows how Nicaragua has consolidated its autocratic regime with help regional institutions, while international pressure forced neighboring Honduras to avert its path toward autocratization.

The cases covered in Chapter 5 focus particularly on three main means of resource redistribution used by dictator clubs to strengthen domestic capacities of co-optation, repression, and legitimation. The first case of Bahrain presented in Chapter 5 shows how the Gulf Cooperation Council (GCC) served as a forum to coordinate material support aimed at *co-opting* reform-oriented factions within the royal family and pro-regime minority groups during large-scale demonstrations in 2011. In combination with military and diplomatic support in the later phases of the conflict, the Bahraini royal family managed to tighten their hold on power, which remains the case today. The GCC continued its financial commitment to the small monarchy by providing further development aid programs through the GCC development fund that were strategically used by the regime to subsidize state pensions and boost their reputation for foreign investors.

While economic cooperation has been at the heart of the first wave of regionalism (Söderbaum 2016b), development assistance channeled through ROs and new sources of South–South cooperation have become central activities, particularly for lower-income ROs in the Global South (Engel and Mattheis 2021). While authoritarian ROs with wealthy members such as the GCC, the Arab League, and the Shanghai Cooperation Organization (SCO) can rely on financial transfers from wealthy to low-income members, lower-income ROs, particularly in Sub-Saharan Africa, have become hubs to coordinate fundraising and Western donors irrespective of regime type (Stapel et al. 2023). In combination with increasing unconditional funds provided by China (Dreher et al. 2011, 2022), the scope for misuse in support of autocratic incumbents has significantly increased.

The second case covered in Chapter 5 focused on the ways in which China has employed the SCO to strengthen its *repression* campaign against Uighur minorities in Xinjiang. When the Uighur issue first surfaced on the international scene in 2009, China employed the SCO "three evils doctrine" to criminalize, pursue, and arrest Uighur activists under charges of terrorism and separatism. Additionally, intelligence collected by the SCO Regional Anti-Terrorist Structure (RATS) department and bilateral extradition agreements were used in the aftermath of the Uighur uprisings to detain and extradite Uighur dissidents to China. With Uighur repression reaching unprecedented heights in the last decade, investigating the continuous role that regional intelligence sharing and backlisting has played in support of China's efforts is a difficult and ongoing effort of current research on transnational repression.

This speaks to further literature on the ways in which authoritarian ROs, particularly in Eurasia, have been found to be heavily engaged in furthering transnational forms of repression through police cooperation, joint anti-terrorism activities, and intelligence sharing to increase their hold over dissidents at home and abroad (Schenkkan and Linzer 2021; Tsourapas 2021). Lemon and Antonov (2020) show that legal harmonization of policies related to the definition and prosecution of extremism, terrorism, and operational searches, which usually relate to the repression of political dissidents, has taken place through information exchange in the Commonwealth of Independent States (CIS) Inter-Parliamentary Assembly. Advances in digital surveillance and regional cooperation on internet content control regulation have also further strengthened the repression capacities of regimes in Eurasia (Flonk 2021; Flonk et al. 2020). A range of authoritarian ROs also regularly engage in joint military maneuvers to signal military strength to potential challengers (cf. Cottiero and Haggard 2023) or even intervene on the side of incumbents to safeguard regimes.

The third case in Chapter 5 has highlighted how ROs can be helpful allies to confer *legitimacy* onto troubled regimes in two ways by focusing on the election crisis in Zimbabwe in 2002. First, regional election monitors provide flawed elections with a relatively clean bill of health, allowing regimes to use favorable reports in their legitimation strategies. Zimbabwean president Mugabe has thereby managed to de-legitimize international and regional critical reports as post-colonial geopolitics by stressing the legitimacy received from SADC monitors. With the rise of international election monitoring as a norm, many autocracies have strategically used international election observers to enhance their legitimacy while still manipulating electoral processes to retain power (Hyde 2011). These shadow election missions are often sent by friendly authoritarian ROs that provide, in general, more favorable reports compared to Western-led missions (Kelley 2009). These strategies seem to be somewhat successful. Perceptions of credibility of regional missions are high and increase trust in elections among the electorate (Bush and Prather 2018, 2022). Regional reports attached to African ROs also retain high standing and can de-legitimize criticism offered by international human rights organizations and Western states (Nganje and Nganje 2019).

The Zimbabwe case also sheds light on a second mechanism: ROs provide a community and identity function for troubled regimes. Mugabe was able to continuously present himself as the former "liberation hero," tying his fate to the identity of the SADC and Sub-Saharan Africa as one of independence and renaissance from colonial rule. The SADC and the African Union (AU) thus continued to offer diplomatic support to the leader, putting solidarity and unity above democratic considerations. Similar acts of loyalty and support have been extended to regimes by other dictator clubs. For example, after the Andijan massacre in Uzbekistan in 2005, officials from the SCO were quick to offer support for the Uzbek regime by framing protestors as illegal terrorists and the Uzbek handling of events as a matter of domestic politics (Aris 2009).

In this vein, dictator clubs can provide an identity function for member regimes. By presenting themselves as part of an ideational community, incumbents can strengthen domestic legitimation narratives and contest the validity of liberal challenges (Costa Buranelli 2020; Russo and Stoddard 2018b). The "Shanghai Spirit"—a loose set of normative values around regional stability, rejection of Western forms of domestic and international governance, and consensual decision-making—has, for instance, helped to legitimize authoritarian practices in Eurasia to reinforce weak state identities after the end of the Cold War while helping to de-legitimize international democracy promotion actors (Ambrosio 2008, 2009; Laruelle 2008). Similarly, the "ASEAN Way" has strengthened elite-led informal decision-making in Southeast Asia and prohibited the development of more inclusive participatory forms of regionalism (Acharya 2003). Gulf and Arab leaders similarly gain legitimacy from regional conceptualizations of Arab identity that they can strategically employ to legitimize their rule domestically and to cast troubling actors as part of an out-group (Yom 2014, p. 2).

Chapters 6 and 7 delve into two lesser-researched areas connected to authoritarian institutions. Chapter 6 turns to the role of ROs as sites of relationship management. Given that many dictator clubs have become more heterogenous during the third wave of democratization, it is crucial to understand how they can manage to sustain authoritarian incumbents in the face of new regional challengers from fellow democratic club members, empowered RO bureaucrats, or critical non-governmental regional groupings. Chapter 6 therefore highlights how dictator clubs establish informal norms for engagement that privilege alliances between incumbent regime members, and how formal decision-making rules institutionalize consensual and often non-transparent proceedings that only include elites in power. The chapter digs deeper into the development of the Mugabe regime, which has managed to withstand a number of regional challengers over the years. Alliances between former liberation parties as well as the consensual style of decision-making forced regional critics such as Zambia and Botswana to conform to regional solidarity norms when they were calling for harsher action against the repressive regime in 2008. Empowered bureaucrats from the court also had to learn that their authority did not matter much when they ruled against the contentious Zimbabwean land reform program that saw the eviction of white farmers without any form of compensation through violent means in 2008. Instead of gaining necessary support from the SADC for their ruling, SADC members were spooked by the "monster" they created and quickly decided to take away large portions of the tribunal's rights, particularly the right of individual access in human rights matters.

Finally, Chapter 7 highlights how financial resources from dictator clubs can help regimes become more independent from international donors. A comparison between Nicaragua under President Ortega and Honduras under President Hernández highlights that membership in a dictator club like ALBA can *shield an autocratic regime from international pressure*, thereby allowing the consolidation of authoritarian rule. Ortega navigated international sanctions with ALBA's support, while Honduras, constrained by aid dependence, succumbed to international pressures, leading to democratic reforms and the end of the autocratization period.

ALBA's assistance, including subsidized oil and finances, alleviated Nicaragua's reliance on aid from multilateral donor institutions, aiding Ortega during the consolidation of his regime. ALBA also launched a campaign challenging the legitimacy of the OAS and its human rights mechanisms, diverting attention from electoral manipulation and reducing OAS's willingness to address ALBA members' transgressions. While ALBA members unsuccessfully advocated for Ortega in the United Nations Human Rights Council (UNHRC), they managed to prevent a United Nations Security Council intervention with the help of Russia and China. Despite ALBA's declining geopolitical significance, Nicaragua found new allies, such as CABEI, and later China and Russia, who offset costs when the regime started to face economic sanctions. In contrast, neighboring Honduras experienced pressure due to its dependency on international aid when the government under Hernández extended term limits and manipulated elections in 2015 and 2017. Under the auspices of the UN and OAS, Honduras underwent electoral and institutional reforms, leading to improved elections in 2021 and the ousting of the autocratic President Hernández. The OAS also established the Mission to Support the Fight against Corruption and Impunity in Honduras (MACCIH), exposing corruption charges and potentially contributing to Hernández's downfall and extradition to the US.

Overall, the evidence presented in this book shows how dictator clubs are important sites to support and sustain autocratic rule across time and space. While authoritarian ROs have previously been considered dysfunctional paper tigers or mere instruments of regional powers, scholarship might have been focusing on formal dimensions and powerful actors too much and missed the important practical outputs of authoritarian ROs. Instead of focusing on the unique aspects of authoritarian cooperation, dictator clubs had for too long been judged by the same standards as democratic institutions.

Implications for the Future of Democracy

As we exit 2023, the level of democracy enjoyed by the average global citizen is down to 1986 levels with a new record of 42 countries undergoing autocratization (V-Dem Institute 2023). The last decade has particularly seen a rise of democratic backsliding and breakdowns in established democracies, resulting in a loss of democratic identity of many ROs in the Global North, from the European Union (EU) to the OSCE and OAS. How will this reconfiguration of membership in democratic ROs affect cooperation in the future? To what extent are democratic ROs able to further contain these types of political regressions? Are they, as some would argue, even responsible for unintentionally empowering backsliding in the first place? Are we likely to see a shift toward nationalist and authoritarian regional orders, also in Europe and the Americas?

The findings from this book offer little reassurance that democratic decline within established democracies can be easily halted by ROs. In contrast, recent EU decisions, such as the shift toward closed European borders with regard to migration and asylum seekers, rather seem to suggest a tough future for political liberties and human rights in the West. All evidence presented in this book points to the fact that transnational cooperation of autocrats has always existed, and will become even more sophisticated and globalized in the coming years to challenge institutionalized controls and guaranteed rights. Populist and right-wing actors have already gained significant ground across EU member states, even successfully entering government in the Netherlands, Italy, Austria, Poland, and Hungary. Even in the absence of right-wing authoritarian parties in government, discourses and party platforms have significantly shifted to the right across all party lines (Abou-Chadi and Krause 2020) and voting for nationalist and isolationist parties has increased overall (Walter 2021a).

These developments are not isolated phenomena. In contrast, authoritarian actors are successfully coordinating across state lines to influence decision-making in the EU and other European institutions, not unlike the regimes covered in this book. In this way they have often successfully managed to block unfavorable decisions. Backsliders in the EU have protected each other from harsher measures taken by the EU Commission in response to major democratic transgressions, for instance by capturing political groupings like the EU Visegrad group (Makarychev 2020; Winzen 2023), and populist parties have joined forces in the parliament of the Council of Europe to draw attention away from human rights matters (Lipps and Jacob 2022). The EU thereby finds itself in an "autocracy trap" whereby the gains from an open single market now help autocrats like Orbán to consolidate autocratic rule (Kelemen 2020).

EU scholars therefore ponder to what extent autocratization processes will eventually mean the end of EU identity and eventual disintegration (Krastev 2012; Sedelmeier 2017; Vollaard 2014). Somewhat surprisingly, Brexit did not result in a large-scale diffusion of withdrawal decisions, but rather seems to have reinforced trust in EU institutions due to the tough exit negotiations of the Commission (Schuette and Dijkstra 2023; Walter 2021b). The EU also seemed to have finally devised an effective tool to pressure backsliders into more conformist behavior through the rule-of-law mechanism that allows asset freezes in response to major violations of European law standards. However, Orbán showed how to successfully use pressure points during negotiations over Ukrainian help to unfreeze some of these assets without meaningful domestic reforms in December 2023, showing that autocrats are adept at using the rules of the game to subvert institutionalized rules to their advantage (Liboreiro 2023).

Further global developments over the last years support this troubling view from Europe: right-wing transnational movements are on the rise since the early 2000s, forming unlikely coalitions to contest liberal policies in international organizations (IOs) (Almeida and Chase-Dunn 2018; Bob 2012; Mccright and Dunlap 2000; Velasco 2020). In consequence, anti-liberal policies diffused dramatically in the last decade, including rollbacks of gender equality and LGBTQ+ rights (Korolczuk and Graff 2018; Lerch et al. 2022). Civil society organizations face hurdles, including stricter laws on funding and international access (Chaudhry 2022; Glasius et al. 2020), and journalists encounter more hostile working conditions than ever due to global surveillance (Gohdes 2020). Rather than fixing these issues, International Governmental Organizations (IGOs) seem to have added to democratic backsliding among their members due to a singular focus on promoting elections over other democratic institutions and cultures (Meyerrose 2020).

As democratic ROs are struggling with newly autocratic members, we also need to pay attention to political developments in hybrid regimes as diverse as Nicaragua, Zambia, and the Philippines, which have seen significant liberalization since the 1990s but are now regressing to authoritarian rule. While I have identified a reinforcement effect of RO membership, it remains an open question to what extent authoritarian ROs are also responsible for reversing the gains of democratization. On the one hand, democratizing coalitions in states that remain members in authoritarian institutions can expect little support from their "bad neighbors." As the case of the SADC has shown, ROs are often willing to overlook authoritarian tactics of their peers or even offer outright support to former autocratic coalitions. ROs might thus be an important factor to explain the current waves of autocratization. On the other hand, ROs might also add to further diffusing authoritarian norms internationally. While the contention of outright autocracy promotion had been rejected by earlier literature on authoritarian regionalism, autocratization could spread even in the absence of outright autocracy promotion. ROs are gaining new members or offer tiered membership to non-regional partners (Hofmann et al. 2023), thereby potentially further diffusing authoritarian discourses and practices beyond their regions.

This also raises the question of policy implications for cooperation with authoritarian ROs and partners. In the wake of the Russian invasion of Ukraine, German chancellor Scholz has declared his intention to work more closely with all types of stable partners, reaching out to long-term autocrats in Central Asia and the Middle East to secure energy supplies and deal with migration issues (Tagesschau 2023). The EU initiated its Global Gateway strategy in 2023 to invest in energy, climate, and infrastructure projects across the globe in an effort to provide alternatives to China's silk road mega project (European Commission 2023). This will pour more finances into autocratic countries and institutions, although these investments are often misused to fund corrupt practices and regimes (Hodzi et al. 2012; Kono and Montinola 2013b; Stapel et al. 2023). At the same time, authoritarian ROs in the Global South serve important functions such as acting as mediators during intra-state conflicts (Haftel 2012; Haftel and Hofmann 2017) or coordinating humanitarian action (Debre and Dijkstra 2021a; Kirchner and Dominguez 2011). These examples show that institutional cooperation is never just normatively good or bad but always represents two sides of the same coin, resulting in difficult decisions with unreconcilable goals for policymakers.

Implications for Global Governance

There is no lack of scholarly writing about the dangers of an international authoritarian order in the not-too-distant future. Across the disciplines of international law and international relations, much has been said about the development toward "authoritarian international law" (Ginsburg 2020), the "challenges" (Lake, Martin, and Risse 2021), and even "the end" (Ikenberry 2018) of the liberal international order. With the proliferation of a reverse wave of autocratization, scholarship has already started to highlight potential international consequences that might result from backlash politics and political backsliding (Copelovitch and Pevehouse 2019; Eilstrup-Sangiovanni and Hofmann 2019; Ferguson et al. 2017; Ikenberry 2018; Pepinsky and Walter 2019), for instance in the form of state withdrawal from IOs (e.g. Choi 2021; von Borzyskowski and Vabulas 2019a, 2021). However, instead of widespread withdrawals, we rather witness efforts to reform and contest global governance from within. The growing backlash, for instance, leads states to cut funding for multilateral projects (Ege and Bauer 2017; Goetz and Patz 2017) and to contest central principles of international cooperation (Börzel and Zürn 2021; Sommerer et al. 2022; Velasco 2020; Walter 2021a).

The elephant in the room, of course, is China's and Russia's rise as global autocratic powerhouses in the last decade. While China has attempted to constrain the international human rights regime since the 1980s (Inboden 2022), its international activism has seen a distinct rise in recent years. Particularly, China has become much more assertive in UN bodies like the Human

Rights Council, where it seeks to shape human rights standards in alignment with more autocratic values (Pauselli et al. 2023; Piccone 2018; Pils 2022). China has also been a central actor to promote stricter content control regulation in global internet governance fora, thereby promoting its vision of cyber sovereignty (Flonk 2021; Flonk et al. 2020). Autocracies in general strategically seek membership in human rights institutions at higher rates than before (Voss 2019), while backsliders and autocracies form coalitions to protect each other from condemnation and sanctions (Meyerrose and Nooruddin 2023).

While China seems to be intent on reshaping the system from within, Russia's invasion of Ukraine marked a gross violation of and departure from international law, reviving debates on the recognition and prosecution of an international crime of aggression (Pollman 2022). But Russia's invasion is only the most recent and egregious act in a longer line of conflicts involving autocratic powers. The South China Sea territorial disputes highlight that China is not unwilling to depart from established international norms by asserting expansive maritime claims and militarizing disputed islands. Saudi Arabia has been waging a long-term proxy war in Yemen, while Venezuela has recently declared its ambition to annex neighboring Guyana after the discovery of vast oil reserves. IOs and established democracies seem relatively powerless in the face of these developments. Instead of harsh sanctions and condemnations, most governments and IOs opted for limited targeted sanctions in reaction to Russia's annexation of Crimea, thereby normalizing violations of international law as relatively costless.

All of these developments point to a crisis of global governance due to growing autocratization of international politics. However, a recent study found that autocratization of IO membership has not increased as dramatically as expected in the last decade based on conventional measurements (Debre and Sommerer 2023). Only a few IOs have come under immediate threat from being controlled by an autocratic majority or have experienced a major decrease in their democratic density, and none of those IOs that are under threat have held stable democratic majorities over time. Instead, the recent wave of autocratization has two main effects. Formerly homogenous democratic clubs like the EU or the North Atlantic Treaty Organization (NATO) have seen increasing backsliding and even democratic breakdowns over the last decade, endangering parts of their foundational identity, while more heterogenous ROs in the Global South like Association of Southeast Asian Nations (ASEAN) and the SADC have become more authoritarian due to breakdowns and consolidation of highly authoritarian systems, as we have seen in Chapter 3.

While global IOs might not yet be dominated by across-the-board autocratic majorities, decision-making, policy output, and legitimacy are already suffering. Empirical data shows that in recent years, at least some important IOs, like the EU, the International Criminal Court, the World Trade Organization (WTO), and the World Health Organization (WHO), have experienced legitimacy crises (Sommerer et al. 2022), and that autocracies specifically have harmed the legitimacy of the Security Council (Zaum 2013). Autocracies are at the forefront of criticizing global governance institutions, often using existing global inequalities to deflect attention from domestic political digressions (Grzymala-Busse 2019; Wonka et al. 2023). While IOs had often responded to legitimacy crisis by using democratic language (Dingwerth et al. 2019), this road to gaining legitimacy might be closed in the future.

Dictator clubs represent major sites of coalition-building for autocracies to successfully lobby on the global stage. As is evident from Chapter 7, ALBA members have intervened on behalf of their members at the UN to attempt to block country-specific targeted resolutions on numerous occasions. The CIS, for instance, has also served as a vehicle to build a successful coalition to promote information security norms and laws at the International Telecommunications Union and United Nations (Debre and Flonk 2022). Fears of an "autocratic alliance" between China and Russia that would serve as a center for authoritarian international law had been circling among policymakers, international lawyers, and scholars alike for several years (Lynch 2018; Myers 2021).

Apart from formal institutions, informal fora and networks might serve as additional sites for autocratic cooperation. In 2021, a number of autocracies founded the "Group of Friends in Defense of the United Nations," aimed at restoring multilateralism, furthering diversity, and ensuring the sovereign equality of UN member states. The UNHRC has seen the re-emergence of the so-called "like-minded group," a loose alliance of mostly autocratic regimes set out to "democratize" the council.[1] As an informal alliance, the group has had a major influence on successfully lobbying for restrictions of monitoring, reporting, and public availability of information on human rights violations and restricting civil society access at the council (Debre 2023; Inboden 2021). At the same time, China has been sponsoring a range of informal human rights fora in the Global South that are aimed at coalition-building and information-gathering among like-minded partners (Stephen 2023).

---

[1] This is according to the statement at the 25th session of the UNHRC by Egypt in 2014, which is considered as the political platform of the group.

These types of authoritarian cooperation also have major consequences for transnational activism. While increasing autocratization has so far not led to meaningful restrictions of formal access rights in IOs (Sommerer and Tallberg 2017), informal practices make the work of activists even harder than before. In ASEAN, for instance, existing participatory arrangements like the ASEAN Civil Society Conference have been under pressure as more and more member states pass stricter financing laws and increase harassments and travel bans (Uhlin 2023). At the UN, China has attacked critical human rights activists (HRW 2021; Human Rights Watch 2017) and autocracies are teaming up in the non-governmental organization (NGO) committee to prevent critical organizations from gaining accreditation (Inboden 2019). These developments come at the heels of increasing transnational repression, with autocracies harassing, detaining, and even targeting dissidents and their families abroad (Dukalskis 2021; Jardine et al. 2021), along with the use of IOs like Interpol (Lemon 2019). China is even establishing a network of extra-territorial police stations across the globe to target political dissidents more effectively (Hawkins 2023).

In combination, the transnational cooperation of authoritarian regimes poses a grave threat to democracy, human rights, and global governance worldwide. While dictator clubs are mostly a Global South occurrence, they have also become an actor on the global stage. In addition, both a decline in democratic quality among established democratic institutions and an expansion of transnational cooperation beyond established institutional fora by autocracies is already set to be one of the main political challenges in years to come. Autocracies will increasingly and more openly attempt to reshape global governance across diplomatic, economic, territorial, and technological realms, posing one of the main challenges to established democratic norms and institutions.

References

Abbott, K. W., & Snidal, D. (1998). Why States Act through Formal International Organizations. *Journal of Conflict Resolution, 42*(1), 3–32. https://doi.org/10.1177/0022002798042001001.

Abdo, G. (2017). *The New Sectarianism: The Arab Uprisings and the Rebirth of the Shi'a-Sunni Divide*. New York: Oxford University Press.

Abou-Chadi, T., & Krause, W. (2020). The Causal Effect of Radical Right Success on Mainstream Parties' Policy Positions: A Regression Discontinuity Approach. *British Journal of Political Science, 50*(3), 829–847. https://doi.org/10.1017/S0007123418000029.

Acemoglu, D., & Robinson, J. A. (2006). *Economic Origins of Dictatorship and Democracy*. Cambridge: Cambridge University Press.

Acharya, A. (1992). Regionalism and Regime Security in the Third World: Comparing the Origins of the ASEAN and the GCC. In B. L. Job (Ed.), *The Insecurity Dilemma National Security of Third World States* (pp. 143–164). Boulder, CO: Lynne Rienner. www.rienner.com/title/The_Insecurity_Dilemma_National_Security_of_Third_World_States.

Acharya, A. (2001). *Constructing a Security Community in Southeast Asia: ASEAN and the Problem of Regional Order* (p. 234). Oxon, New York: Routledge.

Acharya, A. (2003). Democratisation and the Prospects for Participatory Regionalism in Southeast Asia. *Third World Quarterly, 24*(2), 375–390. https://doi.org/10.1080/0143659032000074646.

Acharya, A. (2016). Regionalism Beyond EU-Centrism. In T. A. Börzel & T. Risse (Eds.), *The Oxford Handbook of Comparative Regionalism* (pp. 109–132). Oxford: Oxford University Press.

Acharya, A., & Johnston, A. I. (2007a). *Crafting Cooperation: Regional Institutions in Comparative Perspective*. Cambridge: Cambridge University Press.

Acharya, A., & Johnston, A. I. (2007b). Conclusion: Institutional Features, Cooperation Effects, and the Agenda for Further Research on Comparative Regionalism. In A. Acharya & A. I. Johnston (Eds.), *Crafting Cooperation: Regional Institutions in Comparative Perspective* (pp. 244–278). Cambridge: Cambridge University Press.

Adams, D., & Aburto, W. M. (2018, May 5). Daniel Inc: How Nicaragua's Ortega Financed a Political Dynasty. *Univision*. www.univision.com/univision-news/latin-america/daniel-inc-how-nicaraguas-ortega-financed-a-political-dynasty. Accessed November 27, 2023.

African Union. (2008). *African Union Summit Resolution on Zimbabwe. Adopted at the 11th Ordinary Session of the African Union Assembly, 1 July 2008*. Sharm El Sheikh. www.securitycouncilreport.org/atf/cf/%7B65BFCF9B-6D27-4E9C-8CD3-CF6E4FF96FF9%7D/ZimAUResolution1July08.pdf.

Al Jazeera. (2011, July 11). Polls Close in Nicaragua amid Complaints. *Al Jazeera*. www.aljazeera.com/news/2011/11/7/polls-close-in-nicaragua-amid-complaints. Accessed November 27, 2023.

ALBA. (2019a, March 20). Declaración Conjunta De Los Países De La Alianza Bolivariana Para Los Pueblos De Nuestra América (Alba-Tcp), 40 session. United Nations Human Rights Council. https://hrcmeetings.ohchr.org/HRCSessions/HRCDocuments/29/SP/19431_39_3e48ab87_9823_4d1a_a102_0e579e3cd642.docx. Accessed July 1, 2024.

References **183**

ALBA. (2019b, March 21). Declaración Conjunta Bajo El Tema 10 De La Agenda Del Consejo De Derechos Humanos. https://hrcmeetings.ohchr.org/HRCSessions/HRCDocuments/29/SP/19544_39_5d48129f_3187_40f9_b2c6_b2b3284e6d36.docx. Accessed July 1, 2024.

ALBA. (2019c, August 7). Declaración Conjunta De Los Países De La Alianza Bolivariana Para Los Pueblos De Nuestra América (Alba-Tcp), 41 session (2). https://hrcmeetings.ohchr.org/HRCSessions/HRCDocuments/30/SP/21756_40_340cefa0_2ed4_4a35_b8d8_63240ebe70ac.docx. Accessed July 1, 2024.

ALBA. (2019d, October 7). Declaración Conjunta Bajo El Tema 10 Debate General De La Agenda Del Consejo De Derechos Humanos, 41 session (3).

Aljazeera. (2008, April). Zimbabwe Focus of Regional Summit. *Aljazeera*. www.aljazeera.com/news/africa/2008/04/2008525123616618856.html.

Aljazeera. (2011, February 14). Bahrain Activists in "Day of Rage." *Aljazeera*.

Allen-Ebrahimian, B. (2019, November 24). Exposed: China's Operating Manuals for Mass Internment and Arrest by Algorithm. International Consortium of Investigative Journalists (ICJ). www.icij.org/investigations/china-cables/exposed-chinas-operating-manuals-for-mass-internment-and-arrest-by-algorithm. Accessed December 20, 2022.

Allison, R. (2008). Virtual Regionalism, Regional Structures and Regime Security in Central Asia. *Central Asian Survey*, *27*(2), 185–202. https://doi.org/10.1080/02634930802355121.

Allison, R. (2018). Protective Integration and Security Policy Coordination: Comparing the SCO and CSTO. *The Chinese Journal of International Politics*, *11*(3), 297–338.

Almeida, P., & Chase-Dunn, C. (2018). Globalization and Social Movements. *Annual Review of Sociology*, *44*(1), 189–211. https://doi.org/10.1146/annurev-soc-073117-041307.

Alter, K. J. (2014). *The New Terrain of International Law: Courts, Politics, Rights*. Princeton, NJ: Princeton University Press.

Alter, K. J., & Hooghe, L. (2016). Regional Dispute Settlement. In T. A. Börzel & T. Risse (Eds.), *The Oxford Handbook of Comparative Regionalism* (pp. 539–558). Oxford: Oxford University Press. https://doi.org/10.1093/acprof.

Ambrosio, T. (2008). Catching the "Shanghai Spirit": How the Shanghai Cooperation Organization Promotes Authoritarian Norms in Central Asia. *Europe-Asia Studies*, *60*(8), 1321–1344. https://doi.org/10.1080/09668130802292143.

Ambrosio, T. (2009). *Authoritarian Backlash: Russian Resistance to Democratization in the Former Soviet Union*. Farnham: Ashgate.

Ambrosio, T. (2010). Constructing a Framework of Authoritarian Diffusion: Concepts, Dynamics, and Future Research. *International Studies Perspectives*, *11*(4), 375–392. https://doi.org/10.1111/j.1528-3585.2010.00411.x.

Amnesty International. (2002a). *China's Anti-Terrorism Legislation and Repression in the Xinjiang Uyghur Autonomous Region*. London: Amnesty International.

Amnesty International. (2002b). *People's Republic of China: Serious Human Rights Violations and the Crackdown on Dissent Continue*. London: Amnesty International.

Amnesty International. (2002c). *Amnesty International Report 2002—Zimbabwe*. www.refworld.org/docid/3cf4bc048.html. Accessed December 29, 2022.

Amnesty International. (2010). *"Justice, Justice." The July 2009 Protests in Xinjiang, China*. London: Amnesty International.

Andreas, P. (2005). Criminalizing Consequences of Sanctions: Embargo Busting and Its Legacy. *International Studies Quarterly*, *49*(2), 335–360. https://doi.org/10.1111/j.0020-8833.2005.00347.x.

Aris, S. (2009). The Shanghai Cooperation Organisation: "Tackling the Three Evils." A Regional Response to Non-Traditional Security Challenges or an Anti-Western Bloc? *Europe-Asia Studies*, *61*(3), 457–482.

184 References

Aris, S. (2011). *Eurasian Regionalism. The Shanghai Cooperation Organisation*. Basingstoke: Palgrave Macmillan.

Aris, S. (2012). The Response of the Shanghai Cooperation Organisation to the Crisis in Kyrgyzstan. *Civil Wars*, *14*(3), 451–476. https://doi.org/10.1080/13698249.2012.706954.

Asamba, M. (2017). Raila Odinga Hails Zimbabwe's Bloodless "Coup." *The Standard*. www.standardmedia.co.ke/article/2001260934/raila-odinga-hails-zimbabwe-s-bloodless-coup. Accessed January 5, 2024.

Asharq Al-Awsat. (2021, October 21). GCC Countries Reiterate Support for Bahrain's Fiscal Program. *Asharq AL-awsat*. https://english.aawsat.com/home/article/3258736/gcc-countries-reiterate-support-bahrains-fiscal-program. Accessed December 18, 2022.

Aspinwall, M. (2009). NAFTA-ization: Regionalization and Domestic Political Adjustment in the North American Economic Area. *Journal of Common Market Studies*, *47*(1), 1–24. https://doi.org/10.1111/j.1468-5965.2008.01831.x.

Associated Press. (2022, September 27). Honduras Judge Approves Extradition of Ex-President to U.S. *The New York Times*. https://web.archive.org/web/20220927035326/www.nytimes.com/2022/03/17/world/americas/honduras-extradition-juan-orlando-hernandez.html. Accessed January 6, 2024.

Bach, D. (2005). The Global Politics of Regionalism: Africa. In M. Farrell, B. Hettne, & L. van Langenhove (Eds.), *Global Politics of Regionalism: Theory and Practice* (pp. 171–186). London: Pluto Press.

Bader, J. (2014). *China's Foreign Relations and the Survival of Autocracies*. Abingdon: Routledge.

Bader, J. (2015). Propping Up Dictators? Economic Cooperation from China and its Impact on Authoritarian Persistence in Party and Non-Party Regimes. *European Journal of Political Research*, *54*(4), 655–672. https://doi.org/10.1111/1475-6765.12082.

Bader, J., & Daxecker, U. (2015). A Chinese Resource Curse? The Human Rights Effects of Oil Export Dependence on China versus the United States. *Journal of Peace Research*, *52*(6), 774–790. https://doi.org/10.1177/0022343315593332.

Badza, S. (2009). Zimbabwe's 2008 Harmonized Elections: Regional and International Reaction. In E. V. Masunungure (Ed.), *Defying the Winds of Change: Zimbabwe's 2008 Election* (pp. 149–175). Harare: Weaver Press. https://doi.org/10.1063/1.3284658.

Bahrain News Agency. (2011a, February 18). HM King Hamad Grants HRH Crown Prince Role to Commence Dialogue with all Parties in Bahrain. www.bna.bh/portal/en/news/447586?date=2011-04-9. Accessed December 15, 2017.

Bahrain News Agency. (2011b, March 5). Interior Minister Unveils Plans to Recruit 20000 Employees. www.bna.bh/portal/en/news/449075?date=2011-3-20. Accessed December 15, 2017.

Bahrain News Agency. (2011c, March 7). Housing Minister Unveils Plans to Build 50,000 Units in 5 Years. http://bna.bh/portal/en/news/449278?date=2011-09-28. Accessed December 15, 2017.

Bahrain News Agency. (2011d, March 13). No Compromise on National Security and Safety, HRH Prince Salman Vowed. www.bna.bh/portal/en/news/449823. Accessed December 15, 2017.

Bahrain News Agency. (2011e, April). Peninsula Shield Deployment in Bahrain Legal and Legitimate, Amr Mousa Said. https://advance.lexis.com/api/permalink/aa1ce3ff-b41f-440c-a707-e2a39b828196/?context=1516831.

Baker, B. (2002). When to Call Black White: Zimbabwe's Electoral Reports. *Third World Quarterly*, *23*(6), 1145–1158. https://doi.org/10.1080/0143659022000036603.

Bank, A., & Edel, M. (2015). *Authoritarian Regime Learning: Comparative Insights from the Arab Uprisings*. Working Paper. Hamburg: German Institute of Global and Area Studies (GIGA).

Barker, R. (2001). *Legitimating Identities: The Self-Presentations of Rulers and Subjects*. Cambridge: Cambridge University Press.

Barnett, A., & Gause III, F. G. (1998). Caravans in Opposite Directions. In E. Adler & M. Barnett (Eds.), *Security Communities* (pp. 161–197). Cambridge: Cambridge University Press.

Barnett, A., & Solingen, E. (2007). Designed to Fail or Failure of Design? The Origins and Legacy of the Arab League. In A. Acharya & A. I. Johnston (Eds.), *Crafting Cooperation: Regional Institutions in Comparative Perspective* (pp. 180–220). Cambridge: Cambridge University Press.

Bassiouni, M. C., Rodley, N., Al-Awadhi, B., Kirsch, P., & Arsanjani, M. H. (2011). *Report of the Bahrain Independent Commission of Inquiry*. Manama: Bahraini Independent Commission of Inquiry.

BBC News. (2003, November 3). Was Zimbabwe's Election Fair? http://news.bbc.co.uk/2/hi/africa/3237327.stm. Accessed December 29, 2022.

BBC News. (2008a, April 18). Mugabe Attacks Opposition and UK. http://news.bbc.co.uk/2/hi/africa/7353929.stm. Accessed August 4, 2019.

BBC News. (2008b, May 2). Zimbabwe Announces Poll Results. http://news.bbc.co.uk/2/hi/africa/7380445.stm.

BBC News. (2008c, July 2). African Call for Zimbabwe Unity. http://news.bbc.co.uk/2/hi/africa/7484165.stm.

BBC News. (2009a, July 7). Riots Engulf Chinese Uighur City. http://news.bbc.co.uk/2/hi/asia-pacific/8137824.stm.

BBC News. (2009b, July 9). China Leaders Vow Xinjiang Action. http://news.bbc.co.uk/2/hi/asia-pacific/8141657.stm.

BBC News. (2009c, July 10). Timeline: Xinjiang Unrest. http://news.bbc.co.uk/2/hi/asia-pacific/8138866.stm.

BBC News. (2009d, October 20). Nicaragua Court Backs Re-election. http://news.bbc.co.uk/2/hi/8316167.stm. Accessed November 27, 2023.

BBC News. (2013, August). Zimbabwe Poll "Free and Peaceful" Say Obasanjo and SADC. http://www.bbc.com/news/world-africa-23546050.

BBC News. (2017, October 6). Zimbabwe Succession Row: Grace Mugabe Warns of Coup Plot. www.bbc.com/news/world-africa-41530924. Accessed January 5, 2024.

BBC News. (2018, September 1). Nicaragua Expels UN Team after Critical Report. www.bbc.com/news/world-latin-america-45380265. Accessed November 27, 2023.

Beach, D., & Pedersen, R. (2013). *Process-Tracing Methods: Foundations and Guidelines*. Ann Arbor, MI: University of Michigan Press. https://doi.org/10.3998/mpub.2556282.

Beach, D., & Pedersen, R. (2016). Selecting Appropriate Cases When Tracing Causal Mechanisms. *Sociological Methods & Research*, *47*(4), 1–35. https://doi.org/10.1177/0049124115622510.

Beblawi, H., & Luciani, G. (1987). *The Rentier State*. New York: Croom Helm.

Beetham, D. (1991). *The Legitimation of Power*. Basingstoke: Palgrave Macmillan.

Bell, A. (2011, April 19). SADC Tribunal Review Upholds Unlawful Land Grab Judgement. *SW Radio Africa (London)*. https://advance-lexis-com.zu.idm.oclc.org/api/document?collection=news&id=urn:contentItem:52NM-PJ11-JDVB-N3G6-00000-00&context=1516831. Accessed May 12, 2024.

186 References

Bellin, E. (2004). The Robustness of Authoritarianism in the Middle East: Exceptionalism in Comparative Perspective. *Comparative Politics, 36*(2), 139–157. https://doi.org/10.2307/4150140.

Benjamin, C. (2014, November 14). Khampepe: Zim's 2002 Elections Not Free and Fair. *Mail & Guardian.* https://mg.co.za/article/2014-11-14-khampepe-zimbabwes-2002-elections-not-free-and-fair. Accessed January 4, 2024.

Benuin, G. A. (2022). Xinjiang Victims Database. *shahit.bi.* https://shahit.biz/eng. Accessed December 20, 2022.

Berg, R. C. (2023a, February 6). Why Is CABEI Funding Nicaragua's Dictatorship and What Can the United States Do about It? *CSIS: Center for Strategic and International Studies.* www.csis.org/analysis/why-cabei-funding-nicaraguas-dictatorship-and-what-can-united-states-do-about-it. Accessed January 7, 2024.

Berg, R. C. (2023b, May 8). The Banker to Dictators: A Call to Elect Accountable Leadership at CABEI. *Global Americans.* https://theglobalamericans.org/2023/05/the-banker-to-dictators-a-call-to-elect-accountable-leadership-at-cabei. Accessed November 27, 2023.

Bermeo, N. (2016). On Democratic Backsliding. *Journal of Democracy, 27*(1), 5–19. https://doi.org/10.1353/jod.2016.0012.

Bianculli, A. (2016). *Latin America.* (T. A. Börzel & T. Risse, Eds.). Oxford: Oxford University Press. https://doi.org/10.1093/oxfordhb/9780199682300.013.9.

Biryabarema, E., & Makori, B. (2016, February 21). 'I don't need lectures,' Museveni tells EU after poll criticism. Retrieved from http://www.reuters.com/article/us-uganda-election-idUSKCN0VU0B8

Blaydes, L. (2011). *Elections and Distributive Politics in Mubarak's Egypt.* Cambridge: Cambridge University Press.

Bluhm, K. (2022, March 23). The Ideology Behind Russia's War. *ZOiS Spotlight 11/2022.* www.zois-berlin.de/en/publications/zois-spotlight/the-ideology-behind-russias-war. Accessed December 12, 2022.

Bob, C. (2012). *The Global Right Wing and the Clash of World Politics.* Oxford: Cambridge University Press. www.cambridge.org/core/books/global-right-wing-and-the-clash-of-world-politics/2683ACDB5B99EE461FC008F0E6F4F99C. Accessed April 3, 2023.

Boix, C., & Svolik, M. W. (2013). The Foundations of Limited Authoritarian Government: Institutions, Commitment, and Power-Sharing in Dictatorships. *The Journal of Politics, 75*(02), 300–316. https://doi.org/10.1017/S0022381613000029.

Bolt, J., & van Zanden, J. L. (2020). Maddison Style Estimates of the Evolution of the World Economy: A New 2020 Update. *Maddison Project Database, version 2020.* www.rug.nl/ggdc/historicaldevelopment/maddison/publications/wp15.pdf.

Borger, J., & Rice, X. (2008). Zimbabwe's Neighbours Turn on Mugabe as Election Violence Spreads to New Areas. *The Guardian.* www.theguardian.com/world/2008/jun/19/zimbabwe1.

Börzel, T. A. (2015). The Noble West and the Dirty Rest? Western Democracy Promoters and Illiberal Regional Powers. *Democratization, 22*(3), 519–535. https://doi.org/10.1080/13510347.2014.1000312.

Börzel, T. A. (2016). Theorizing Regionalism: Cooperation, Integration, and Governance. In T. A. Börzel & T. Risse (Eds.), *The Oxford Handbook of Comparative Regionalism* (pp. 41–63). Oxford: Oxford University Press.

Börzel, T. A., & Risse, T. (2003). Conceptualizaing the Domestic Impact of Europe. In K. Featherstone & C. M. Radaelli (Eds.), *The Politics of Europeanization* (pp. 57–82). Oxford: Oxford University Press.

Börzel, T. A., & Risse, T. (2016a). *The Oxford Handbook of Comparative Regionalism.* Oxford: Oxford University Press.

Börzel, T. A., & Risse, T. (2016b). Introduction. In T. A. Börzel & T. Risse (Eds.), *The Oxford Handbook of Comparative Regionalism* (pp. 3–15). Oxford: Oxford University Press.

Börzel, T. A., & Risse, T. (2016c). Three Cheers for Comparative Regionalism. In T. A. Börzel & T. Risse (Eds.), *The Oxford Handbook of Comparative Politics* (pp. 621–648). Oxford: Oxford University Press.

Börzel, T. A., & van Hüllen, V. (2015). *Governance Transfer by Regional Organizations: Patching Together a Global Script*. Basingstoke: Palgrave Macmillan.

Börzel, T. A., & Zürn, M. (2021). Contestations of the Liberal International Order: From Liberal Multilateralism to Postnational Liberalism. *International Organization, 75*(2), 282–305. https://doi.org/10.1017/S0020818320000570.

Boutton, A. (2019). Coup-Proofing in the Shadow of Intervention: Alliances, Moral Hazard, and Violence in Authoritarian Regimes. *International Studies Quarterly, 63*(1), 43–57. https://doi.org/10.1093/isq/sqy056.

Brinks, D., & Coppedge, M. (2006). Diffusion Is No Illusion, Neighbor Emulation in the Third Wave of Democracy. *Comparative Political Studies, 39*(4), 463–489.

Brownlee, J. (2007a). *Authoritarianism in an Age of Democratization*. New York: Cambridge University Press. http://202.28.199.34/multim/3120423.pdf.

Brownlee, J. (2007b). *Authoritarianism in an Age of Democratization*. New York: Cambridge University Press.

Brownlee, J. (2012). *Democracy Prevention: The Politics of the U.S.–Egyptian Alliance*. Cambridge: Cambridge University Press.

Bruszt, L., & Palestini, S. (2016). Regional Development Governance. In T. A. Börzel & T. Risse (Eds.), *The Oxford Handbook of Comparative Regionalism* (pp. 374–404). Oxford: Oxford University Press.

Bueno de Mesquita, B., Smith, A., Randolph, S. M., & Morrow, J. D. (2003). *The Logic of Political Survival*. Cambridge, MA: MIT Press.

Burnell, P. (2000). *Democracy Assistance*. London: Frank Cass.

Bush, S. S., & Prather, L. (2018). Who's There? Election Observer Identity and the Local Credibility of Elections. *International Organization, 72*(3), 659–692. https://doi.org/10.1017/S0020818318000140.

Bush, S. S., & Prather, L. (2022). *Monitors and Meddlers: How Foreign Actors Influence Local Trust in Elections* (1st ed.). Cambridge: Cambridge University Press. https://doi.org/10.1017/9781009204262.

CABEI. (2014, May 5). CABEI to Finance Expansion of Nicaraguan National Police. www.bcie.org/en/news-and-media/news/article/cabei-to-finance-expansion-of-nicaraguan-national-police. Accessed November 27, 2023.

CABEI. (2020, March 23). CABEI and Nicaraguan Government Agree to Deobligate Police Loan. www.bcie.org/en/news-and-media/news/article/cabei-and-nicaraguan-government-agree-to-deobligate-police-loan. Accessed January 7, 2024.

CABEI. (2022, March 16). CABEI Inaugurates Modern Facilities in Nicaragua. www.bcie.org/en/news-and-media/news/article/bcie-inaugura-modernas-instalaciones-en-nicaragua. Accessed November 27, 2023.

Carothers, T. (2004). *Critical Mission: Essays on Democracy Promotion*. Washington, DC: Carnegie Endowment for International Peace.

Carroll, R. (2008, November 20). Fresh Violence Feared after Ortega Accused of Vote Rigging. *The Guardian*. www.theguardian.com/world/2008/nov/20/nicaragua-sandainista-daniel-ortega. Accessed November 27, 2023.

Carter Center. (2002). Carter Center Urges Zimbabweans to Vote. *News & Events*.

188 References

Cassani, A., & Tomini, L. (2020). Reversing Regimes and Concepts: From Democratization to Autocratization. *European Political Science, 19*(2), 272–287. https://doi.org/10.1057/s41304-018-0168-5.

Chamorro, C. F. (2016, April 14). The Right to Know about Albanisa. *El Confidencial.* https://confidencial.digital/english/the-right-to-know-about-albanisa. Accessed November 27, 2023.

Chaudhry, S. (2022). The Assault on Civil Society: Explaining State Crackdown on NGOs. *International Organization, 76*(3), 549–590. https://doi.org/10.1017/S0020818321000473.

Cheibub, J. A., Gandhi, J., & Vreeland, J. R. (2010). Democracy and Dictatorship Revisited. *Public choice, 143*(1/2), 67–101.

Cheibub, J. A., & Vreeland, J. R. (2011). Economic Development and Democratization. In N. J. Brown (Ed.), *The Dynamics of Democratization. Dictatorship, Development, and Diffusion* (pp. 145–182). Baltimore, MD: The Johns Hopkins University Press.

China Cables Exposes Chilling Details of Mass Detention in Xinjiang. (2019). International Consortium of Investigative Journalists. www.icij.org/investigations/china-cables/watch-china-cables-exposes-chilling-details-of-mass-detention-in-xinjiang. Accessed December 17, 2022.

China Daily. (2009, July 18). Xinjiang Riot Hits Regional Anti-Terror Nerve. *China Daily.* www.chinadaily.com.cn/china/2009-07/18/content_8445811.htm.

Choi, S.-W. (2021). Nationalism and Withdrawals from Intergovernmental Organizations: Connecting Theory and Data. *The Review of International Organizations, 17*, 205–215. https://doi.org/10.1007/s11558-021-09417-1.

Christie, S. (2011a, August 19). Killed Off by "Kings and Potentates." *Mail & Guardian.* https://advance-lexis-com.zu.idm.oclc.org/api/document?collection=news&id=urn:contentItem:54MV-RC91-JDV6-X18M-00000-00&context=1516831. Accessed May 12, 2024.

Christie, S. (2011b, October 6). The SADC Tribunal's Last Gasp. *Mail & Guardian.* https://mg.co.za/article/2011-06-10-the-sadc-tribunals-last-gasp. Accessed January 5, 2024.

Chulov, M., Finn, T., & Kamali, S. (2011, February 19). Bahrain Protesters Reclaim Pearl Roundabout in Central Manama. *The Guardian.* www.theguardian.com/world/2011/feb/19/bahrain-protesters-reclaim-city-centre-manama.

Clark, J. F. (2016). South Africa: Africa's Reluctant and Conflicted Regional Power. *Air and Space Power Journal: Africa and Francophonie, 7*(1), 30–47.

Clarke, Michael. (2010). Widening the Net: China's Anti-Terror Laws and Human Rights in the Xinjiang Uyghur Autonomous Region. *International Journal of Human Rights, 14*(4), 542–558. https://doi.org/10.1080/13642980802710855.

Clarke, Micheal. (2013). Ethnic Separatism in the People's Republic of China: History, Causes and Contemporary Challenges. *European Journal of East Asian Studies, 12,* 109–133.

Coe, B. (2015). Sovereignty Regimes and the Norm of Noninterference in the Global South: Regional and Temporal Variation. *Global Governance, 21*(2015), 275–298.

Collins, K. (2009). Economic and Security Regionalism among Patrimonial Authoritarian Regimes: The Case of Central Asia. *Europe-Asia Studies, 61*(2), 249–281. https://doi.org/10.1080/09668130802630854.

Colombo, S. (2012). The GCC and the Arab Spring: A Tale of Double Standards. *The International Spectator, 47*(4), 110–126. https://doi.org/10.1080/03932729.2012.733199.

Confidencial. (2021, July 7). The Lethal Blow to the Companies Owned by the "Family," Sanctioned by the US. *Confidencial.* https://confidencial.digital/english/the-lethal-blow-to-the-companies-owned-by-the-family-sanctioned-by-the-us. Accessed November 27, 2023.

Confidencial. (2023, December 22). Ortega Says Free Trade with China "Frees Us from Sanctions." *Confidencial.* https://confidencial.digital/english/ortega-says-free-trade-with-china-frees-us-from-sanctions. Accessed January 7, 2024.

Connectas. (2019). Petrofraud Investigation: The Chavista Continental Disaster with Venezuelan Money. *Connectas.* www.connectas.org/especiales/petrofraude/introduccion.html. Accessed November 28, 2023.

Constitución Política De La República De Nicaragua. Political Constitution of the Republic of Nicaragua (1987).

Cooley, A. (2012). *Great Games, Local Rules: The New Great Power Contest in Central Asia.* New York: Oxford University Press. https://doi.org/10.1093/acprof.

Cooley, A., & Heathershaw, J. (2017). *Dictators without Borders: Power and Money in Central Asia.* New Haven, CT: Yale University Press.

Copelovitch, M., & Pevehouse, J. C. W. (2019). International Organizations in a New Era of Populist Nationalism. *The Review of International Organizations*, 14(2), 169–186. https://doi.org/10.1007/s11558-019-09353-1.

Coppedge, M., Gerring, J., Altman, D., Bernhard, M., Fish, S., Hicken, A., et al. (2011). Conceptualizing and Measuring Democracy: A New Approach. *Perspectives on Politics*, 9(02), 247–267. https://doi.org/10.1017/S1537592711000880.

Coppedge, M., Gerring, J., Knutsen, C. H., Lindberg, S. I., Teorell, J., Altman, D., et al. (2020). V-Dem [Country–Year/Country–Date] Dataset v10. *Varieties of Democracy (V-Dem) Project.* https://doi.org/10.23696/vdemds20.

Coppedge, M., Gerring, J., Lindberg, S. I., Skaaning, S.-E., Teorell, J., Altman, D., et al. (2023). V-Dem Dataset v13. Varieties of Democracy (V-Dem) Project. www.v-dem.net/en/data/data-version-7-1.

Coppedge, M., Lindberg, S., Skaaning, S.-E., & Teorell, J. (2015). Measuring High Level Democratic Principles Using the V-Dem Data. *International Political Science Review*, 37(5), 580–593. https://doi.org/10.1177/0192512115622046.

Cordoba, J. (2009, June 26). Honduras Lurches Toward Crisis Over Election. *Wall Street Journal.* www.wsj.com/articles/SB124597369604957305. Accessed November 27, 2023.

Costa Buranelli, F. (2020). Authoritarianism as an Institution? The Case of Central Asia. *International Studies Quarterly*, 64(4), 1005–1016. https://doi.org/10.1093/isq/sqaa058.

Cottiero, C. (2023). Protection for Hire: Cooperation through Regional Organizations. *International Studies Quarterly*, 67(4).

Cottiero, C., & Haggard, S. (2023). Stabilizing Authoritarian Rule: The Role of International Organizations. *International Studies Quarterly*, 67(2), sqad031. https://doi.org/10.1093/isq/sqad031.

Council of the EU. (2021, August 11). Nicaragua: Declaration by the High Representative on behalf of the European Union. www.consilium.europa.eu/en/press/press-releases/2021/11/08/nicaragua-declaration-by-the-high-representative-on-behalf-of-the-european-union. Accessed November 27, 2023.

Cox, R. D. (1972). Regression Models and Life-Tables. *Journal of the Royal Statistical Society. Series B (Methodological)*, 34(2), 187–220.

Dahl, R. A. (1971). *Polyarchy. Participation and Opposition.* New Haven, CT: Yale University Press.

Debre, M. J. (2021). Legitimation, Regime Survival, and Shifting Alliances in the Arab League: Explaining Sanction Politics during the Arab Spring. *International Political Science Review*, 42(4), 516–530. https://doi.org/10.1177/0192512120937749.

Debre, M. J. (2023). Authoritarian Networks in Global Governance: How authoritarian Regimes Undermine Human Rights. Presented at the ECPR Joint Sessions of Workshops, Toulouse.

190 References

Debre, M. J., & Dijkstra, H. (2021a). COVID-19 and Policy Responses by International Organizations: Crisis of Liberal International Order or Window of Opportunity? *Global Policy*, *12*(4), 443–454. https://doi.org/10.1111/1758-5899.12975.

Debre, M. J., & Dijkstra, H. (2021b). Institutional Design for a Post-Liberal Order: Why Some International Organizations Live Longer Than Others. *European Journal of International Relations*, *27*(1), 311–339. https://doi.org/10.1177/1354066120962183.

Debre, M. J., & Flonk, D. (2022). Authoritarianism Gone Global: How Autocratic Coalitions Undermine Liberal International Norms. Presented at the International Studies Association Conference 2022, online.

Debre, M. J., & Morgenbesser, L. (2017). Out of the Shadows: Autocratic Regimes, Election Observation and Legitimation. *Contemporary Politics*, *23*(3), 328–347. https://doi.org/10.1080/13569775.2017.1304318.

Debre, M. J., & Sommerer, T. (2023). *Weathering the Storm? The Third Wave of Autocratization and International Organization Membership*. https://ucigcc.org/wp-content/uploads/2023/11/Debre-Sommerer-Working-Paper-11.21.23.pdf. Accessed January 21, 2024.

Delegation of Venezuela. (2019, October 7). Declaración De La Delegación De Venezuela A Nombre De Los Países De La Alianza Bolivariana Para Los Pueblos De Nuestra América (Alba-Tcp). https://hrcmeetings.ohchr.org/HRCSessions/HRCDocuments/30/SP/21941_40_3319f4c2_8efb_420f_a735_28fcef1afdb3.docx. Accessed July 1, 2024.

Dell'orto, G. (2023, November 16). Nicaragua's Exiled Clergy and Faithful in Miami Keep Up Struggle for Human Rights at Mass. *AP News*. https://apnews.com/article/nicaragua-catholic-priests-exile-ortega-miami-b401f7d0649135f45448034cc1a0e0da. Accessed November 27, 2023.

Diamond, L. (2002). Thinking about Hybrid Regimes. *Journal of Democracy*, *13*(2), 21–35.

Dingwerth, K., Witt, A., Lehmann, I., Reichel, E., Weise, T., Dingwerth, K., et al. (2019). *International Organizations under Pressure: Legitimating Global Governance in Challenging Times*. Oxford: Oxford University Press.

Donno, D. (2010). Who Is Punished? Regional Intergovernmental Organizations and the Enforcement of Democratic Norms. *International Organization*, *64*(4), 593–625. https://doi.org/10.1017/S0020818310000202.

Dowden, R. (2008). *Africa: Altered States, Ordinary Miracles*. New York: PublicAffairs.

Dowding, K., & Kimber, R. (1983). The Meaning and Use of "Political Stability." *European Journal of Political Research*, *11*(1983), 229–243. https://doi.org/10.1111/j.1475-6765.1983.tb00060.x.

Dreher, A., Fuchs, A., Parks, B. C., Strange, A. M., & Tierney, M. J. (2022). *Banking on Beijing: The Aims and Impacts of China's Overseas Development Program*. Cambridge: Cambridge University Press.

Dreher, A., Nunnenkamp, P., & Thiele, R. (2011). Are "New" Donors Different? Comparing the Allocation of Bilateral Aid between nonDAC and DAC Donor Countries. *World Development*, *39*(11), 1950–1968. https://doi.org/10.1016/j.worlddev.2011.07.024.

Drezner, D. W. (2011). Sanctions Sometimes Smart: Targeted Sanctions in Theory and Practice. *International Studies Review*, *13*(1), 96–108. https://doi.org/10.1111/j.1468-2486.2010.01001.x.

Dugger, C. W. (2008, May 18). Mugabe Opponent Cancels Return to Zimbabwe. *The New York Times*. www.nytimes.com/2008/05/18/world/africa/18zimbabwe.html. Accessed December 6, 2023.

Dugger, C. W., & Bearak, B. (2008, June 23). Mugabe Rival Quits Zimbabwe Runoff, Citing Attacks. *The New York Times*. www.nytimes.com/2008/06/23/world/africa/23zimbabwe.html.

Dukalskis, A. (2021). *Making the World Safe for Dictatorship*. Oxford: Oxford University Press.

References 191

Dukalskis, A., Furstenberg, S., Gorokhovskaia, Y., Heathershaw, J., Lemon, E., & Schenkkan, N. (2022). Transnational Repression: Data Advances, Comparisons, and Challenges. *Political Research Exchange*, *4*(1), 2104651. https://doi.org/10.1080/2474736X.2022.2104651.

Dukalskis, A., & Gerschewski, J. (2017). What Autocracies Say (And What Citizens Hear): Proposing Four Mechanisms of Autocratic Legitimation. *Contemporary Politics*, *23*(3), 251–268. https://doi.org/10.1080/13569775.2017.1304320.

DW. (2002, February 15). As Mugabe Wins, Critics Cry Foul. *DW*. www.dw.com/en/as-mugabe-wins-critics-cry-foul/a-472748. Accessed December 29, 2022.

Dzirutwe, M. (2016, August 8). Zimbabwe War Veterans Leaders Boycott Mugabe Heroes Speech. *Reuters*. www.reuters.com/article/idUSKCN10J11B. Accessed January 5, 2024.

Early, B. R. (2011). Unmasking the Black Knights: Sanctions Busters and Their Effects on the Success of Economic Sanctions. *Foreign Policy Analysis*, *7*(4), 381–402. https://doi.org/10.1111/j.1743-8594.2011.00143.x.

Easton, D. (1965). *A Systems Analysis of Political Life*. Chicago, IL: Wiley.

Ege, J., & Bauer, M. W. (2017). How Financial Resources Affect the Autonomy of International Public Administrations. *Global Policy*, *8*(August), 75–84. https://doi.org/10.1111/1758-5899.12451.

Eilstrup-Sangiovanni, M., & Hofmann, S. C. (2019). Of the Contemporary Global Order, Crisis, and Change. *Journal of European Public Policy*, *27*(7), 1077–1089. https://doi.org/10.1080/13501763.2019.1678665.

EISA. (2002). Zimbabwe: Excerpts from 2002 African Observer Mission Reports. www.eisa.org/wep/zim2002om1.htm. Accessed December 29, 2022.

Engel, U., & Mattheis, F. (2021). *Finances of Regional Organisations in the Global South: Follow the Money*. London: Routledge.

Escribà-Folch, A. (2013). Repression, Political Threats, and Survival under Autocracy. *International Political Science Review*, *34*(5), 543–560. https://doi.org/10.1177/0192512113488259.

Escribà-Folch, A., & Wright, J. (2010). Dealing with Tyranny: International Sanctions and the Survival of Authoritarian Rulers. *International Studies Quarterly*, *54*(2), 335–359. https://doi.org/10.1111/j.1468-2478.2010.00590.x.

EU Election Observation Mission. (2006). *Final Report: Presidential and Parliamentary Elections Nicaragua 2006*. EU Election Observation Mission. www.eods.eu/library/FR%20NICARAGUA%202006_en.pdf. Accessed July 12, 2024.

European Commission. (2023, March 1). Global Gateway. https://commission.europa.eu/strategy-and-policy/priorities-2019-2024/stronger-europe-world/global-gateway_de. Accessed January 21, 2024.

European Parliament. European Parliament Resolution of 26 November 2009 on Nicaragua. Pub. L. No. P7_TA(2009)0103 (2009). www.europarl.europa.eu/doceo/document/TA-7-2009-0103_EN.html. Accessed January 7, 2024.

European Union Election Observation Mission Nicaragua. (2011). *Final Report General Elections and Parlacen Elections 2011*. www.eods.eu/library/FR%20NICARAGUA%2022.02.2012_en.pdf. Accessed November 27, 2023.

Facon, I. (2013). Moscow's Global Foreign and Security Strategy: Does the Shanghai Cooperation Organization Meet Russian Interests? *Asian Survey*, *53*(3), 461–483. https://doi.org/10.1525/as.2013.53.3.461.

Farah, D., & Yates, C. (2019). *Maduro's Last Stand: Venezuela's Survival Through the Bolivarian Joint Criminal Enterprise*. www.ibiconsultants.net/_upload/mediaandpublications/document/maduros-last-stand.pdf. Accessed December 31, 2022.

192 References

Fawn, R. (2006). Battle over the Box: International Election Observation Missions, Political Competition and Retrenchment in the Post-Soviet Space. *International Affairs, 82*(6), 1133–1153. https://doi.org/10.1111/j.1468-2346.2006.00592.x.

Fawn, R. (2013). *International Organizations and Internal Conditionality: Making Norms Matter*. Basingstoke: Palgrave Macmillan.

Fearon, J. D. (1997). Signaling Foreign Policy Interests. *Journal of Conflict Resolution, 41*(1), 68–90. https://doi.org/10.1177/0022002797041001004.

Fearon, J. D. (1998). Domestic Politics, Foreign Policy, and Theories of International Relations. *Annual Review of Political Science, 1*, 289–313.

Ferguson, N., Zakaria, F., & Griffiths, R. (2017). *Is This the End of the Liberal International Order? Niall Ferguson vs. Fareed Zakaria*. Toronto: House of Anansi Press.

Ferry, L. L., Hafner-Burton, E. M., & Schneider, C. J. (2020). Catch Me If You Care: International Development Organizations and National Corruption. *Review of International Organizations, 15*(4), 767–792. https://doi.org/10.1007/s11558-019-09371-z.

Fishman, R. M. (1990). Rethinking State and Regime: Southern Europe's Transition to Democracy. *World Politics, 42*(03), 422–440. https://doi.org/10.2307/2010418.

Flonk, D. (2021). Emerging Illiberal Norms: Russia and China as Promoters of Internet Content Control. *International Affairs, 97*(6), 1925–1944. https://doi.org/10.1093/ia/iiab146.

Flonk, D., Jachtenfuchs, M., & Obendiek, A. S. (2020). Authority Conflicts in Internet Governance: Liberals vs. Sovereigntists? *Global Constitutionalism, 9*(2), 364–386. https://doi.org/10.1017/S2045381720000167.

France 24. (2016, June 9). How the Bahraini Monarchy Crushed the Country's Arab Spring. https://observers.france24.com/en/20160906-bahrain-monarchy-arab-spring-repression-revolution. Accessed October 2, 2019.

France 24. (2017a, November 15). Zimbabwe Army "Coup" Weakens Mugabe's Power. www.france24.com/en/20171115-explosions-heard-zimbabwe-capital-harare-coup-mugabe. Accessed January 5, 2024.

France 24. (2017b, November 18). Thousands of Zimbabweans Rally for Mugabe's Resignation. www.france24.com/en/20171118-zimbabwe-robert-mugabe-protests-army-house-arrest-grace-military. Accessed January 5, 2024.

Freedom House. (2021). *Zimbabwe: Freedom in the World Country Report 2020* (Freedom in the World). https://freedomhouse.org/country/zimbabwe/freedom-world/2021. Accessed May 12, 2024.

Freedom House. (2023). *Nicaragua: Freedom in the World 2023 Country Report* (Freedom in the World). https://freedomhouse.org/country/nicaragua/freedom-world/2023. Accessed November 27, 2023.

Fukuyama, F. (1989). The End of History? *The National Interest, 16*, 3–18.

Galbreath, D. J. (2007). *The Organization for Security and Co-operation in Europe (OSCE)*. London: Routledge. www.routledge.com/The-Organization-for-Security-and-Co-operation-in-Europe-OSCE/Galbreath/p/book/9780415407649. Accessed May 9, 2021.

Gandhi, J. (2008). *Political Institutions under Dictatorship*. Cambridge: Cambridge University Press.

Gandhi, J., & Przeworski, A. (2006). Cooperation, Cooptation, and Rebellion under Dictatorships. *Economics and Politics, 18*, 1–26.

Gandhi, J., & Przeworski, A. (2007). Authoritarian Institutions and the Survival of Autocrats. *Comparative Politics, 11*, 1279–1301.

Gandhi, J., & Reuter, O. J. (2013). The Incentives for Pre-Electoral Coalitions in Non-Democratic Elections. *Democratization, 20*(1), 137–159. https://doi.org/10.1080/13510347.2013.738865.

References 193

Gasiorowski, M. J. (1995). Economic Crisis and Political Regime Change: An Event History Analysis. *The American Political Science Review, 89*(4), 882–897. https://doi.org/10.2307/2082515.

Gat, A. (2007). The Return of Authoritarian Great Powers. *Foreign Affairs, 86*(4), 59–69.

Gawrich, A. (2015). Too Little, Too Late? Governance Transfer and the Eastern Enlargement of the Council of Europe. In T. A. Börzel & V. van Hüllen (Eds.), *Governance Transfer by Regional Organizations: Patching Together a Global Script* (pp. 211–226). London: Palgrave Macmillan UK. https://doi.org/10.1057/9781137385642_12.

GCC. (1981). *Charter of the Gulf Cooperation Council (GCC)*. Abu Dhabi City, United Arab Emirates.

Geddes, B. (2003). *Paradigms and Sand Castles: Theory Building and Research Design in Comparative Politics.* Ann Arbor, MI: University of Michigan Press.

Geddes, B., Wright, J., & Frantz, E. (2014). Autocratic Breakdown and Regime Transitions: A New Data Set. *Perspectives on Politics, 12*(02), 313–331. https://doi.org/10.1017/S1537592714000851.

Geddes, B., Wright, J., & Frantz, E. (2018). *How Dictatorships Work: Power, Personalization, and Collapse.* Cambridge: Cambridge University Press. https://doi.org/10.1017/9781316336182.

Gerring, J. (2007). *Case Study Research: Principles and Practices.* Cambridge: Cambridge University Press. https://books.google.de/books/about/Case_Study_Research.html?id=xECY0nnkTvMC&redir_esc=y.

Gerschewski, J. (2013). The Three Pillars of Stability: Legitimation, Repression, and Co-Optation in Autocratic Regimes. *Democratization, 20*(1), 13–38. https://doi.org/10.1080/13510347.2013.738860.

Getachew, A. (2019). *Worldmaking after Empire: The Rise and Fall of Self-Determination.* Princeton, NJ: Princeton University Press.

Gibney, J. (2014, January 30). Nicaragua's Revolution Heads toward Dictatorship. *Bloomberg.com.* www.bloomberg.com/view/articles/2014-01-30/nicaragua-s-revolution-heads-toward-dictatorship-. Accessed November 27, 2023.

Gilpin, R. (1981). *War and Change in World Politics.* Cambridge: Cambridge University Press. https://doi.org/10.1017/CBO9780511664267.

Gilpin, R. (1987). *The Political Economic of International Relations.* Princeton, NJ: Princeton University Press.

Ginsburg, T. (2020). Authoritarian International Law? *American Journal of International Law, 114*(2), 221–260. https://doi.org/10.1017/ajil.2020.3.

Girvan, N. (2011). ALBA, Petrocaribe, and Caricom: Issues in a New Dynamic. In R. S. Clem & A. P. Maingot (Eds.), *Venezuela's Petro-Diplomacy: Hugo Chávez's Foreign Policy* (pp. 116–134). Gainesville, FL: University Press of Florida. https://doi.org/10.5744/florida/9780813035307.003.0009.

Glasius, M., Schalk, J., & De Lange, M. (2020). Illiberal Norm Diffusion: How Do Governments Learn to Restrict Nongovernmental Organizations? *International Studies Quarterly, 64*(2), 453–468. https://doi.org/10.1093/isq/sqaa019.

Gleditsch, K. S., & Ward, M. D. (2006). Diffusion and the International Context of Democratization. *International Organization, 60*(04), 911–933. https://doi.org/10.1017/S0020818306060309.

Goddard, S. E., Krebs, R. R., Kreuder-Sonnen, C., & Rittberger, B. (2024). Contestation in a World of Liberal Orders. *Global Studies Quarterly, 4*(2), ksae026. https://doi.org/10.1093/isagsq/ksae026.

194   References

Goetz, K. H., & Patz, R. (2017). Resourcing International Organizations: Resource Diversification, Organizational Differentiation, and Administrative Governance. *Global Policy*, *8*(August), 5–14. https://doi.org/10.1111/1758-5899.12468.

Gohdes, A. R. (2020). Repression Technology: Internet Accessibility and State Violence. *American Journal of Political Science*, *64*(3), 488–503. https://doi.org/10.1111/ajps.12509.

Goldstein, J. (1996). International Law and Domestic Institutions: Reconciling North American "Unfair" Trade Laws. *International Organization*, *50*(4), 541–564.

Grauvogel, J., & von Soest, C. (2014). Claims to Legitimacy Count: Why Sanctions Fail to Instigate Democratisation in Authoritarian Regimes. *European Journal of Political Research*, *53*(4), 635–653. https://doi.org/10.1111/1475-6765.12065.

Gray, J. (2018). Life, Death, or Zombie? The Vitality of International Organizations. *International Studies Quarterly*, *62*(1), 1–13. https://doi.org/10.1093/isq/sqx086.

Gray, J., & Slapin, J. B. (2012). How Effective Are Preferential Trade Agreements? Ask the Experts. *Review of International Organizations*, *7*, 309–333. http://link.springer.com/article/10.1007%2Fs11558-011-9138-1.

Greenhill, B. (2015). *Transmitting Rights: International Organizations and the Diffusion of Human Rights Practices*. New York: Oxford University Press.

Grigorescu, A. (2007). Transparency of Intergovernmental Organizations: The Roles of Member States, International Bureaucracies and Nongovernmental Organizations. *International Studies Quarterly*, *51*(3), 625–648.

Grigorescu, A. (2015). *Democratic Intergovernmental Organizations? Normative Pressure and Decision-Making Rules*. Cambridge: Cambridge University Press.

Grzymala-Busse, A. (2019). Introduction. *Polity*, *51*(4). https://doi.org/10.1086/705292.

Gulf News. (2011, September 17). Saudi Arabia Ratifies GCC Security Treaty: Pact Aims to Boost Cooperation to Achieve Collective Security. *Gulf News (United Arab Emirates)*.

Gulf News. (2016, July 27). Kuwaiti MP Gets 11 Years in Jail for Offending Saudi Arabia. Dashti Was Also Sentenced to Three More Years for Comments against Bahrain. *Gulf News (United Arab Emirates)*.

Gulf News (United Arab Emirates). (2011, June 16). GCC Condemns Iran's Interference in Affairs of Its Member States. https://advance.lexis.com/api/permalink/c297af7d-2ee1-4dcb-a9b9-1ac1e42d3ef7/?context=1516831. Accessed August 4, 2019.

Haber, S., & Menaldo, V. (2011). Do Natural Resources Fuel Authoritarianism? A Preappraisal of the Resource Curse. *American Political Science Review*, *105*(1), 1–26. https://doi.org/10.1017/S0003055410000584.

Hackenesch, C., & Bader, J. (2020). The Struggle for Minds and Influence: The Chinese Communist Party's Global Outreach. *International Studies Quarterly*, *64*(3), 723–733. https://doi.org/10.1093/isq/sqaa028.

Hadenius, A., & Teorell, Jan. (2007). Pathways from Authoritarianism. *Journal of Democracy*, *18*(1), 143–157. https://doi.org/10.1353/jod.2007.0009.

Hafner-Burton, E. M. (2008). Sticks and Stones: Naming and Shaming the Human Rights Enforcement Problem. *International Organization*, *62*(4), 689–716. https://doi.org/10.1017/S0020818308080247.

Hafner-Burton, E. M. (2009). *Forced to Be Good: Why Trade Agreements Boost Human Rights* (1st ed.). Ithaca, NY: Cornell University Press. www.jstor.org/stable/10.7591/j.ctt7zdx1. Accessed April 3, 2021.

Hafner-Burton, E. M., Mansfield, E. D., & Pevehouse, J. C. W. (2015). Human Rights Institutions, Sovereignty Costs and Democratization. *British Journal of Political Science*, *45*(1), 1–27. https://doi.org/10.1017/S0007123413000240.

References 195

Hafner-Burton, E. M., & Schneider, C. J. (2019). The Dark Side of Cooperation: International Organizations and Member Corruption. *International Studies Quarterly*, *63*(4), 1108–1121. https://doi.org/10.1093/isq/sqz064.

Haftel, Y. Z. (2012). *Regional Economic Institutions and Conflict Mitigation*. Ann Arbor, MI: University of Michigan Press. https://doi.org/10.3998/mpub.4314887.

Haftel, Y. Z., & Hofmann, S. C. (2017). Institutional Authority and Security Cooperation within Regional Economic Organizations. *Journal of Peace Research*, *54*(4), 484–498. https://doi.org/10.1177/0022343316675908.

Hartmann, C. (2016). Sub-Saharan Africa. In T. A. Börzel & T. Risse (Eds.), *The Oxford Handbook of Comparative Regionalism* (pp. 271–294). Oxford: Oxford University Press.

Hawkins, A. (2023, April 20). Explainer: China's covert overseas "police stations." *The Guardian*. www.theguardian.com/world/2023/apr/20/explainer-chinas-covert-overseas-police-stations. Accessed January 21, 2024.

Hawkins, D. G., Lake, D. A., Nielson, D. L., & Tierney, M. J. (Eds.) (2006). *Delegation and Agency in International Organizations*. Cambridge: Cambridge University Press. https://doi.org/10.1017/CBO9780511491368.

Heldt, E. (2017). Regaining Control of Errant Agents? Agency Slack at the European Commission and the World Health Organization. *Cooperation and Conflict*, *52*(4), 469–484. https://doi.org/10.1177/0010836717703673.

Hellquist, E. (2015). Interpreting Sanctions in Africa and Southeast Asia. *International Relations*, *29*(3), 319–333. https://doi.org/10.1177/0047117815600934.

Herb, M. (1999). *All in the Family: Absolutism, Revolution, and Democracy in Middle Eastern Monarchies*. Albany, NY: SUNY Press.

Herbst, J. (2007). Crafting Regional Cooperation in Africa. In A. Acharya & A. I. Johnston (Eds.), *Crafting Cooperation: Regional Institutions in Comparative Perspective* (pp. 129–180). Cambridge: Cambridge University Press.

Heydemann, S. (2007). Upgrading Authoritarianism in the Arab World (13). www.brookings.edu/wp-content/uploads/2016/06/10arabworld.pdf.

Heydemann, S., & Leenders, R. (2011). Authoritarian Learning and Authoritarian Resilience: Regime Responses to the "Arab Awakening." *Globalizations*, *8*(5), 647–653. https://doi.org/10.1080/14747731.2011.621274.

Hinnebusch, R. (2012). Syria: From "Authoritarian Upgrading" to Revolution? *International Affairs*, *88*(July 2000), 95–113. https://doi.org/10.1111/j.1468-2346.2012.01059.x.

Hobson, C., & Kurki, M. (2012). *The Conceptual Politics of Democracy Promotion*. New York: Routledge.

Hodzi, O., Hartwell, L., & de Jager, N. (2012). "Unconditional Aid": Assessing the Impact of China's Development Assistance to Zimbabwe. *South African Journal of International Affairs*, *19*(1), 79–103. https://doi.org/10.1080/10220461.2012.670435.

Hofmann, S. C., Andreska, A., Burai, E., & Uribe, J. (2023). Porous Organizational Boundaries and Associated States: Introducing Memberness in International Organizations. *European Journal of International Relations*, *29*(4), 929–959. https://doi.org/10.1177/13540661231163988.

Hohlstein, F. (2022). *Regional Organizations and Their Responses to Coups: Measures, Motives and Aims*. Bristol: Bristol University Press. https://bristoluniversitypressdigital.com/display/book/9781529224108/9781529224108.xml. Accessed December 13, 2022.

Holthaus, L. (2010). *Regimelegitimität und regionale Kooperation im Golf-Kooperationsrat (Gulf Cooperation Council)*. New York: Peter Lang.

Honduran News. (2008, July 31). Honduras Joins ALBA. www.hondurasnews.com/honduras-joins-alba. Accessed November 27, 2023.

196 References

Hooghe, L., Lenz, T., & Marks, G. (2019). *A Theory of International Organization*. Oxford: Oxford University Press.

Hooghe, L., Marks, G., Lenz, T., Bezuijen, J., Ceka, B., & Derderyan, S. (2017). *Measuring International Authority, Volume III*. Oxford: Oxford University Press.

HRIC. (2011a). *Counter-Terrorism and Human Rights: The Impact of the Shanghai Cooperation Organization*. Hong Kong: Human Rights in China (HRIC).

HRIC. (2011b). *Counter-Terrorism and Human Rights: The Impact of the Shanghai Cooperation Organization*. Hong Kong: Human Rights in China (HRIC).

HRW. (2021, March 11). China's "Slanders and Smears" at UN Human Rights Council. *Human Rights Watch*. www.hrw.org/news/2021/03/11/chinas-slanders-and-smears-un-human-rights-council. Accessed July 8, 2022.

Hufbauer, G. C., Schott, J., Elliott, K. A., & Oegg, B. (2009). *Economic Sanctions Reconsidered* (3rd ed.). Washington, DC: Peterson Institute for International Economics.

Hulse, M., & van der Vleuten, A. (2015). Agent Run Amuck: The SADC Tribunal and Governance Transfer Rollback. In T. A. Börzel & V. van Hüllen (Eds.), *Governance Transfer by Regional Organizations: Patching Together a Global Script* (pp. 89–106). Basingstoke: Palgrave Macmillan.

Human Rights Watch. (2002a). *Fast Track Land Reform in Zimbabwe*. www.hrw.org/reports/2002/zimbabwe/ZimLand0302-03.htm#P425_104154. Accessed December 29, 2022.

Human Rights Watch. (2002b). *Organized Violence by State Agents and Ruling Party Supporters*. www.hrw.org/legacy/backgrounder/africa/zimbabwe/Zim3-05.htm. Accessed December 29, 2022.

Human Rights Watch. (2008a). *All Over Again: Human Rights Abuses and Flawed Electoral Conditions in Zimbabwe's Coming General Elections*. Report number: Human Rights Watch Report, Vol.20, No.2(A). doi: 10.1163/2210-7975_HRD-2156-0567.

Human Rights Watch. (2008b, April 19). Zimbabwe: ZANU-PF Sets Up "Torture Camps." Opposition Voters Tell of Beatings, Intimidation. http://pantheon.hrw.org/legacy/english/docs/2008/04/19/zimbab18604.htm. Accessed December 16, 2017.

Human Rights Watch. (2009a, October 15). China: Xinjiang Trials Deny Justice: Proceedings Failed Minimum Fair Trial Standards. www.hrw.org/news/2009/10/15/china-xinjiang-trials-deny-justice. Accessed December 16, 2017.

Human Rights Watch. (2009b, October 21). China: Detainees "Disappeared" after Xinjiang Protests: Chinese Government Should Account for Every Detainee. www.hrw.org/news/2009/10/21/china-detainees-disappeared-after-xinjiang-protests. Accessed December 16, 2017.

Human Rights Watch. (2014, April 26). GCC: Joint Security Agreement Imperils Rights: Vaguely Worded Provisions Endanger Free Expression, Privacy. www.hrw.org/news/2014/04/26/gcc-joint-security-agreement-imperils-rights.

Human Rights Watch. (2017). The Costs of International Advocacy: China's Interference in United Nations Human Rights Mechanisms. www.hrw.org/report/2017/09/05/costs-international-advocacy/chinas-interference-united-nations-human-rights. Accessed July 4, 2022.

Huntington, S. P. (1993). *The Third Wave: Democratization in the Late Twentieth Century*. Norman, OK: University of Oklahoma Press.

Huntington, S. P. (2006). *Political Order in Changing Societies*. New Haven, CT: Yale University Press.

Hurwitz, L. (1973). Contemporary Approaches to Political Stability. *Comparative Politics*, 5(3), 449–463.

Hyde, S. D. (2011). *The Pseudo-Democrat's Dilemma: Why Election Monitoring Became an International Norm*. Ithaca, NY: Cornell University Press. https://doi.org/10.7591/cornell/9780801449666.001.0001.

Hyde, S. D., & Marinov, N. (2014). Information and Self-Enforcing Democracy: The Role of International Election Observation. *International Organization*, *68*(2), 329–359. https://doi.org/10.1017/S0020818313000465.

ICG. (2005). *Bahrain's Sectarian Challenge*. Amman: International Crisis Group.

ICG. (2008). *Ending Zimbabwe's Nightmare: A Possible Way Forward*. Pretoria: International Crisis Group.

ICG. (2011). *Popular Protest in North Africa and the Middle East (VIII): Bahrain's Rocky Road to Reform*. Manama: International Crisis Group.

IJRC. (2012, November 20). Understanding the IACHR Reform Process. *International Justice Resource Center*. https://ijrcenter.org/2012/11/20/iachr-reform-process. Accessed November 27, 2023.

IJRC. (2013, March 25). OAS Concludes Formal Inter-American Human Rights "Strengthening" Process, but Dialogue Continues on Contentious Reforms. *International Justice Resource Center*. https://ijrcenter.org/2013/03/24/oas-concludes-formal-inter-american-human-rights-strengthening-process-but-dialogue-continues-on-contentious-reforms. Accessed January 7, 2024.

Ikenberry, G. J. (2001). *After Victory: Institutions, Strategic Restraint, and the Rebuilding of Order after Major Wars*. Princeton, NJ: Princeton University Press.

Ikenberry, G. J. (2011). *Liberal Leviathan: The Origins, Crisis, and Transformation of the American World Order*. Princeton, NJ: Princeton University Press.

Ikenberry, G. J. (2018). The End of Liberal International Order? *International Affairs*, *94*(1), 7–23. https://doi.org/10.1093/ia/iix241.

Ikenberry, G. J. (2020). *A World Safe for Democracy: Liberal Internationalism and the Crises of Global Order*. New Haven, CT: Yale University Press.

Inboden, R. S. (2019). *Authoritarian States: Blocking Civil Society Participation in the United Nations*. The University of Texas at Austin: Robert Strauss Center. https://strausscenter.org/wp-content/uploads/strauss/18-19/RSInboden_AuthoritarianStates.pdf. Accessed September 6, 2021.

Inboden, R. S. (2021). China at the UN: Choking Civil Society. *Journal of Democracy*, *32*(3), 124–135.

Inboden, R. S. (2022). *China and the International Human Rights Regime*. Cambridge: Cambridge University Press.

Inter-American Commission on Human Rights. (2023). Statistics of the Inter-American Commission on Human Rights: Petitions, Cases, and Precautionary Measures. www.oas.org/en/iachr/multimedia/statistics/statistics.html. Accessed November 27, 2023.

International Crisis Group. (2008). *Negotiating Zimbabwe's Transition*. Pretoria: International Crisis Group.

International Crisis Group. (2019). *Fight and Flight: Tackling the Roots of Honduras' Emergency* (No. 77). International Crisis Group. www.crisisgroup.org/latin-america-caribbean/central-america/honduras/077-fight-and-flight-tackling-roots-honduras-emergency. Accessed January 6, 2024.

International Crisis Group. (2021). *Handling the Risks of Honduras' High-Stakes Poll* (No. 45). International Crisis Group. www.crisisgroup.org/latin-america-caribbean/central-america/honduras/b045-handling-risks-honduras-high-stakes-poll. Accessed January 6, 2024.

Jardine, B., Lemon, E., & Hall, N. (2021). *No Space Left to Run: China's Transnational Repression of Uyghurs*. Uyghur Human Rights Project and Oxus Society for Central Asian

198 References

Affairs. https://uhrp.org/report/no-space-left-to-run-chinas-transnational-repression-of-uyghurs. Accessed August 1, 2023.

Jetschke, A., & Katada, S. N. (2016). Asia. In T. A. & Börzel (Ed.), *The Oxford Handbook of Comparative Regionalism* (pp. 225–248). Oxford: Oxford University Press.

Jetschke, A., Theiner, P., Marggraf, C., & Münch, S. (2016). *The Comparative Regional Organizations Project: Generating a New Dataset*. Heidelberg: German, Swiss and Austrian Political Science Association.

Josua, M., & Edel, M. (2014). To Repress or Not to Repress: Regime Survival Strategies in the Arab Spring. *Terrorism and Political Violence*, 27(2), 289–309. https://doi.org/10.1080/09546553.2013.806911.

Kagan, R. (2008). *The Return of History and the End of Dreams*. Washington, DC: Carnegie Endowment for International Peace. http://carnegieendowment.org/2008/04/30/return-of-history-and-end-of-dreams-pub-20089.

Kagan, R. (2012). *The World America Made* (1st ed.). New York: Alfred A. Knopf.

Kan, S. A. (2010). *U.S.–China Counterterrorism Cooperation: Issues for U.S. Policy*. Washington, DC: Congressional Research Service. https://fas.org/sgp/crs/terror/RL33001.pdf.

Kararach, G. (2014). *Development Policy in Africa: Mastering the Future?* Basingstoke: Palgrave Macmillan.

Katzman, K. (2017). *Bahrain: Reform, Security, and U.S. Policy*. Washington, DC: Congressional Research Service.

Kelemen, R. D. (2020). The European Union's Authoritarian Equilibrium. *Journal of European Public Policy*, 27(3), 481–499. https://doi.org/10.1080/13501763.2020.1712455.

Kelley, J. G. (2004). *Ethnic Politics in Europe: The Power of Norms and Incentives*. Princeton, NJ: Princeton University Press.

Kelley, J. G. (2009). D-Minus Elections: The Politics and Norms of International Election Observation. *International Organization*, 63(4), 765–765. https://doi.org/10.1017/S0020818309990117.

Kelley, J. G. (2012). *Monitoring Democracy: When International Election Observation Works, and Why It Often Fails*. Princeton, NJ: Princeton University Press.

Kellogg, P. (2007). Regional Integration in Latin America: Dawn of an Alternative to Neoliberalism? *New Political Science*, 29(2), 187–209. https://doi.org/10.1080/07393140701431888.

Keohane, R. O. (1984). *After Hegemony: Cooperation and Discord in the World Political Economy*. Princeton, NJ: Princeton University Press.

Khampepe, S., & Moseneke, D. (2002). *Report on the 2002 Presidential Elections of Zimbabwe*. www.veritaszim.net/sites/veritas_d/files/Khampepe%20Report%20on%202002%20Presidential%20Election%20in%20Zimbabwe.pdf. Accessed January 4, 2024.

Kirchner, E. Joseph, & Dominguez, R. (2011). *The Security Governance of Regional Organizations*. London: Routledge.

Knecht, S., & Debre, M. J. (2018). Die "digitale IO": Chancen und Risiken von Online-Daten für die Forschung zu Internationalen Organisationen. *Zeitschrift für Internationale Beziehungen (ZIB)*, 25(1), 175–188.

Kneuer, M., Demmelhuber, T., Peresson, R., & Zumbrägel, T. (2018). Playing the Regional Card: Why and How Authoritarian Gravity Centres Exploit Regional Organisations. *Third World Quarterly*, 40(3), 451–470. https://doi.org/10.1080/01436597.2018.1474713.

Köllner, P. (2008). Autoritäre Regime: Ein Überblick über die jüngere Literatur. *Zeitschrift für Vergleichende Politikwissenschaft*, 2(2), 351–366. https://doi.org/10.1007/s12286-008-0013-2.

Kono, D. Y., & Montinola, G. R. (2013). The Uses and Abuses of Foreign Aid: Development Aid and Military Spending. *Political Research Quarterly*, 66(3), 615–629. https://doi.org/10.1177/1065912912456097.

Korany, B. (1986). Political Petrolism and Contemporary Arab Politics 1967–1983. *Journal of Asian and African Studies, 21*(2), 66–80.

Koremenos, B., Lipson, C., & Snidal, D. (2001). The Rational Design of International Institutions. *International Organization, 55*(4), 761–799.

Korolczuk, E., & Graff, A. (2018). Gender as "Ebola from Brussels": The Anticolonial Frame and the Rise of Illiberal Populism. *Signs: Journal of Women in Culture and Society, 43*(4), 797–821. https://doi.org/10.1086/696691.

Kragh, M. (2022, April 21). Ukraine as Putin's Ideological Project. *Stockholm Centre for Eastern European Studies.* www.ui.se/globalassets/ui.se-eng/publications/sceeus/ukraine-as-putins-ideological-project.pdf.

Krastev, I. (2012). European Disintegration? A Fraying Union. *Journal of Democracy, 23*(4), 1–16.

KUNA. (2011). GCC Interior Meeting Begins, Kuwait Warns of External Dangers. www.kuna.net.kw/ArticlePrintPage.aspx?id=2207267&language=en. Accessed December 6, 2015.

Kurmanaev, A., & Trigo, M. S. (2020, June 7). A Bitter Election: Accusations of Fraud—And Now Second Thoughts. *The New York Times.* www.nytimes.com/2020/06/07/world/americas/bolivia-election-evo-morales.html. Accessed January 6, 2024.

Lacey, M. (2009, July 1). Leader's Ouster Not a Coup, Says the Honduran Military. *The New York Times.* www.nytimes.com/2009/07/02/world/americas/02coup.html. Accessed November 27, 2023.

Laruelle, M. (2008). *Russian Eurasianism: An Ideology of Empire.* Washington, DC: Woodrow Wilson Center Press. www.amazon.de/Russian-Eurasianism-Ideology-Empire-Woodrow/dp/080189073X.

Laurie, C. (2017). *The Land Reform Deception: Political Opportunism in Zimbabwe's Land Seizure Era.* Oxford: Oxford University Press.

Legrenzi, M. (2011). *GCC and the International Relations of the Gulf: Diplomacy, Security and Economy Coordination in a Changing Middle East.* New York: I.B. Tauris.

Lemon, E. (2019). Weaponizing Interpol. *Journal of Democracy, 30*(2), 15–29. https://doi.org/10.1353/jod.2019.0019.

Lemon, E., & Antonov, O. (2020). Authoritarian Legal Harmonization in the Post-Soviet Space. *Democratization, 27*(7), 1221–1239. https://doi.org/10.1080/13510347.2020.1778671.

Lenz, T., Bezuijen, J., Hooghe, L., & Marks, G. (2015). Patterns of International Organization: Task-Specific vs. General Purpose. In E. da Conceicao-Heldt, M. Koch, & A. Liese (Eds.), *Internationale Organisationen. Politische Vierteljahresschrift, Sonderheft 49* (pp. 131–155). Baden-Baden: Nomos.

Lerch, J., Schofer, E., Frank, D. J., Longhofer, W., Ramirez, F. O., Wotipka, M., & Valesco, K. (2022). Women's Participation and Challenges to the Liberal Script: A Global Perspective. *International Sociology, 37*(3). https://journals.sagepub.com/doi/full/10.1177/02685809211060911. Accessed March 30, 2023.

Levitsky, S., & Way, L. A. (2002). The Rise of Competitive Authoritarianism. *Journal of Democracy, 13*(2), 51–65. https://doi.org/10.1353/jod.2002.0026.

Levitsky, S., & Way, L. A. (2006). Linkage versus Leverage. Rethinking the International Dimension of Regime Change. *Comparative Politics, 38*(4), 379–400. https://doi.org/10.2307/20434008.

Levitsky, S., & Way, L. A. (2010). *Competitive Authoritarianism: Hybrid Regimes after the Cold War.* Cambridge: Cambridge University Press.

Levitsky, S., & Way, L. A. (2013). The Durability of Revolutionary Regimes. *Journal of Democracy, 24*(3), 5–17. https://doi.org/10.1353/jod.2013.0043.

200 References

Libman, A., & Obydenkova, A. (2014). International Trade as a Limiting Factor in Democratization: an Analysis of Subnational Regions in Post-Communist Russia. *Studies in Comparative International Development*, *49*(2), 168–196. https://doi.org/10.1007/s12116-013-9130-2.

Libman, A., & Obydenkova, A. V. (2018). Understanding Authoritarian Regionalism. *Journal of Democracy*, *29*(4), 151–165. https://doi.org/10.1353/jod.2018.0070.

Liboreiro, J. (2023, December 13). Hungary Gets €10 Billion in Frozen EU Funds amid Orbán's Threats. *euronews*. www.euronews.com/my-europe/2023/12/13/brussels-releases-10-billion-in-frozen-eu-funds-for-hungary-amid-orbans-threats. Accessed January 21, 2024.

Lieberman, E. S. (2005). Nested Analysis as a Mixed-Method Strategy for Comparative Research. *American Political Science Review*, *99*(03), 435–452. https://doi.org/10.1017/S0003055405051762.

Linz, J. J. (2000). *Totalitarian and Authoritarian Regimes*. Boulder, CO: Lynne Rienner Publishers.

Lipps, J., & Jacob, M. S. (2022). Undermining Liberal International Organizations from Within: Evidence from the Parliamentary Assembly of the Council of Europe. University of California Institute on Global Conflict and Cooperation. https://ucigcc.org/wp-content/uploads/2022/08/lipps-and-jacob_v3.pdf.

Lipset, S. M. (1959). Some Social Requisites of Democracy: Economic Development and Political Legitimacy. *The American Political Science Review*, *53*(1), 69–105. https://doi.org/10.2307/1951731.

Little, A., & Meng, A. (2023, January 17). Subjective and Objective Measurement of Democratic Backsliding. SSRN Scholarly Paper, Rochester, NY. https://doi.org/10.2139/ssrn.4327307.

Lohaus, M., & Stapel, S. (2022). Who Commits to Regional Human Rights Treaties? Reputational Benefits, Sovereignty Costs, and Regional Dynamics. *Journal of Human Rights*, *22*(3), 386–405. https://doi.org/10.1080/14754835.2022.2135369.

Louër, L. (2011, June 29). Bahrain's National Dialogue and the Ever-Deepening Sectarian Divide. *Carnegie Endowment for International Peace*. http://carnegieendowment.org/sada/?fa=44882.

Lucas, V., & Richter, T. (2013). *Public Wages, Social Spending and Taxation: Are There Different Mechanisms of Mass-Cooptation Safeguarding Authoritarian Rule?* Chicago, IL: American Political Science Association.

Lührmann, A., & Lindberg, S. I. (2019). A Third Wave of Autocratization Is Here: What Is New about It? *Democratization*, *26*(7), 1095–1113. https://doi.org/10.1080/13510347.2019.1582029.

Lusaka Times. (2017, November 16). Zambia: The Illegal Takeover of Power in Zimbabwe Is Not in Tune with Modern Politics—President Lungu. www.lusakatimes.com/2017/11/16/illegal-takeover-power-zimbabwe-not-tune-modern-politics-president-lungu. Accessed January 5, 2024.

Lust-Okar, E. (2005). *Structuring Conflict in the Arab World: Incumbents, Opponents, and Institutions*. Cambridge: Cambridge University Press.

Lynch, C. (2018). At the U.N., China and Russia Score Win in War on Human Rights. Foreign Policy, 26 March 2018, 2018. https://foreignpolicy.com/2018/03/26/at-the-u-n-china-and-russia-score-win-in-war-on-human-rights/.

Maddison, A. (2010). World Population, GDP and Per Capita GDP, 1–2008 AD. www.ggdc.net/maddison.

Mahdavi, H. (1970). The Patterns and Problems of Economic Development in Rentier States: The Case of Iran. In M. A. Cook (Ed.), *Studies in the Economic History of the Middle East* (pp. 428–467). Oxford: Oxford University Press.

Mail & Guardian. (2008, December 18). Botswana Denies Plot to Unseat Mugabe. https://mg.co.za/article/2008-12-16-botswana-denies-plot-to-unseat-mugabe. Accessed August 4, 2019.

Mail & Guardian. (2008, February 25). DA Calls on Mbeki to Release Khampepe Report. https://mg.co.za/article/2008-02-25-da-calls-on-mbeki-to-release-khampepe-report. Accessed January 4, 2024.

Mail & Guardian. (2014a, November 19). Tsvangirai: SA Aided Subversion of Zim Democratic Process. https://mg.co.za/article/2014-11-19-tsvangirai-sa-wittingly-or-unwittingly-aided-subversion-of-zim-democratic-process. Accessed January 4, 2024.

Mail & Guardian. (2014b, November 21). Mbeki Betrayed Democracy. https://mg.co.za/article/2014-11-21-editorial-mbeki-betrayed-democracy. Accessed January 4, 2024.

Mail & Guardian. (2024). Khampepe Commission. https://mg.co.za/tag/khampepe-commission. Accessed January 4, 2024.

Makarychev, A. (2020). Introduction: "Bad Weather" Regionalism and the Post-Liberal International Order at Europe's Margins. *Polity, 52*(2), 221–234. https://doi.org/10.1086/707789.

Malkin, E. (2017a, December 13). U.S. at a Crossroad as It Confronts Turmoil in Honduras. *The New York Times.* www.nytimes.com/2017/12/13/world/americas/honduras-election-juan-orlando-hernandez.html. Accessed November 27, 2023.

Malkin, E. (2017b, December 18). Honduran President Declared Winner, but O.A.S. Calls for New Election. *The New York Times.* www.nytimes.com/2017/12/17/world/americas/honduran-presidential-election.html. Accessed November 27, 2023.

Mansfield, E. D., Milner, H. V., & Pevehouse, J. C. (2008). Democracy, Veto Players and the Depth of Regional Integration. *World Economy, 31*(1), 67–96. https://doi.org/10.1111/j.1467-9701.2007.01082.x.

Mansfield, E. D., Milner, H. V., & Rosendorff, B. P. (2000). Free to Trade: Democracies, Autocracies, and International Trade. *The American Political Science Review, 94*(2), 305–321. https://doi.org/10.2307/2586014.

Mansfield, E. D., & Pevehouse, J. C. (2006). Democratization and International Organizations. *International Organization, 60*(01), 137–167. https://doi.org/10.1017/S002081830606005X.

Mansfield, E. D., & Pevehouse, J. C. (2008). Democratization and the Varieties of International Organizations. *Journal of Conflict Resolution, 52*(2), 269–294. https://doi.org/10.1177/0022002707313691.

Marshall, M. G., Gurr, T. R., & Jaggers, K. (2016). Political Regime Characteristics and Transitions, 1800–2013. *Polity IV Dataset.* Center for Systemic Peace and Societal-Systems Research Inc.

Marshall, M. G., Gurr, T. R., & Jaggers, K. (2018). Polity IV Project: Political Regime Characteristics and Transitions, 1800–2017. www.systemicpeace.org/inscr/p4manualv2017.pdf.

Martin, L. L. (1993). Credibility, Costs, and Institutions: Cooperation on Economic Sanctions. *World Politics, 45*(3), 406–432. https://doi.org/10.2307/2950724.

Martin, L. L. (2000). *Democratic Commitments: Legislatures and International Cooperation.* Princeton, NJ: Princeton University Press. https://press.princeton.edu/titles/6865.html.

Martin, L. L. (2017). International Institutions: Weak Commitments and Costly Signals. *International Theory, 9*(3), 353–380. https://doi.org/10.1017/S1752971917000082.

202 References

Mattli, W. (1999). *The Logic of Regional Integration*. Cambridge: Cambridge University Press.

Mbeki, T. (2014, November 27). Mbeki: We Owe No One an Apology. *Mail & Guardian*. https://mg.co.za/article/2014-11-27-mbeki-we-owe-no-one-an-apology. Accessed January 4, 2024.

Mccright, A. M., & Dunlap, R. E. (2000). Challenging Global Warming as a Social Problem: An Analysis of the Conservative Movement's Counter-Claims. *Social Problems, 47*(4), 499–522. https://doi.org/10.2307/3097132.

McGreal, C. (2008, November 10). Tsvangirai Isolated after African Summit Calls for Zimbabwe Deal. *The Guardian*. www.theguardian.com/world/2008/nov/10/zimbabwe.

Mearsheimer, J. J. (2014). Why the Ukraine Crisis Is the West's Fault: The Liberal Delusions That Provoked Putin. *Foreign Affairs, 93*(5 (September/October)), 1–12.

Mearsheimer, J. J. (2019). Bound to Fail: The Rise and Fall of the Liberal International Order. *International Security, 43*(4), 7–50. https://doi.org/10.1162/ISEC_a_00342.

Mearsheimer, J. J. (2022, March 19). Why the West Is Principally Responsible for the Ukrainian Crisis. *The Economist*. www.economist.com/by-invitation/2022/03/11/john-mearsheimer-on-why-the-west-is-principally-responsible-for-the-ukrainian-crisis. Accessed December 12, 2022.

MercoPress. (2021, October 12). Nicaragua Severs Ties with Taiwan, "Rogue Chinese Territory." https://en.mercopress.com/2021/12/10/nicaragua-severs-ties-with-taiwan-rogue-chinese-territory. Accessed January 7, 2024.

Meyer, P. J., & Sullivan, M. P. (2012). *U.S. Foreign Assistance to Latin America and the Caribbean: Recent Trends and FY2013 Appropriations*. Congressional Research Service. https://sgp.fas.org/crs/row/R42582.pdf. Accessed November 27, 2023.

Meyerrose, A. M. (2020). The Unintended Consequences of Democracy Promotion: International Organizations and Democratic Backsliding. *Comparative Political Studies, 53*(10–11), 1547–1581. https://doi.org/10.1177/0010414019897689.

Meyerrose, A. M., & Nooruddin, I. (2023). Trojan Horses in Liberal International Organizations? How Democratic Backsliders Undermine the UNHRC. *The Review of International Organizations*. https://doi.org/10.1007/s11558-023-09511-6.

Millennium Challenge Corporation. (2009). *Congressional Notification Transmittal Sheet* (Congressional Notification). https://assets.mcc.gov/content/uploads/2017/05/cn-061709-nicaragua-partialtermination.pdf. Accessed November 27, 2023.

Millward, J. A. (2007). *Eurasian Crossroads: A History of Xinjiang*. London: C. Hurst & Co. (Publishers) Ltd.

Mogielnicki, R. (2018, October 30). The Politics of Aid: GCC Support for Bahrain. Middle East Institute. MEI@75. www.mei.edu/publications/politics-aid-gcc-support-bahrain. Accessed December 18, 2022.

Moore, B. (1966). *Social Origins of Dictatorship and Democracy: Lord and Peasant in the Making of the Modern World*. Boston, MA: Beacon Press. https://books.google.it/books/about/Social_Origins_of_Dictatorship_and_Democ.html?id=Ip9W0yWtVO0C&pgis=1.

Moravcsik, A. (1997). Taking Preferences Seriously: A Liberal Theory of International Politics. *International Organization, 51*(4), 513–553. https://doi.org/10.1162/002081897550447.

Moravcsik, A. (2000). The Origins of Human Rights Regimes: Democratic Delegation in Postwar Europe. *International Organization, 54*(2), 217–252. https://doi.org/DOI:10.1162/002081800551163.

Morse, B. Y. L. (2012). The Era of Electoral Authoritarianism. *World Politics, 1*(1), 161–198. https://doi.org/10.1017/S0043887111000281.

Murdie, A., & Peksen, D. (2013). The Impact of Human Rights INGO Activities on Economic Sanctions. *The Review of International Organizations, 8*(1), 33–53. https://doi.org/10.1007/s11558-012-9146-9.

Myers, S. L. (2021, March 29). An Alliance of Autocracies? China Wants to Lead a New World Order. *The New York Times*. https://www.nytimes.com/2021/03/29/world/asia/china-us-russia.html. Accessed 4 July 2022.

Myerson, R. B. (2008). The Autocrat's Credibility Problem and Foundations of the Constitutional State. *American Political Science Review, 102*(01), 125–139. https://doi.org/10.1017/S0003055408080076.

Nandi-Ndaitwah, N. (2017). Statement on the Current Political Situation in Zimbabwe. Botschaft der Republik Namibia in Deutschland. www.namibia-botschaft.de/index.php/53-uncategorised/814-namibia-statement-on-the-current-political-situation-in-zimbabwe. Accessed May 12, 2024.

Nathan, L. (2012). *Community of Insecurity: SADC's Struggle for Peace and Security in Southern Africa*. Farnham: Ashgate.

NBC News. (2008, September 15). Zimbabwe Power-Sharing Deal Signed. www.nbcnews.com/id/26715920/ns/world_news-africa/t/zimbabwe-power-sharing-deal-signed/#.Wuu9ptMvxbU.

NBC News. (2009, July 15). Chinese Muslims Target of Propaganda Effort. www.nbcnews.com/id/31927269/ns/world_news-asia_pacific/t/chinese-muslims-target-propaganda-effort/#.WjgybVSdVbU.

New York Times. (2009, July 11). Rumbles on the Rim of China's Empire. www.nytimes.com/2009/07/12/weekinreview/12wong.html.

New Zimbabwe. (2008, December 6). Zimbabwe: Mugabe Says Does Not Regret Taking White Farmers' Farms. *BBC Monitoring Africa: Political Supplied by BBC Worldwide Monitoring*. https://advance-lexis-com.zu.idm.oclc.org/api/document?collection=news&id=urn:contentItem:4V36-0VM0-TX34-N0S1-00000-00&context=1516831. Accessed May 12, 2024.

News24. (2008a, April 13). Zim Summit Ends at Dawn. www.news24.com/Africa/Zimbabwe/Zim-summit-ends-at-dawn-20080413.

News24. (2008b, November 28). Mbeki Slams Tsvangirai. www.news24.com/SouthAfrica/News/Mbeki-slams-Tsvangirai-20081128-2.

Nganje, F., & Nganje, K. (2019). Liberal Internationalism Meets Third Worldism: The Politics of International Election Observation in the DRC's Post-War Elections. *Third World Quarterly, 40*(3), 521–541. https://doi.org/10.1080/01436597.2018.1549941.

Ngcobo, C. President of the Republic of South Africa and Others v M & G Media Limited., No. Case CCT 03/11 [2011] ZACC 32 (The Constitutional Court of South Africa 29 November 2011). http://hdl.handle.net/20.500.12144/3638. Accessed January 4, 2024.

Niebel, I. (2008, April 1). Berlin legt Managua die Daumenschrauben an. *amerika21*. https://amerika21.de/nachrichten/inhalt/2008/apr/berlin_vs_managua. Accessed January 7, 2024.

Niebel, I. (2009, April 3). Nicaragua stoppt Verhandlungen mit der EU. *amerika21*. https://amerika21.de/nachrichten/inhalt/2009/apr/0403nicaraguastoppteu. Accessed January 7, 2024.

Nooruddin, I. (2017). *Analysis for the Organization of American States (OAS)*. Washington, DC: Georgetown University Press. www.oas.org/fpdb/press/Nooruddin-Analysis-for-OAS-Honduras-2017.pdf.

NORDEM. (2002). *Norwegian Election Observation Mission: Presidential Elections in Zimbabwe 2002*. Oslo: Norwegian Resource Bank for Democracy and Human Rights.

Norris, P., Frank, R. W., & Martínez I Coma, F. (2014). Measuring Electoral Integrity around the World: A New Dataset. *PS: Political Science & Politics, 47*(04), 789–798. https://doi.org/doi:10.1017/S1049096514001061.

204 References

Norris, P., Nai, A., & Grömping, M. (2016). Perceptions of Electoral Integrity: US 2016 (PEI_US_1.0). Harvard Dataverse. https://doi.org/10.7910/DVN/YXUV3W.

Nyamanhindi, R. (2008, April 1). SADC Calls on All Parties to Accept Results of Zimbabwe Elections. *SARDC*. www.sardc.net/en/southern-african-news-features/sadc-calls-on-all-parties-to-accept-results-of-zimbabwe-elections.

OAS. (2009a, June 28). OAS Permanent Council Condemns Coup D'etat in Honduras, Calls Meeting of Ministers and Entrusts Secretary General with Carrying Out Consultations. *OAS: Organization of American States*. www.oas.org/en/media_center/press_release.asp?sCodigo=E-214/09. Accessed November 27, 2023.

OAS. (2009b, August 1). Secretary General Insulza Expresses OAS' Concern at Nicaraguan Developments. *OAS: Organization of American States Press Release*. www.oas.org/en/media_center/press_release.asp?sCodigo=E-434/08. Accessed November 27, 2023.

OAS. (2013). Proyecto De Resolución Del Cuadragésimo Cuarto Período Extraordinario De Sesiones De La Asamblea General. https://t.co/wnK1wLSkqY. Accessed July 1, 2024.

OAS. (2016a). Agreement between the Government of the Republic of Honduras and the General Secretariat of the Organization of American States for the Establishment of the Mission to Support the Fight against Corruption and Impunity in Honduras. www.oas.org/en/spa/dsdsm/docs/maccih_%20agreement_e.pdf. Accessed June 1, 2024.

OAS. (2016b, October 16). Statement of the General Secretariat on the Electoral Process in Nicaragua. *OAS: Organization of American States Press Release*. www.oas.org/en/media_center/press_release.asp?sCodigo=E-111/16. Accessed November 27, 2023.

OAS. (2017, December 17). Organization of American States: Democracy for Peace, Security, and Development. *OAS: Organization of American States*. www.oas.org/en/media_center/press_release.asp?sCodigo=E-092/17. Accessed November 27, 2023.

Obydenkova, A. V., & Libman, A. (2019). *Authoritarian Regionalism in the World of International Organizations: Global Perspective and the Eurasian Enigma*. Oxford: Oxford University Press.

Odinius, D., & Kuntz, P. (2015). The Limits of Authoritarian Solidarity: The Gulf Monarchies and Preserving Authoritarian Rule during the Arab Spring. *European Journal of Political Research*, 54(4), 639–654. https://doi.org/10.1111/1475-6765.12085.

O'Donnell, G. A. (1973). *Modernization and Bureaucratic-Authoritarianism: Studies in South American Politics*. Berkeley, CA: Institute of International Studies, University of California.

O'Donnell, G. A., Schmitter, P. C., & Whitehead, Laurence. (1986). *Transitions from authoritarian rule. Prospects of Democracy*. Baltimore, MD: Johns Hopkins University Press.

OHCHR. (2022). *OHCHR Assessment of Human Rights Concerns in the Xinjiang Uyghur Autonomous Region, People's Republic of China*. United Nations Human Rights Office of the High Commissioner.

Olivares, I. (2022, September 14). The Banker Who Funds Dictators Seeks Reelection. *Confidencial*. https://confidencial.digital/english/the-banker-who-funds-dictators-seeks-reelection. Accessed January 7, 2024.

Oloruntoba, S. O. (Ed.). (2020). *Pan Africanism, Regional Integration and Development in Africa*. Cham: Springer International Publishing. https://doi.org/10.1007/978-3-030-34296-8.

Organized Crime and Corruption Reporting Project (OCCRP). (2023, October 31). The Dictators' Bank: How Central America's Main Development Bank Enabled Corruption and Authoritarianism. www.occrp.org/en/the-dictators-bank/the-dictators-bank-how-central-americas-main-development-bank-enabled-corruption-and-authoritarianism. Accessed January 7, 2024.

Oxford Public International Law. Gramara (Private) Limited and ors v Government of Zimbabwe and Attorney-General of Zimbabwe., No. HH 169/2009, ILDC 1746 (ZW

2010) (Zimbabwe High Court 29 January 2010). https://opil.ouplaw.com/display/10.1093/law:ildc/1746zw10.case.1/law-ildc-1746zw10. Accessed December 5, 2023.

Palestini, S. (2021). Regional Organizations and the Politics of Sanctions against Undemocratic Behaviour in the Americas. *International Political Science Review*, *42*(4), 469–483. https://doi.org/10.1177/0192512120911700.

Panke, D., Lang, S., & Wiedemann, A. (2015). Regional Actors in the United Nations: Exploring the Regionalization of International Negotiations. *Global Affairs*, *1*(4–5), 431–440. https://doi.org/10.1080/23340460.2015.1109384.

Panke, D., & Stapel, S. (2016). Exploring Overlapping Regionalism. *Journal of International Relations and Development*, *21*, 635–662. https://doi.org/10.1057/s41268-016-0081-x.

Panke, D., Stapel, S., & Starkmann, A. (2020). *Comparing Regional Organizations: Global Dynamics and Regional Particularities*. Bristol: Bristol University Press.

Papada, E., Angiolillo, F., Gastaldi, L., Köhler, L., Lundstedt, M., Natsika, N., et al. (2023). *Democracy Report 2023: Defiance in the Face of Autocratization*. Gothenburg: V-Dem Institute, University of Gothenburg. www.v-dem.net/publications/democracy-reports. Accessed November 27, 2023.

Partlow, J. (2018a, July 17). "They Are Shooting at a Church": Inside the 15-Hour Siege by Nicaraguan Paramilitaries on University Students. *Washington Post*. www.washingtonpost.com/world/students-in-nicaragua-trapped-in-church-amid-gunfire-by-pro-government-militias/2018/07/14/c7f04512-86e3-11e8-9e06-4db52ac42e05_story.html. Accessed November 27, 2023.

Partlow, J. (2018b, August 3). "They Took My Humanity": Pro-Government Paramilitaries Terrorize Nicaraguan Protesters. *Washington Post*. www.washingtonpost.com/world/the_americas/they-took-my-humanity-pro-government-paramilitaries-terrorize-nicaraguan-protesters/2018/08/02/349f8914-900a-11e8-ae59-01880eac5f1d_story.html. Accessed November 27, 2023.

Partrick, N. (2011). *The GCC: Gulf State Integration or Leadership Cooperation?* (No. 19). London: The London School of Economics and Political Science.

Pauselli, G., Urdínez, F., & Merke, F. (2023). Shaping the Liberal International Order from the Inside: A Natural Experiment on China's Influence in the UN Human Rights Council. *Research & Politics*, *10*(3), 20531680231193513. https://doi.org/10.1177/20531680231193513.

Peksen, D., & Drury, A. C. (2010). Coercive or Corrosive: The Negative Impact of Economic Sanctions on Democracy. *International Interactions*, *36*(3), 240–264. https://doi.org/10.1080/03050629.2010.502436.

Peksen, D., Peterson, T. M., & Drury, A. C. (2014). Media-Driven Humanitarianism? News Media Coverage of Human Rights Abuses and the Use of Economic Sanctions. *International Studies Quarterly*, *58*(4), 855–866. https://doi.org/10.1111/isqu.12136.

Pelz, D. (2017, November 24). "The Crocodile": The Man Who Snapped Back. *DW*. www.dw.com/en/emmerson-mnangagwa-the-crocodile-who-snapped-back/a-41396645. Accessed January 5, 2024.

Pepinsky, T. (2014). The Institutional Turn in Comparative Authoritarianism. *British Journal of Political Science*, *44*(3), 631–653. https://doi.org/10.1017/S0007123413000021.

Pepinsky, T. B., & Walter, S. (2019). Introduction to the Debate Section: Understanding Contemporary Challenges to the Global Order. *Journal of European Public Policy*, *27*(7), 1074–1076. https://doi.org/10.1080/13501763.2019.1678663.

Permanent Representative of Cuba to the United Nations. (2019, November 11). Intervención del Representante Permanente de Cuba, Embajador Pedro L. Pedroso Cuesta, en nombre de los países miembros de la Alianza Bolivariana para los Pueblos de Nuestra América. United Nations Human Rights Council. https://hrcmeetings.ohchr.org/HRCSessions/

206 References

HRCDocuments/26/SP/16647_38_0fbbcad0_1a52_4a4e_b7e7_2d09156c8d87.doc. Accessed July 1, 2024.

Pevehouse, J. C. (2005). *Democracy from Above: Regional Organizations and Democratization.* Cambridge: Cambridge University Press. https://doi.org/10.1017/CBO9780511491078.

Pevehouse, J. C. (2016). Regional Human Rights and Democracy Governance. In T. A. Börzel & T. Risse (Eds.), *The Oxford Handbook of Comparative Regionalism* (pp. 486–512). Oxford: Oxford University Press.

Pevehouse, J. C., Nordstrom, T., McManus, R. W., & Jamison, A. S. (2020). Tracking Organizations in the World: The Correlates of War IGO Data, Version 3.0. *Journal of Peace Research, 57*(3), 492–503. https://doi.org/10.1177/0022343319881175.

Piccone, T. (2018). *China's Long Game on Human Rights at the United Nations.* Brookings Institute. https://perma.cc/WW4J-KZLU. Accessed April 14, 2023.

Pillay, A. G., Kambavo, R., Tshosa, O. B., & Chomba, F. (2011, June 13). Three Illegal and Ultra Vires Decisions. www.politicsweb.co.za/documents/three-illegal-and-ultra-vires-decisions. Accessed May 12, 2024.

Pils, E. (2022). Autocratic Challenges to International Human Rights Law: A Chinese Case Study. *Current Legal Problems, 75*(1), 189–236. https://doi.org/10.1093/clp/cuac007.

Plurinational State of Bolivia. (2015, March 13). Estado Plurinacional de Bolivia a nombre de la Alianza Bolivariana para los Pueblos de Nuestra América Tratado de Comercio de los Pueblos (ALBA-TCP), sobre las sanciones unilaterales adoptadas pos los Estados Unidos, contra la Repúlica Bolivariana de Venezuela. United Nations Human Rights Council. https://hrcmeetings.ohchr.org/HRCSessions/RegularSessions/28thSession/OralStatements/39_Bolivia_GD2-3_27.pdf. Accessed July 1, 2024.

Poast, P., & Urpelainen, J. (2018). *Organizing Democracy: How International Organizations Assist New Democracies.* Chicago, IL: The University of Chicago Press.

Pollman, E. 2022. The crime of aggression and the case of Ukraine. *American Yearbook of International Law, 1*(1), 694–729.

Powers, K., & Goertz, G. (2011). The Economic-Institutional Construction of Regions: Conceptualisation and Operationalisation. *Review of International Studies, 37*(5), 2387–2415. https://doi.org/DOI:10.1017/S0260210510001762.

Prentice, R. L., Williams, B. J., & Peterson, A. V. (1981). On the Regression Analysis of Multivariate Failure Time Data. *Biometrika, 68*(2), 373–379.

Przeworski, A., Alvarez, M. E., Cheibub, J. A., & Limongi, F. (2000). *Democracy and Development: Political Institutions and Well-Being in the World, 1950–1990.* Cambridge: Cambridge University Press. https://books.google.com/books?id=uiFH5dh12p0C&pgis=1.

Putnam, R. D. (1988). Diplomacy and Domestic Politics: The Logic of Two-Level Games. *International Organization, 42*(3), 427–460.

Ramzy, A., & Buckley, C. (2019, November 16). "Absolutely No Mercy": Leaked Files Expose How China Organized Mass Detentions of Muslims. *The New York Times.* www.nytimes.com/interactive/2019/11/16/world/asia/china-xinjiang-documents.html. Accessed December 17, 2022.

Repucci, S., & Slipowitz, A. (2022). *Freedom in the World 2022. The Global Expansion of Authoritarian Rule.* Freedom House. https://freedomhouse.org/sites/default/files/2022-02/FIW_2022_PDF_Booklet_Digital_Final_Web.pdf. Accessed December 31, 2022.

Reuters. (2009, September 10). EU to Warn Honduras of Further Sanctions over Coup. www.reuters.com/article/idUSLA269022. Accessed January 6, 2024.

Reuters. (2010, February 11). World Bank Restores Development Aid to Honduras. www.reuters.com/article/idUSN10203057. Accessed January 6, 2024.

References **207**

Reuters. (2011, June 7). Kazakh Deports Uighur to China, Rights Groups Cry Foul. *Thomson Reuters News Agency*. http://news.trust.org//item/?map=kazakh-deports-uighur-to-china-rights-groups-cry-foul.

Ricks, T. E. (2017, June). Could the Chinese Communist Party Survive Dropping South China Sea Claims? *Foreign Policy*. http://foreignpolicy.com/2017/06/29/could-the-chinese-communist-party-survive-dropping-south-china-sea-claims. Accessed April 30, 2018.

Riggirozzi, Pia, & Tussie, D. (2012). The Rise of Post-Hegemonic Regionalism in Latin America. In Pía Riggirozzi & D. Tussie (Eds.), *The Rise of Post-Hegemonic Regionalism: The Case of Latin America* (pp. 1–16). Heidelberg: Springer. https://doi.org/10.1007/978-94-007-2694-9.

Risse, T., & Babayan, N. (2015). Democracy Promotion and the Challenges of Illiberal Regional Powers: Introduction to the Special Issue. *Democratization*, *22*(3), 381–399. https://doi.org/10.1080/13510347.2014.997716.

Risse, T., & Sikkink, K. (1999). The Socialization of International Human Rights Norms into Domestic Practices: Introduction. In Thomas Risse, Stephen C. Ropp, Kathryn Sikkink (Eds.), *The Power of Human Rights: International Norms and Domestic Change* (pp. 1–38). Cambridge: Cambridge University Press. https://doi.org/10.2307/20049553.

Risse-Kappen, T. (2017). Collective Identity in a Democratic Community. In Thomas Risse (Ed.), *Domestic Politics and Norm Diffusion in International Relations* (pp. 78–113). Abingdon: Routledge.

Robinson, C. (2019, October 11). Big Loans Provide New Oxygen for Ortega in Nicaragua. *Havana Times*. https://havanatimes.org/nicaragua/big-loans-provide-new-oxygen-for-ortega-in-nicaragua. Accessed November 27, 2023.

Robinson, C. (2022, March 28). Ortega Has So Far Won the Battle against the Nica Act... *Havana Times*. https://havanatimes.org/features/ortega-has-so-far-won-the-battle-against-the-nica-act. Accessed November 27, 2023.

Ross, M. L. (2001). Does Oil Hinder Democracy? *World Politics*, *53*(3), 325–361. https://doi.org/10.1353/wp.2001.0011.

Ross, M. L. (2012). *The Oil Curse: How Petroleum Wealth Shapes the Development of Nations*. Princeton, NJ: Princton University Press.

RTE News. (2017, November 22). "People Have Spoken" According to Zimbabwe's Mnangagwa. www.rte.ie/news/world/2017/1122/921922-zimbabwe-mugabe-mnangagwa. Accessed January 5, 2024.

Russett, B. M., & Oneal, J. R. (2001). *Triangulating Peace: Democracy, Interdependence, and International Organizations*. New York: Norton. https://books.wwnorton.com/books/webad.aspx?id=10720.

Russo, A., & Stoddard, E. (2018). Why Do Authoritarian Leaders Do Regionalism? Ontological Security and Eurasian Regional Cooperation. *The International Spectator I*, *53*(3), 20–37. https://doi.org/10.1080/03932729.2018.1488404.

SADC. (2001). *Summit of the SADC Task Force on Developments in Zimbabwe Communiqué. Zimbabwe, Harary: 10–11 September, 2001*. Harare, Zimbabwe.

SADC. (2002). *SADC Extra-ordinary Summit Communiqué Malawi: Blantyre: 14 January, 2002*. Blantyre, Malawi.

SADC. (2007). *Communiqué 2007 Extra-Ordinary SADC Summit of Heads of State and Government, 28th–29th March 2007*. Dar-es-Salaam, Tanzania.

SADC. (2008a). *Communiqué of the 2008 First Extra-Ordinary SADC Summit of Heads of State and Government*. Lusaka, Zambia.

SADC. (2008b). *Communiqué of the Extraordinary Summit of the SADC Organ*. Sandton, South Africa.

208 References

SADC. (2008c). *SADC Election Observation Mission (SEOM) Preliminary Statement.* Harare, Zimbabwe.

SADC. (2008d). *2008 SADC Summit for Heads of State and Government, Sandton South Africa, 16–17 August 2008.* Sandton, South Africa.

SADC. (2008e). *Agreement between the Zimbabwe African National Union-Patriotic Fron (ZANU-PF) and the two Movement for Democratic Change (MDC) Formations, on Resolving the Challenges Facing Zimbabwe.* Harare, Zimbabwe.

SADC. (2009a). *Communiqué Extraordinary Summit of the SADC Heads of State and Government: Presidential Guest House, Pretoria, Republic of South Africa, 26–27 January 2009.* Pretoria, South Africa.

SADC. (2009b). *Communiqué of the 29th Summit of SADC Head of State and Government, September 07 to 08, 2009.* Kinshasa, Democratic Republic of Congo. https://reliefweb. int/report/madagascar/communique-29th-summit-sadc-head-state-and-government. Accessed December 6, 2023.

SADC. (2010, August 19). Communiqué of the 30th Jubilee Summit of SADC Heads of State and Government. www.gov.za/news/media-statements/communiqu%C3%A9-30th-jubilee-summit-sadc-heads-state-and-government-19-aug-2010. Accessed January 5, 2024.

SADC. (2012). *Final Communiqué of the 32nd Summit of SADC Heads of State and Government.* Maputo, Mozambique. www.afdb.org/fileadmin/uploads/afdb/Documents/Generic-Documents/Communique_32nd_Summit_of_Heads_of_States.pdf. Accessed May 12, 2024.

SADC. (2013). *SADC Election Observation Mission to the Republic of Zimbabwe Preliminary Statement.*

SADC Troika. (2017). *SADC Organ Troika Plus Council Chairperson Ministerial Meeting discusses the Political Situation in Zimbabwe.* Gaborone, Botswana: SADC. www.sadc. int/latest-news/press-release-sadc-organ-troika-plus-council-chairperson-ministerial-meeting-discusses. Accessed May 12, 2024.

Sáenz, E. (2019, April 30). Sanctions, Bancorp and the Ortega Family Wealth. *Confidencial.* https://confidencial.digital/english/sanctions-bancorp-and-the-ortega-family-wealth. Accessed November 27, 2023.

Salehyan, I. (2008). The Externalities of Civil Strife: Refugees as a Source of International Conflict. *American Journal of Political Science*, 52(4), 787–801.

Sasa, M. (2009, September 2). Zim Pulls Out of SADC Tribunal. *The Herald.* www. zimbabwesituation.com/old/sep3_2009.html. Accessed January 5, 2024.

Satubaldina, A. (2022, January 20). CSTO Peacekeepers Complete Their Mission, Withdraw from Kazakhstan. *The Astana Time.* https://astanatimes.com/2022/01/csto-peacekeepers-complete-their-mission-withdraw-from-kazakhstan. Accessed August 1, 2023.

Schedler, A. (2006). *Electoral Authoritarianism: The Dynamics of Unfree Competition.* Boulder, CO: Lynne Rienner Publishers.

Schenkkan, N., & Linzer, I. (2021). *Out of Sight, Not Out of Reach. The Global Scale and Scope of Transnational Repression.* Washington, DC: Freedom House. https://freedomhouse. org/sites/default/files/2021-02/Complete_FH_TransnationalRepressionReport2021_rev020221.pdf.

Schimmelfennig, F. (2003). *The EU, NATO and the Integration of Europe: Rules and Rhetoric.* Cambridge: Cambridge University Press. https://doi.org/10.1017/CBO9780511492068.

Schimmelfennig, F. (2016). Europe. In T. A. Börzel & T. Risse (Eds.), *The Oxford Handbook of Comparative Regionalism* (pp. 178–201). Oxford: Oxford University Press.

Schimmelfennig, F., & Sedelmeier, U. (2005). *The Europeanization of Central and Eastern Europe.* Ithaca, NY: Cornell University Press. https://books.google.de/books/about/The_Europeanization_of_Central_and_Easte.html?id=YYvXpCRYFj8C&redir_esc=y.

Schmidt, B. (2009, November 16). In Nicaragua, Opposition Sees an End Run. *The New York Times*. www.nytimes.com/2009/11/16/world/americas/16nicaragua.html. Accessed November 27, 2023.

Schneider, C. J. (2008). *Conflict, Negotiation and European Union Enlargement*. Cambridge: Cambridge University Press. https://doi.org/10.1017/CBO9780511575235.

Schuette, L., & Dijkstra, H. (2023). The Show Must Go On: The EU's Quest to Sustain Multilateral Institutions since 2016. *JCMS: Journal of Common Market Studies*, 61(5), 1318–1226. https://doi.org/10.1111/jcms.13466.

SCO. (2001). *Declaration on the Establishment of the Shanghai Cooperation Organization*. Shanghai, China.

SCO. (2002). *Charter of the Shanghai Cooperation Organization*. St. Petersburg, Russia.

SCO. (2009). *Convention of the Shanghai Cooperation Organization against Terrorism*. Yekaterinburg, Russia.

SCO. (2010, April 29). РАТС ШОС: сообща против терроризма [RATS SCO: Together against Terrorism]. *Shanghai Cooperation Organization*. http://infoshos.ru/ru/?idn=5810. Accessed December 17, 2017.

Scoones, I., Marongwe, N., Mavedzenge, B., Mahenehene, J., Murimbarimba, F., & Sukume, C. (2010). *Zimbabwe's Land Reform: Myths and Realities*. Woodbridge: James Currey.

Seawright, J. (2016). *Multi-Method Social Science: Combining Qualitative and Quantitative Tools*. Cambridge: Cambridge University Press. www.cambridge.org/gb/academic/subjects/social-science-research-methods/qualitative-methods/multi-method-social-science-combining-qualitative-and-quantitative-tools?format=HB&isbn=9781107097711#2oTIz8xTUJJsPqGr.97.

Sedelmeier, U. (2017). Political Safeguards against Democratic Backsliding in the EU: The Limits of Material Sanctions and the Scope of Social Pressure. *Journal of European Public Policy*, 24(3), 337–351. https://doi.org/10.1080/13501763.2016.1229358.

Sejersen, M. (2019). Democratic Sanctions Meet Black Knight Support: Revisiting the Belarusian Case. *Democratization*, 26(3), 502–520.

Sentencia [S.] No. 504, de las 5:00 p.m., No. Boletín Judicial [B.J.] (Corte Suprema de Justicia, Sala de lo Constitutional) [Supreme Court of Justice, Constitutional Chamber], October 19, 2009.

Shambaugh, D. L. (2013). *China Goes Global: The Partial Power*. New York: Oxford University Press. https://books.google.com/books/about/China_Goes_Global.html?id=ZUhhLwg85YEC.

Silitski, V. (2010). "Survival of the Fittest": Domestic and International Dimensions of the Authoritarian Reaction in the Former Soviet Union Following the Colored Revolutions. *Communist and Post-Communist Studies*, 43(4), 339–350. https://doi.org/10.1016/j.postcomstud.2010.10.007.

Simmons, B. A. (2009). *Mobilizing for Human Rights: International Law in Domestic Politics*. New York: Cambridge University Press.

Simmons, B. A., & Danner, A. (2010). Credible Commitments and the International Criminal Court. *International Organization*, 64(2), 225–256. https://doi.org/10.1017/S0020818310000044.

Singer, J. D. (1988). Reconstructing the Correlates of War Dataset on Material Capabilities of States, 1816–1985. *International Interactions*, 14(2), 115–132. https://doi.org/10.1080/03050628808434695.

Skaaning, S.-E. (2020). Waves of Autocratization and Democratization: A Critical Note on Conceptualization and Measurement. *Democratization*, 27(8), 1533–1542. https://doi.org/10.1080/13510347.2020.1799194.

210 References

Sky News. (2017, November 15). Youth Wing Leader of Mugabe's Party Says Sorry amid Zimbabwe "Coup." *Sky News*. https://news.sky.com/story/robert-mugabes-wife-grace-flees-zimbabwe-amid-army-takeover-11127740. Accessed January 5, 2024.

Söderbaum, F. (2004). *The Political Economy of Regionalism: The Case of Southern Africa*. Basingstoke: Palgrave Macmillan.

Söderbaum, F. (2004b). Modes of Regional Governance in Africa: Neoliberalism, Sovereignty Boosting, and Shadow Networks. *Global Governance, 10*(4), 419–436.

Söderbaum, F. (2013). Rethinking Regions and Regionalism. *Georgetown Journal of International Affairs, 14*(2), 9–18.

Söderbaum, F. (2016). Old, New, and Comparative Regionalism: The History and Scholarly Development of the Field. In T. A. Börzel & T. Risse (Eds.), *The Oxford Handbook of Comparative Regionalism* (pp. 16–38). Oxford: Oxford University Press.

Sommerer, T., Agné, H., Zelli, F., & Bes, B. (2022). *Global Legitimacy Crises: Decline and Revival in Multilateral Governance*. Oxford: Oxford University Press.

Sommerer, T., & Tallberg, J. (2017). Transnational Access to International Organizations 1950–2010: A New Data Set. *International Studies Perspectives, 18*(3), 247–266. https://doi.org/10.1093/isp/ekv022.

Southern Africa Litigation Centre. (2010, November 11). SADC Tribunal in Limbo. www.southernafricalitigationcentre.org/2010/11/11/salc-in-the-news-sadc-tribunal-in-limbo. Accessed January 4, 2024.

Southern African Legal Information Institute (SAFLII). Mike Campbell (PVT) Limited and Another v Republic of Zimbabwe., No. SADCT: 2/07 (Southern African Development Community (SADC) Tribunal 13 December 2007). www.saflii.org/sa/cases/SADCT/2007/1.html. Accessed January 4, 2024.

Southern African Legal Information Institute (SAFLII). Mike Campbell (PVT) Ltd and Others v Republic of Zimbabwe., No. SADC (T) Case No. 2/2007 (Southern African Development Community (SADC) Tribunal 28 November 2008). www.saflii.org/sa/cases/SADCT/2008/2.html.

Southern African Legal Information Institute (SAFLII). Campbell and Another v Republic of Zimbabwe., No. SADC (T) 03/2009 (Southern African Development Community (SADC) Tribunal 6 May 2009). www.saflii.org/sa/cases/SADCT/2009/1.html. Accessed May 12, 2024.

Special Monitoring Mission for Nicaragua. (2023). Special Monitoring Mechanism for Nicaragua. www.oas.org/en/iachr/jsform/Default.asp?File=/en/iachr/MESENI/informes.asp. Accessed November 27, 2023.

Stapel, S., Panke, D., & Söderbaum, F. (2023). Regional International Organizations in Africa as Recipients of Foreign Aid: Why Are Some More Attractive to Donors Than Others? *Cooperation and Conflict, 58*(4), 522–541 001083672211477. https://doi.org/10.1177/00108367221147791.

Stephen, M. (2023). Competitive Regime Creation through Informal Forums: The Case of China's South-South Human Rights Forum. Presented at the Authoritarian States and International Organizations Workshop, The Hague.

Sudworth, J., & The V. J. Team. (2022). Xinjiang Police Files: Inside a Chinese Internment Camp. *BBC News*. www.bbc.co.uk/news/resources/idt-8df450b3-5d6d-4ed8-bdcc-bd99137eadc3. Accessed December 17, 2022.

Sunday Standard. (2008, July 2). Botswana Prepares for War? www.sundaystandard.info/botswana-prepares-for-war. Accessed December 6, 2023.

Svolik, M. W. (2009). Power Sharing and Leadership Dynamic in Authoritarian Regimes. *American Journal of Political Science, 53*(3), 477–494.

References 211

Svolik, M. W. (2012). *The Politics of Authoritarian Rule*. New York: Cambridge University Press.

Tagesschau. (2023, September 29). Deutschland schmiedet Partnerschaft mit zentralasiatischen Ländern. www.tagesschau.de/inland/gesellschaft/scholz-asien-100.html. Accessed January 21, 2024.

Tallberg, J., Lundgren, M., Sommerer, T., & Squatrito, T. (2020). Why International Organizations Commit to Liberal Norms. *International Studies Quarterly*, *64*(3), 626–640. https://doi.org/10.1093/isq/sqaa046.

Tallberg, J., Sommerer, T., & Squatrito, T. (2016). Democratic Memberships in International Organizations: Sources of Institutional Design. *The Review of International Organizations*, *11*(1), 59–87. https://doi.org/10.1007/s11558-015-9227-7.

Tallberg, J., Sommerer, T., Squatrito, T., & Jonsson, C. (2013). *The Opening Up of International Organizations*. Cambridge: Cambridge University Press. https://doi.org/10.1017/cbo9781107325135.

Tamayo, J. O. (2011, December 2). Obama Administration Consulting Other Nations on Nicaragua. *The Miami Herald*. www.mcclatchydc.com/news/politics-government/article24719920.html. Accessed November 27, 2023.

Tanneberg, D., Stefes, C., & Merkel, W. (2013). Hard Times and Regime Failure: Autocratic Responses to Economic Downturns. *Contemporary Politics*, *19*(1), 115–129. https://doi.org/10.1080/13569775.2013.773206.

Tansey, O. (2016a). *The International Politics of Authoritarian Rule*. Oxford: Oxford University Press. https://global.oup.com/academic/product/international-politics-of-authoritarian-rule-9780199683628?cc=de&lang=en&.

Tansey, O. (2016b). The Problem with Autocracy Promotion. *Democratization*, *23*(1), 141–163. https://doi.org/10.1080/13510347.2015.1095736.

teleSUR. (2018, December 13). Honduran UN-Backed Dialogue Ends "Without Formal Agreements." www.telesurenglish.net/news/Honduran-UN-Backed-Dialogue-Ends-Without-Formal-Agreements-20181213-0013.html. Accessed January 6, 2024.

The Economist. (2017). An Unhappy Isle: Bahrain Is Still Hounding Its Shia. https://www.economist.com/middle-east-and-africa/2017/01/19/bahrain-is-still-hounding-its-shia.

The Guardian. (2002, February 18). EU Imposes Sanctions on Zimbabwe. www.theguardian.com/world/2002/feb/18/zimbabwe.

The Guardian. (2015, April 24). Honduran Judges Throw Out Single-Term Limit on Presidency. www.theguardian.com/world/2015/apr/24/honduran-judges-throw-out-single-term-limit-on-presidency. Accessed November 27, 2023.

The Herald. (2002a, February 27). US, Britain Double Standards Slammed. *Africa News*. https://advance.lexis.com/api/document?collection=news&id=urn:contentItem:457M-6MS0-0040-T3GN-00000-00&context=1516831. Accessed December 29, 2022.

The Herald. (2002b, March 15). Sharp Divisions between Western Countries, Africa Emerge over Poll Result. *Africa News*. https://advance.lexis.com/api/document?collection=news&id=urn:contentItem:45C1-RC60-0040-T44J-00000-00&context=1516831. Accessed December 29, 2022.

The Herald. (2002c, March 16). EU Agrees Funding Two Observer Groups. *Africa News*. https://advance.lexis.com/api/document?collection=news&id=urn:contentItem:45C7-W3R0-0040-T4BX-00000-00&context=1516831. Accessed December 20, 2022.

The Herald. (2002d, March 16). SADC Endorses "Substantially Free and Fair" Zimbabwe Vote. *Africa News*. https://advance.lexis.com/api/document?collection=news&id=urn:contentItem:45CF-NRR0-0040-T4D2-00000-00&context=1516831. Accessed December 29, 2022.

212 References

The Herald. (2002e, March 17). President Mugabe's Inauguration Speech. *Africa News.* https://advance.lexis.com/api/document?collection=news&id=urn:contentItem:45CV-GHK0-0040-T0C3-00000-00&context=1516831.　　　　Accessed　　　December 29, 2022.

The Herald. (2002f, March 18). Mugabe's Victory a Step in the Right Direction. *Africa News.* https://advance.lexis.com/api/document?collection=news&id=urn:contentItem:45CN-MXX0-0040-T00S-00000-00&context=1516831. Accessed December 29, 2022.

The Herald. (2002g, March 20). MDC Backtracks on Reconciliation Talks. *Africa News.* https://advance.lexis.com/api/document?collection=news&id=urn:contentItem:45D3-K9N0-0040-T1SW-00000-00&context=1516831. Accessed December 29, 2022.

The Herald. (2011, August 19). Zimbabwe; SADC Must Wean Itself from Donors, Control Own Budget. *Africa News.* https://advance-lexis-com.zu.idm.oclc.org/api/document?collection=news&id=urn:contentItem:53KF-5NJ1-JC86-C2TX-00000-00&context=1516831. Accessed May 12, 2024.

The Hindu. (2022, October 14). SCO-RATS Decides to Counter Threats from International Terror Groups Operating from Afghanistan. www.thehindu.com/news/national/sco-rats-decides-to-counter-threats-from-international-terror-groups-operating-from-afghanistan/article66009451.ece. Accessed December 20, 2022.

The Irish Times. (2008, August 16). Mugabe Faces Boycott at Regional Summit. *The Irish Times.* https://advance-lexis-com.zu.idm.oclc.org/api/document?collection=news&id=urn:contentItem:4T77-17B0-TX39-J16T-00000-00&context=1516831.

The Star. (2008, April 16). Little Real Agreement at Bloc Party. *The Star (South Africa).* https://advance.lexis.com.

The Telegraph. (2008, April 12). Zimbabwe Is Not in Crisis, Says Thabo Mbeki. www.telegraph.co.uk/news/worldnews/1584902/Zimbabwe-is-not-in-crisis-says-Thabo-Mbeki.html.

The Tico Times. (2008a, June 27). Ortega Walking Thin Line with Foreign Donors. https://ticotimes.net/2008/06/27/ortega-walking-thin-line-with-foreign-donors. Accessed January 7, 2024.

The Tico Times. (2008b, December 12). EU Suspends Budget Support to Nicaragua. https://ticotimes.net/2008/12/12/eu-suspends-budget-support-to-nicaragua. Accessed January 7, 2024.

The World Bank. (2024). GDP Growth (Annual %): Nicaragua. World Bank national accounts data and OECD National Accounts data files. https://data.worldbank.org/indicator/NY.GDP.MKTP.KD.ZG?locations=NI. Accessed July 4, 2024.

The Zimbabwe Situation. (2014, March 8). AU Human Rights Court Criticised over "Devastating" SADC Decision. www.zimbabwesituation.com/news/zimsit_au-human-rights-court-criticised-over-devastating-sadc-tribunal-decision. Accessed January 5, 2024.

The Zimbabwean. (2008, May 27). Campbell Case: Head of Argument Summary. www.thezimbabwean.co/2008/05/campbell-case-heads-of-argument-summary. Accessed January 4, 2024.

Tolstrup, J. (2015). Black Knights and Elections in Authoritarian Regimes: Why and How Russia Supports Authoritarian Incumbents in Post-Soviet States. *European Journal of Political Research, 54*(4), 673–690. https://doi.org/10.1111/1475-6765.12079.

Tomini, L. (2021). Don't Think of a Wave! A Research Note about the Current Autocratization Debate. *Democratization, 28*(6), 1191–1201. https://doi.org/10.1080/13510347.2021.1874933.

Tsourapas, G. (2021). Global Autocracies: Strategies of Transnational Repression, Legitimation, and Co-Optation in World Politics. *International Studies Review, 23*(3), 616–644. https://doi.org/10.1093/isr/viaa061.

Uhlin, A. (2023). Civil Society Activism beyond the Nation State: Legitimating ASEAN? In E. Hansson & M. L. Weiss (Eds.), *Routledge Handbook of Civil and Uncivil Society in Southeast Asia* (pp.139–152). London: Routledge.

UN Human Rights Council. (2023). *Detailed Conclusions of the Group of Human Rights Experts on Nicaragua* (No. A/HRC/52/CRP.5). Huma Rights Council. www.ohchr.org/sites/default/files/documents/hrbodies/hrcouncil/sessions-regular/session52/A-HRC-52-CRP-5-EN.pdf. Accessed November 27, 2023.

UN News. (2018, December 21). Nicaragua: UN Rights Chief "Alarmed" by Imminent Expulsion of Key Human Rights Groups. https://news.un.org/en/story/2018/12/1029111. Accessed November 27, 2023.

UN Peacebuilding. (2021). Success Story: Honduras. www.un.org/peacebuilding/content/success-story-honduras. Accessed January 6, 2024.

UN Press. (2009, June 30). General Assembly, Acting Unanimously, Condemns Coup d'État in Honduras, Demands Immediate, Unconditional Restoration of President. https://press.un.org/en/2009/ga10842.doc.htm. Accessed January 6, 2024.

UNHRC. (2019). Annual Report of the United Nations High Commissioner for Human Rights and reports of the Office of the High Commissioner and the Secretary-General: Promotion and Protection of Human Rights in Nicaragua. https://documents-dds-ny.un.org/doc/UNDOC/LTD/G19/070/46/PDF/G1907046.pdf?OpenElement.

UNHRC. (2022). Resolution adopted by the Human Rights Council on 31 March 2022 - Promotion and Protection of Human Rights in Nicaragua. https://documents-dds-ny.un.org/doc/UNDOC/GEN/G22/303/66/PDF/G2230366.pdf?OpenElement. Accessed January 7, 2024

UNHRC. (2023). Resolution Adopted by the Human Rights Council on April 3, 2023 - Promotion and Protection of Human Rights in Nicaragua. https://documents-dds-ny.un.org/doc/UNDOC/GEN/G23/072/95/PDF/G2307295.pdf?OpenElement. Accessed July 1, 2024.

United Nations. (2008). *Security Council 5933rd Meeting.* New York.

United Nations General Assembly. (2009). Report of the Special Rapporteur on the Promotion and Protection of Human Rights and Fundamental Freedoms While Countering Terrorism, Martin Scheinin, Tenth Sess. Human Rights Council. https://doi.org/10.1017/S0020818300007499.

United Nations Security Council. (2018). Cooperation between the United Nations and Regional and Subregional Organizations in Maintaining International Peace and Security: The Situation in Nicaragua. S/PV.8340. www.securitycouncilreport.org/atf/cf/%7B65BFCF9B-6D27-4E9C-8CD3-CF6E4FF96FF9%7D/s_pv_8340.pdf. Accessed July 1, 2024.

US Department of State. (2002, March 13). Zimbabwe; Statement on the Zimbabwe Electoral Process by Walter Kansteiner, US Assistant Secretary for African Affairs. *Africa News.* https://advance.lexis.com/api/document?collection=news&id=urn:contentItem:45BK-T4M0-0040-T2MH-00000-00&context=1516831. Accessed December 29, 2022.

US Department of State. (2012). *Kazakhstan 2012 Human Rights Report.* Washington, DC: US Bureau of Democracy, Human Rights and Labor.

US Department of the Treasury. (2023a, November 15). Treasury Sanctions Nicaraguan Financial Institution and Officials Supporting Ortega Regime. Press Release. https://home.treasury.gov/news/press-releases/sm1149. Accessed November 27, 2023.

US Department of the Treasury. (2023b, December 14). Treasury Sanctions Nicaraguan National Police and Police Commissioners Involved in Human Rights Abuse. Press Release. https://home.treasury.gov/news/press-releases/sm930. Accessed January 7, 2024.

US Senate. Reinforcing Nicaragua's Adherence to Conditions for Electoral Reform Act of 2021 or the RENACER Act., Pub. L. No. 117–154 (2021).

214 References

van der Vleuten, A. (2007). Contrasting Cases: Explaining Interventions by SADC and ASEAN. In A. Ribeiro Hoffmann & A. van der Vleuten (Eds.), *Closing or Widening the Gap? Legitimacy and Democracy in Regional Integration Organizations* (pp. 157–174). Aldershot: Ashgate Publishing, Ltd.

van der Vleuten, A., & Hulse, M. (2013). Governance Transfer by the Southern African Development Community (SADC). A B2 Case Study Report (No. 48). Berlin: Collaborative Research Center (SFB) 700. www.sfb-governance.de/en/publikationen/sfb-700-working_papers/wp48/SFB-Governance-Working-Paper-48.pdf. Accessed May 12, 2024.

van Wie Davis, E. (2008). Uyghur Muslim Ethnic Separatism in Xinjiang, China. *Asian Affairs: An American Review, 35*(1), 15–30. https://doi.org/10.3200/AAFS.35.1.15-30.

Vanderhill, R. (2012). Learning to Be Bad: How Autocratic Leaders Adopt Strategies from Abroad to Maintain Power. http://ssrn.com/abstract=2108791.

Vanderhill, R. (2013). *Promoting Authoritarianism Abroad*. Boulder, CO: Lynne Rienner Publishers.

V-Dem Institute. (2023). *Defiance in the Face of Autocratization*. V-Dem Institute, University of Gothenburg. https://v-dem.net/documents/29/V-dem_democracyreport2023_lowres.pdf.

Velasco, K. (2020, July 24). Transnational Backlash and the Deinstitutionalization of Liberal Norms: LGBT+ Rights in a Contested World. SocArXiv. https://doi.org/10.31235/osf.io/3rtje.

Voeten, E. (2019). Making Sense of the Design of International Institutions. *Annual Review of Political Science, 22*(1), 147–163. https://doi.org/10.1146/annurev-polisci-041916-021108.

Voice of America. (2018, February 27). In Honduras, US Envoy Haley Tempers Trump Threat Over Drug Trafficking. www.voanews.com/a/honduran-leader-should-talk-to-opposition-haley-says/4273317.html. Accessed January 6, 2024.

Vollaard, H. (2014). Explaining European Disintegration. *Journal of Common Market Studies, 52*(5), 1142–1159. https://doi.org/10.1111/jcms.12132.

von Borzyskowski, I., & Vabulas, F. (2019a). Hello, Goodbye: When Do States Withdraw from International Organizations? *Review of International Organizations, 14*, 335–366. https://doi.org/10.1007/s11558-019-09352-2.

von Borzyskowski, I., & Vabulas, F. (2019b). Credible Commitments? Explaining IGO Suspensions to Sanction Political Backsliding. *International Studies Quarterly, 63*(1), 139–152. https://doi.org/10.1093/isq/sqy051.

von Borzyskowski, I., & Vabulas, F. (2021). On IGO Withdrawal by States vs Leaders, and Exogenous Measures for Inference. *The Review of International Organizations, 17*, 217–222. https://doi.org/10.1007/s11558-021-09419-z.

von Soest, C. (2015). Democracy Prevention: The International Collaboration of Authoritarian Regimes. *European Journal of Political Research, 54*(4), 623–638. https://doi.org/10.1111/1475-6765.12100.

von Soest, C., & Grauvogel, J. (2017). Identity, Procedures and Performance: How Authoritarian Regimes Legitimize Their Rule. *Contemporary Politics, 23*(3), 287–305. https://doi.org/10.1080/13569775.2017.1304319.

von Soest, C., & Wahman, M. (2014). Are Democratic Sanctions Really Counterproductive? *Democratization* (February), 1–24. https://doi.org/10.1080/13510347.2014.888418.

Voss, M. J. (2019). The Use (or Misuse) of Amendments to Contest Human Rights Norms at the UN Human Rights Council. *Human Rights Review, 20*(4), 397–422. https://doi.org/10.1007/s12142-019-00574-w.

Waddell, B. (2018, August 21). Venezuelan Oil Fueled the Rise and Fall of Nicaragua's Ortega Regime. *The Conversation*. http://theconversation.com/venezuelan-oil-fueled-the-rise-and-fall-of-nicaraguas-ortega-regime-100507. Accessed November 27, 2023.

References   215

Walter, S. (2021a). The Backlash Against Globalization. *Annual Review of Political Science*, *24*(1), 421–442. https://doi.org/10.1146/annurev-polisci-041719-102405.

Wahman, M., Teorell, J., & Hadenius, A. (2013). Authoritarian Regime Types Revisited: Updated Data in Comparative Perspective. *Contemporary Politics*, *19*(1), 19–34. https://doi.org/10.1080/13569775.2013.773200.

Walter, S. (2021b). Brexit Domino? The Political Contagion Effects of Voter-Endorsed Withdrawals from International Institutions. *Comparative Political Studies*, *54*(13), 2382–2415. https://doi.org/10.1177/0010414021997169.

Waltz, K. N. (1979). *Theory of International Politics*. Reading, MA: Addison-Wesley Pub. Co. https://books.google.de/books/about/Theory_of_international_politics.html?id=Z17uAAAAMAAJ.

Washington Post. (2011, March 10). GCC Pledges $20 Billion in Aid for Oman, Bahrain. www.washingtonpost.com/wp-dyn/content/article/2011/03/10/AR2011031003629.html. Accessed December 15, 2017.

Way, L. A. (2015). The Limits of Autocracy Promotion: The Case of Russia in the "Near Abroad." *European Journal of Political Research*, *54*(4), 691–706. https://doi.org/10.1111/1475-6765.12092.

Weber, P. M., & Schneider, G. (2022). Post-Cold War Sanctioning by the EU, the UN, and the US: Introducing the EUSANCT Dataset. *Conflict Management and Peace Science*, *39*(1), 97–114. https://doi.org/10.1177/0738894220948729.

Weeks, J. L. (2008). Autocratic Audience Costs: Regime Type and Signaling Resolve. *International Organization*, *62*(1), 35–64.

Weinhardt, C., & ten Brink, T. (2020). Varieties of Contestation: China's Rise and the Liberal Trade Order. *Review of International Political Economy*, *27*(2), 258–280. https://doi.org/10.1080/09692290.2019.1699145.

Weiss, J. C., & Wallace, J. L. (2021). Domestic Politics, China's Rise, and the Future of the Liberal International Order. *International Organization*, 1–30. https://doi.org/10.1017/S002081832000048X.

Weitz, R. (2010). China's Growing Clout in the SCO: Peace Mission 2010. *China Brief*, *10*(20), 7–10.

Weller, N., & Barnes, J. (2016). Pathway Analysis and the Search for Causal Mechanisms. *Sociological Methods & Research*, *45*(3), 424–457. https://doi.org/10.1177/0049124114544420.

Weyland, K. (2010). The Diffusion of Regime Contention in European Democratization, 1830–1940. *Comparative Political Studies*, *43*(8/9), 1148–1176. https://doi.org/10.1177/0010414010370439.

Weyland, K. (2012). The Arab Spring: Why the Surprising Similarities with the Revolutionary Wave of 1848? *Perspectives on Politics*, *10*(4), 917–934. https://doi.org/10.1017/S1537592712002873.

Whitehead, L. (1996). *The International Dimensions of Democratization: Europe and the Americas*. Oxford: Oxford University Press.

Whitehead, L. (2014). Antidemocracy Promotion: Four Strategies in Search of a Framework. *Taiwan Journal of Democracy*, *10*(2), 1–24.

Wikileaks. (2008). *Botswana Presents Its Request List for Military Assistance, and a Tacit Appeal for Partnership* (Wikileaks Public Library of US Diplomacy No. 08GABORONE577_a). Gaborone, Botswana. https://wikileaks.org/plusd/cables/08GABORONE577_a.html. Accessed December 6, 2023.

Wines, M. (2010, August 2). In Restive Chinese Area, Cameras Keep Watch. *New York Times*. www.nytimes.com/2010/08/03/world/asia/03china.html.

Wintrobe, R. (1998). *The Political Economy of Dictatorship*. Cambridge: Cambridge University Press.

216 References

Winzen, T. (2023). How Backsliding Governments Keep the European Union Hospitable for Autocracy: Evidence from Intergovernmental Negotiations. *The Review of International Organizations,75*(2), 635–6644. https://doi.org/10.1007/s11558-023-09518-z.

Wong, E. (2010, February 13). China Hints at Trials for 20 Seeking Asylum. *New York Times.* www.nytimes.com/2010/02/14/world/asia/14uighur.html.

Wonka, A., Gastinger, M., & Blauberger, M. (2023). The Domestic Politics of EU Action against Democratic Backsliding: Public Debates in Hungarian and Polish Newspapers. *Journal of European Public Policy*, 1–24. https://doi.org/10.1080/13501763.2023.2279245.

World Bank. (2023). Total Natural Resources Rents (% of GDP). *The World Bank Data.* https://data.worldbank.org/indicator/NY.GDP.TOTL.RT.ZS. Accessed August 1, 2023.

World Legal Information Institute (WorldLII). The Republic of Nicaragua v. The United States of America: Military and Paramilitary Activities in and against Nicaragua., No. ICJ Rep 14 (International Criminal Court 27 June 1986). www.worldlii.org/int/cases/ICJ/1986/1. html. Accessed January 7, 2024.

Wright, J. (2008). Do Authoritarian Institutions Constrain? How Legislatures Affect Economic Growth and Investment. *American Journal of Political Science, 52*(2), 322–343. https://doi.org/10.1111/j.1540-5907.2008.00315.x.

Wright, J., Frantz, E., & Geddes, B. (2015). Oil and Autocratic Regime Survival. *British Journal of Political Science, 45*(2), 287–306. https://doi.org/10.1017/S0007123413000252.

Yom, S. L. (2014). Authoritarian Monarchies as an Epistemic Community. *Taiwan Journal of Democracy, 10*(1), 43–62.

Yom, S. L. (2016). Collaboration and Community amongst the Arab Monarchies. In M. Lynch (Ed.), *Transnational Diffusion and Cooperation in the Middle East* (POMEPS Stu, pp. 33–37). Washington, DC: Institute for Middle East Studies, George Washington University.

Zaum, D. (Ed.). (2013). *Legitimating International Organizations.* Oxford: Oxford University Press.

ZESN. (2002). *Post-Election Assessment.* Zimbabwe Election Support Network (ZESN). http://archive.kubatana.net/html/archive/elec/020312zesn.asp?sector=ELEC&range_start=481. Accessed December 29, 2022.

Zimbabwe Independent. (2008, May 16). Mbeki "Shocked" at Zim Violence. www.theindependent.co.zw/2008/05/16/mbeki-shocked-at-zim-violence.

Zumbrägel, T. (2020). Kingdom of Gravity: Autocratic Promotion and Diffusion in Saudi Arabia. In Marianne Kneuer & Thomas Demmelhuber (Eds.), *Authoritarian Gravity Centers* (pp. 55–88). London: Routledge.

Zürn, M. (2018). *A Theory of Global Governance: Authority, Legitimacy, and Contestation.* Oxford: Oxford University Press.

Zürn, M., Tokhi, A., & Binder, M. (2021). The International Authority Database. *Global Policy, 12*(4), 430–442. https://doi.org/10.1111/1758-5899.12971.

Index

African Union 58, 59, 79, 110, 180
ALBA *see* Bolivarian Alliance for the Peoples of Our America 147, 148, 180
Arab League *see* League of Arab States
ASEAN *see* Association of Southeast Asian Nations
Association of Southeast Asian Nations 58, 180
AU *see* African Union
Authoritarianism 11, 23, 30–34, 59
  Authoritarian learning 34, 147–148
  Authoritarian resilience 30–34, 99, 180
  Authoritarian regionalism 58, 147, 148
  Autocracy *see* Authoritarianism
  Autocrat *see* Authoritarianism
  Transnational authoritarianism *see* authoritarian regionalism
Authority 12–16, 19–20, 35, 43, 58–59, 69, 99
Autocratic density 9, 58, 59
Autocratic norms 9, 23, 58
Autocratic Stability 23, 34, 58
Autocratization 23, 59, 110

Backsliding *see* Democratic Backsliding
Bahrain 99, 172, 180
Black knight 99, 112
Bolivarian Alliance for the Peoples of Our America 147–148, 180

Chávez, Hugo 147
China 59, 100, 180
CIS *see* Commonwealth of Independent States 59, 180
Co-optation 30, 34, 99
Collective security 58, 99, 112
Collective Security Treaty Organization 59, 112, 180
COMESA *see* Common Market for Eastern and Southern Africa
Common Market for Eastern and Southern Africa 59, 180
Common Market of the South 47, 57, 147

Commonwealth of Independent States 59, 112, 180
Corruption 99, 112, 138
CSTO *see* Collective Security Treaty Organization

Democratization 11, 23, 30–34
Democratic Backsliding 30, 99, 100
Dictator clubs 58, 99, 147
Digital authoritarianism 99, 100, 112
Domestic survival *see* Survival

EAC *see* East African Community
East African Community 112
Economic Community of West African States 59, 180
Economic regionalism 58–59, 99
ECOWAS *see* Economic Community of West African States
Election manipulation 30, 112, 138
Election monitoring 35, 112
Emmerson Mnangagwa 112
EU *see* European Union
European Union 11, 59, 180

Foreign aid 99, 138, 180
Functionalist theory 22, 23

Gaddafi, Muammar 22
GCC *see* Gulf Cooperation Council
Geopolitics 14, 34, 37
Grace Mugabe 138–140
Gulf Cooperation Council 58, 59, 99, 172

Homogeneity 9, 37, 58
Human rights violation 31, 120, 151, 160
Hybrid Regimes 9, 14, 23, 31

IGAD *see* Intergovernmental Authority on Development
Institutional design 58, 59
Intelligence sharing 100
Intergovernmental Authority on Development 2

218 Index

International Democracy Promotion 58–59, 99
International organization 58, 99, 112
International sanctions 99, 100, 112

Khama, Seretse Ian 138, 140
King Hamad bin Isa Al Khalifa 97–98, 100

League of Arab States 58, 180
Legitimacy 29–30, 35, 98
  Legitimacy crisis 97, 116
  Legitimation Strategies 29–30, 34, 97
Levy Mwanawasa 130, 131
LOAS *see* League of Arab States

Maduro, Nicolas 147, 180
Mbeki, Thabo 116, 121–131
MERCOSUR *see* Common Market of the South
Mohammed bin Salman 98
Mugabe, Robert 110, 116, 126, 131
Museveni, Yoweri 2

Nazarbayev, Nursultan 59, 100, 180
Non-interference 58, 99
Norm diffusion 58, 100

OAS *see* Organization of American States
Organization for Security and Cooperation in Europe 58, 100
Organization of American States 58, 100
Ortega, Daniel 147, 180
OSCE *see* Organization for Security and Cooperation in Europe

Pan-Africanism 168
Patronage Networks 3, 30, 72, 170
Political survival *see* survival

Regime 22–27, 88, 98
  Regime change 4, 11, 62
  Regime-Boosting Regionalism 33–35
Regional anti-terrorism structure 102, 104
Regional court 5, 17, 39, 61, 133, 135

Regional integration 21, 47, 130
Regional sanctions 37, 147
Regionalism 8, 34, 35
Repression 30, 34, 172
Resource redistribution 34, 35, 93, 172

SADC *see* Southern African Development Community
Saudi Arabia 4, 84, 96, 100
SCO *see* Shanghai Cooperation Organization
RATS *see* regional anti-terrorism structure
Russia 4, 8, 96, 166
Shanghai Cooperation Organization 2, 58, 102, 104, 105, 106, 107, 108
South Africa 17, 75
Southern African Development Community 120, 121, 126, 128, 129, 133
Sovereignty 4, 12–22, 33–39, 87, 99, 121, 137, 161
  Sovereignty costs 8, 21, 167
Surveillance 108, 172, 177
Survival 9, 11–17, 22–33, 70–90
  Survival analysis 67–68

Tsvangirai, Morgan 110, 126, 130
Turkey 23, 107

Uighurs 1, 103–107
UK *see* United Kingdom
UNASUR *see* Union of South American Nations
Union of South American Nations 57, 147
United Kingdom 57, 152, 156
United States of America 20, 93, 112–113, 147, 162
USA *see* United States of America

Venezuela 147, 148, 154, 161

Xingjiang 1, 92, 94, 102–108, 172

Zimbabwe 1, 17, 61, 82, 85, 88, 92–95, 108–142